A SALUTE TO CHOCOLATE

A SALUTE TO
CHOCOLATE

by
Sylvia Balser Hirsch
and
Morton Gill Clark

GRAMERCY BOOKS • NEW YORK

A SALUTE TO CHOCOLATE

Contents

Chocolate, Past and Present

Although vanilla is undoubtedly America's most useful flavoring, adaptable as it is and amenable to use with other flavors, chocolate is certainly America's favorite. Like vanilla, it may be combined with other flavors to great advantage—orange, almond or rum, for instance —but its taste, unlike that of vanilla, invariably remains predominant. In 1965, the latest year for which figures are available, the United States consumed 720,000,000 pounds of chocolate in cakes, cookies, pies, ice creams, puddings, syrups, sauces and candies. Here we have not yet learned (as they did centuries ago in Mexico) that chocolate is also excellent when used in small quantities with meats and birds. When we do, we will no doubt add to our annual consumption.

Chocolate was discovered for Europeans in 1519 by Cortez in Mexico. Montezuma, the last Aztec ruler, personally consumed some fifty "pitchers" of a chocolate drink each day and had two thousand "pitchers" prepared for members of his household. It gave strength, so it was said; it gave courage, wisdom. Rare aphrodisiacal powers were attributed to it (as was also the case later in Europe). Cortez took beans of the cacao tree back to Spain with him for the court to taste and ponder, and, for a hundred years, chocolate was a Spanish "secret."

During that time Spanish cooks changed the royal Aztec drink from a cold one to a hot one; they improved its quality by the addition of sugar, and the flavor by the addition of vanilla. The bars that they made of the crude chocolate, which would subsequently be grated for the drink, often included a flour of some sort as a binder. Nut powders or flours were often used instead of grain flours. Spices were included—ginger, cinnamon, cloves and the native American pimentos, which came to be known as allspice. The cracked or pounded cacao bean would be melted and mixed with these other ingredients according to household formula, then hardened into cakes similar to those which are even today used by Mexicans.

From the Spanish court, chocolate quite naturally moved to the Austrian court. (The Emperor Charles V called it a "divine drink" to "build up resistance and fight fatigue.") And from there it was taken to the French court, by either Anne of Austria, Queen of Louis XIII, or Marie Thérèse, the Austrian princess who became the Queen of Louis XIV.

From France, the taste for chocolate passed to England. And here, for the first time, it was introduced in a limited way to the masses. In June of 1657, the first chocolate house was opened in London. "In Bishopsgate Street," ran the advertisement, "in Queen's Head Alley, at a Frenchman's house, is an excellent West India drink called Chocolate to be sold. . . ." It was expensive, of course; nevertheless, other chocolate houses soon sprang up, some of great elegance. And in time, many of them, like White's, which flourished in Queen Anne's day, combined chocolate drinking with gambling and "intellectual discussions" which often centered on the merits of chocolate itself. One housewife, for instance, was reported to have been "brought to bed of twins three times for drinking it."

Chocolate was first imported into the American Colonies in 1755 by Massachusetts traders who took sacks of cacao beans in the West Indies in exchange for rum. Its popularity as a drink can be judged by the number of advertisements that appeared in early periodicals in Boston, New York, Philadelphia and Charleston. But the price remained high until mass production began to eliminate some of the tedious handwork that had been involved in the chocolate-making process before. Dr. James Baker financed the first serious attempt to manufacture chocolate on a large scale in a rented grist mill on the Neponset River in Massachusetts in 1765. And his success in the venture was assured when the pre-Revolution tax on tea made many colonists turn to chocolate as a standard household beverage. "The superiority of chocolate, both for health and nourishment," said Thomas Jefferson at the time, "will soon give it the preference over tea and coffee in America which it has in Spain."

That Jefferson's prophecy was never realized can be attributed in no small measure to the success that Dr. Baker's grandson achieved with new methods of chocolate manufacture when he took over the factory in the early nineteenth century. A cocoa press now made possible the separation of cocoa butter from cocoa powder. And while this process made for a better cocoa that would give the world a smoother drink, it also made for better chocolate which, because of the fact that it was enriched by the very same cocoa butter that had been extracted to make cocoa, now melted to a velvet smoothness of both flavor and consistency. (Until then, cooking chocolate had often had a granular texture.) And so vastly superior and dependable and delicious were the bars now sold that in short order chocolate became linked in most minds not with beverages at all but with cakes, creams, desserts and candies. Such a mental association made it virtually impossible to think of chocolate in the same terms as coffee or tea. This association was cemented by the invention of the milk chocolate process in 1876 by Daniel Peter of Vevey, Switzerland. But whatever chocolate may have lost in popularity as a beverage, it more than made up for by what it gained in prestige as a flavor.

The word *chocolate* comes from a combination of Mexican Indian words, the most probable being *xoco* (meaning *sour*) and *atl* (meaning *water*). It referred in the beginning to the drink, of course, not the bean from which the drink was made, the bean being the seed of the cacao tree. *Cocoa,* as a word, first appeared in print in Dr. Johnson's Dictionary in 1775. It was either a typesetter's error or the Doctor's.

The cacao tree—*Theobroma cacao,* meaning "food of the gods"—is native to Central and South America but grows today in many scattered areas of a belt running around the earth to 20 degrees latitude on both sides of the equator. It requires a warm, humid atmosphere with considerable but well-distributed rainfall and a heavy but well-drained soil. And though individual trees are known to have lived to as ripe an old age as two hundred years, all are temperamental in infancy and indeed are inclined to delicacy throughout their long and useful lifetimes.

As for its looks, the cacao tree is a decorative thing but in an oddly artificial way. Standing as it does about thirty feet at maximum growth, it seems to have been put together from bits of different trees. Its glossy oval leaves, reddish when young, turn to a rich dark green on maturity. Mosses, lichens and orchids cling to its bark. All the year round clusters of five-petaled blossoms, sometimes white, sometimes pink, sometimes yellow, sometimes two colors at once, gleam through the foliage and mosses from the trunk of the tree and the woodier portions of older branches from which they grow directly, looking for all the world as though they'd been glued there.

The major portion of the world's cacao beans today come from Africa—Ghana, Nigeria and the Cameroons in particular—where the plantations for the most part are small holdings of not more than five acres each. Brazil accounts for the next largest share, with the state of Bahia producing ninety-five percent of the total on plantations averaging about 250 acres each. The best of the cacao beans are the *criollos* of Central and South America, but the most important from a commercial standpoint are the *forasteros,* sometimes called *amelo-*

nados. An average cacao tree in the course of a year, despite its hundreds of blossoms, yields only between two and three pounds of commercial beans, an average pod, or fruit, containing about four ounces of pulp-covered beans which, when dried and cured and ready for sale, will weigh about one and one-half ounces.

The harvest of cacao beans, unlike that of other crops, lasts throughout the entire year. Peak seasons occur at different times of the year in different countries although the climates of the different countries may be vastly similar. The world over, harvesting is a matter of hand labor for the most part. Pickers called *tumbadores* are sent out into the plantations armed with long-handled, hook-bladed knives to clip the ripe fruits from the trees. They are followed by women and children with baskets, who gather the fruits up, dump them in huge stacks, sort them and open them with lethal machetes. Within the fruits, the cacao beans nestle in a soft mucilaginous pulp which is scooped out by hand or wooden spatula. A good worker can open 500 cacao pods an hour. As a rule it requires about 400 beans to make one pound of chocolate.

Between the breaking of the pod and the appearance of the chocolate there are many months and many miles. Beans and pulp together must undergo a natural fermentation which lasts from two to nine days. Then the beans must be dried. The same drying method is in use today as was used four hundred years ago by the Indian slaves of Montezuma. The beans are spread on trays of bamboo matting in the sun. In some places, hot-air pipes have been put to use to accomplish or facilitate the drying; but, while the hot air dries the beans, it lacks the sun's power to develop flavor. And finally, when at last sorted by hand, the beans are poured into sacks, stamped with the grower's name and point of origin, and carted to shipping centers, from which they go to manufacturers in all parts of the world who buy not from one source alone but many, using different cacao beans from different parts of the world with an eye to a blend of flavor. It is in fact the blend, in conjunction with the particular chocolate-making process that each manufacturer follows, that determines the quality and flavor of the chocolate which at last reaches the consumer. Blend gives the individual characteristics that make one chocolate different from another and, in the long run, determine the taste of the cakes, cookies, pies and creams that appear day in, day out, the world over, at a million tables. Blend accounts for the personality that chocolate makers stamp on their products. And it gives us, of course, not only diversity but endless pleasure.

Chocolate—
Its Kinds and Uses

Nibs, which are the "meat" of cracked, roasted cocoa beans, are the source of all chocolate and cocoa and cocoa butter. These nibs, when ground under considerable pressure, are liquefied by the heat of the grinding process itself. The resulting chocolate liquid, often called *chocolate liquor,* is composed of fine cocoa powder in suspension and a fat known as *cocoa butter. Commercial chocolate* is resolidified chocolate liquor with extra cocoa butter added for richness and smoothness. *Commercial cocoa* is that portion of the chocolate liquor which remains after most of the cocoa butter has been extracted.

Cooking chocolate is available in most markets in several distinct types. The chocolate offered by each manufacturer represents a personal taste and a personal blend. It is for you to decide which suits your taste best.

Bitter chocolate, often referred to as unsweetened or baking or cooking chocolate, is made without sugar, as its name implies. It is sold in cakes of eight ounces each which are in turn, for convenience, marked off in eight one-ounce squares. It is also sold in a semiliquid form in sealed one-ounce envelopes as *no-melt chocolate,* or by trade name. In our testing, we have used the cake chocolate throughout unless otherwise stated. Bitter chocolate, because of its deep, rich chocolate flavor, is the kind most frequently called for in cakes and other baked or steamed desserts.

Semisweet chocolate is lightly sweetened and, while it is sold in eight-ounce cakes similar to those made of bitter chocolate, it is also sold packaged in bits or pieces. The weight of these packages varies, of

5

course, but is clearly marked on each envelope. Measurements for bits have sometimes been given by package weight, sometimes by cup. It seems to us that this should not cause too much confusion. This chocolate, because of its sheen when melted, is generally used for candy-dipping. It is also used for cake frostings and fillings and sauces and many creams.

Sweet chocolate, as its name implies, is definitely sweet. When it is used in any dish, sauce, filling or frosting, little additional sugar is needed. Like the semisweet chocolate, it too is available both in bars and packaged bits and pieces. It may be eaten as is, of course, but it lacks the smooth melting quality that typifies *milk chocolate.*

Milk chocolate is the everyday eating chocolate best known in candy bars. It is made by combining chocolate liquor with extra cocoa butter, sugar, flavorings and milk or cream. It may be melted as is and used for frosting or filling or sauce or in a variety of "made" dishes—pies, puddings and creams.

Cocoa powder, as we have mentioned, is the dry portion of the chocolate liquor that is left when most of the cocoa butter has been removed. The term includes various kinds of cocoa such as breakfast cocoa (which may be sweetened or not), medium and low-fat cocoas and Dutch process cocoa, which has been treated with alkali to neutralize the natural acids. *Dutch process cocoa,* which has nothing to do with Holland or the Dutch, is darker than other cocoas and has an individual flavor.

Chocolate syrup, of course, is both flavored and sweetened, and is itself used as a flavoring and sweetener. *Chocolate sauce,* on the other hand, is a more or less finished product and is used on cakes, puddings and ice creams as needed.

White chocolate, so called, is not chocolate at all but an artificial preparation of vegetable fats with coloring and flavors.

All chocolate of whatever kind should be stored in a cool, dry place at a temperature of about 60° F. If chocolate becomes warm, the cocoa butter rises to the surface and a grayish film or "bloom" appears. This does not harm the chocolate insofar as its cooking qualities are concerned, but it does affect its eating quality. With the fat on the surface, the remaining chocolate below becomes crumbly. Well-wrapped, properly stored chocolate should keep for a year. Cocoa will also keep well for a year under similar temperature conditions if in a tightly covered container. All chocolate contains an appreciable amount of fats and carbohydrates. It is therefore a good source of quick energy. It is also an excellent source of calories. Weight watchers should remember therefore that

1 ounce bitter chocolate contains 144 calories

1 ounce semisweet contains about 147 calories
1 ounce sweet chocolate contains about 155 calories

Milk chocolate has somewhat fewer calories than sweet despite its milk or cream.

One square of cooking chocolate equals one ounce and four tablespoons of cocoa equal one ounce. When substituting cocoa for chocolate, however, bear in mind that extra fat must be added: one ounce of chocolate equals three tablespoons cocoa plus one half tablespoon butter.

Cake or bar chocolate may be used melted, grated or shaved. For culinary purposes it is most frequently melted. All chocolate burns easily, however, so great care should be taken when exposing it to heat.

TO MELT CHOCOLATE

For safety and ease, always melt chocolate in the top of a double boiler over hot, *not boiling,* water, unless *boiling* for some special reason is specifically directed. Boiling water is bound to steam. The steam rising around the upper part of the double boiler is bound to condense. And when chocolate is being melted alone, it will "tighten" if even one drop of water falls into it—an unfortunate state of affairs which is a separation of the chocolate solids and its fat content. Oddly enough, this happens only with water in minute quantity. Chocolate may be melted with perfect safety in a quantity of water—even a few spoonfuls, or with butter, or coffee or any liquid for that matter. A drop or two, however, will ruin it.

"Tightened" chocolate may be made usable again by the addition of one or two tablespoons of some tasteless cooking oil which has no water content—corn oil, for instance. Merely add and stir vigorously until the chocolate becomes smooth once more. Do NOT add butter.

Aside from its being the chocolate for use as flavoring, melted chocolate has some special uses, too, as in the making of such delectable fancies as these *Colettes*, chocolate cups which may be filled with fruits or creams or both for special occasions.

COLETTES

12 ounces sweet chocolate (1½ cakes) or 1 package chocolate bits	16 paper baking cups

Melt chocolate in the top of a double boiler over hot (not boiling) water; remove from heat and cool slightly. While chocolate is cooling, prepare 8 double paper cups by placing one inside another. Put 2 tablespoons of the cooled chocolate in each of the 8 cups. Using the back of a teaspoon, spread it around the cup so that the entire inside is coated. When all are done, set them in a muffin pan and chill until the chocolate is firm. Then handling the cups as quickly and gently as possible, peel off the paper. Return cups to muffin pan. Keep chilled until needed.

To serve, fill with ice cream or some rich custard or pastry cream and top with chopped nuts or shredded coconut and a grating of semisweet or bitter chocolate.

Or make a special dessert on the order of the following Parisian Fancy.

PARISIAN FANCY

8 chocolate cups
8 champagne biscuits
3 tablespoons kirsch
1 cup fresh strawberries, sliced and lightly sugared (or whole fresh raspberries)

1 cup heavy cream
2 tablespoons powdered sugar
1 teaspoon vanilla
   Shaved bitter chocolate curls

Crumble 1 biscuit coarsely in each of the chocolate cups. Sprinkle with a few drops of Kirsch. Add sugared berries with a few drops of their natural syrup. Whip cream until stiff and sweeten with the powdered sugar; add vanilla. Put a generous spoonful on top of the sliced berries. Top with a few extra strawberry slices, some bitter chocolate curls and few extra drops of kirsch. Serve 8.

Marie Josés are somewhat similar to the Parisian Fancy, but for these, put a layer of plain cake in the bottom of each cup, sprinkle this with maraschino and then top with vanilla-flavored whipped cream piped on with a pastry bag to make elaborate rosettes. Garnish with a whole or halved maraschino cherry.

Grated chocolate is thought of as being used chiefly for decoration, but it is called for in many recipes and in some it is absolutely essential.

TO GRATE CHOCOLATE

Have chocolate cold and firm and the grater dry. Use a regular tinware grater, or an electric blender flicked on for a few seconds; or a mouli grater—a little French gadget procurable at any shop dealing in specialty kitchenwares.

Use grated chocolate (sweet, semisweet or bitter, as desired) over frosted cakes, creams, pies and puddings; or use it to give a special kind of finish as with these *Schlosserkuchen*—Prune Fritters:

SCHLOSSERKUCHEN

1 pound largest prunes
2 cups dry white wine
1 cup blanched almonds (approximately)

1 cup flour
1 pinch salt
1 cup grated sweet chocolate
Vegetable oil for frying

Put prunes in a deep bowl, cover with white wine and soak overnight. Drain in the morning, reserving the wine. Cover prunes with water. Cook gently until just tender. Drain. Remove pits carefully. Insert a whole almond in each prune. Chill.

Make a batter of the flour and 1 cup of the reserved wine. (Add more wine if necessary to make 1 cup.) Add pinch of salt. Beat batter until smooth. Heat vegetable oil to 390° F. for frying. Dip prunes in batter to coat them evenly. Fry a few at a time until crisp and golden brown. Drain on paper. While still hot, roll in the grated chocolate to coat them evenly. Serve immediately. Serves 6-8.

Or grated chocolate may be used to give a festive touch to such a simple dessert as this Apple Bonbon.

APPLE BONBON

2 pounds tart cooking apples
2 tablespoons water
⅔ cup sugar

½ cup heavy cream
1 tablespoon powdered sugar
3 ounces grated bitter chocolate

Peel, core and slice the apples. Combine them in a heavy saucepan with water and cook, covered, over low heat until just tender. Add sugar and cook until the sugar is melted. Press through a sieve into a serving dish or casserole. Cool, then chill. Whip cream and sweeten with the powdered sugar. Spread over apples and top with the grated chocolate. Keep in the refrigerator until needed. Serves 4.

Chocolate curls, though they have a flavor of their own, are pure decoration. Use them on cakes, creams and custards; gain an effect of elegance by arranging them at intervals around the edge of a dish or cake. Use just a few of them to top whipped cream on pies and refrigerator cakes. Use them for contrast with fruits—strawberries, raspberries, peaches.

TO MAKE CHOCOLATE CURLS

Shave cold, hard chocolate in long strokes with a vegetable parer or with the broad grating blade of a stand-up grater. Handle the resulting curls gently for they break easily. Their length and curliness is what gives the wanted effect.

Chocolate may also be used to make special decorations such as these Ivy Leaves for cakes and desserts.

CHOCOLATE IVY LEAVES

18 to 20 fresh, small English-ivy leaves

½ cup semisweet chocolate bits
1 tablespoon butter plus one teaspoon

Wash and dry the ivy leaves. Melt chocolate in the top of a double boiler over hot (not boiling) water; add butter and blend. Remove from heat but leave over hot water.

Spread wax paper over a cookie sheet large enough to hold all the ivy leaves in a single layer. Using a spatula, spread a thin layer of chocolate over the under side of each leaf. Lay leaves chocolate-side-up on cookie sheet. Refrigerate until chocolate is absolutely firm.

Take ivy leaf by stem. Insert the point of a knife at the stem end between leaf and chocolate just far enough to loosen the leaf. Gently peel the leaf away from chocolate. Return chocolate leaves to paper covered cookie sheet with the side that was next to the leaves uppermost; this should have a leaf vein pattern on it. Return to refrigerator until needed. Use to encircle cake or cream.

For other special uses of chocolate see "Bread and Such" and "Chocolate with Meat and Other Main Dishes" in Table of Contents.

Some General Information

All measurements unless otherwise stated are for level standard measuring spoons and cups.

Flour in all cases means all-purpose flour except where some special kind is specifically mentioned. It should always be sifted before measuring; then simply fill spoon or cup to overflowing and, with a sheet of wax paper to catch the overflow, level the surface with a knife.

Butter measurements given in cups are also given in pounds or sticks, each stick being ¼ pound, of course. Bear in mind also that

¼ pound butter equals ½ cup
8 tablespoons equal ½ cup
3 teaspoons equal 1 tablespoon

If you must measure your butter from a 1-pound brick, however, simply fill a measuring cup with cold water to the level of your required butter measurement. Now add dabs of cold butter and when the water has risen to twice its original level, you will have added the required amount of butter. Pour off the water and the butter is ready for use.

Butter has been specified as the shortening or fat in virtually all recipes for we feel that it gives the best results insofar as taste and general quality are concerned. Margarine may be substituted for butter in many cases, of course, and at a considerable saving in money, but we feel that this economy is reflected proportionately in any cake or dessert made with economy primarily in mind.

Vegetable oil, where specified, means any tasteless oil. Vegetable shortening means any solidified vegetable cooking fat other than margarine.

Sugar, unless otherwise specified, means white granulated sugar. Where other kinds are stipulated, use the precise type given. Bear in mind especially that powdered and confectioners' sugars differ from one another in that the latter contains a percentage of cornstarch.

Baking powder, unless otherwise stated, means double acting baking powder. Soda, where specified, means plain baking soda (bicarbonate).

Cream in all cases refers to any light cream other than the so-called coffee cream on sale in most markets. Heavy cream, however, means the heaviest available. This, of course, is considerably less heavy than the heavy cream that rises naturally from rich whole milk if left to its own devices. In the old days in this country, plain heavy cream was often of such thickness that it was ladled out, not poured. This kind of heavy cream may be approximated on special occasions if you will buy a quart of commercial heavy cream, pour it into a clean pan and let it rise (as though it were whole milk) for twenty-four hours in the refrigerator. Or, if you like, you can make a reasonable facsimile of the *crème fraiche* that is the popular heavy cream of France. This has a very faint and delicious sour taste to it, but a hint only. It is excellent with fruits of all kinds, or when used in conjunction with a kind of sweetness which, by itself, might be cloying.

CRÈME FRAICHE

Combine 1 teaspoon buttermilk with 1 cup heaviest cream in a glass jar. Blend. Let stand, covered, for 6 to 8 hours at 75° F. Stir and refrigerate until needed.

Milk, where referred to in the following recipes, means whole milk which has, of course, a certain percentage of butterfat. In all probability, unless purchased direct from a farmer, this milk will be homogenized—treated in a way that prevents the butterfat from rising as cream.

Many of the following recipes require a sugar syrup boiled to some specified degree of heat. This may be judged approximately by various tests which involve dropping bits of the boiling syrup into cold water. A candy thermometer, however, is not only easier but more accurate. Use one by all means. If you have none, the cold water tests are as follows:

At 234° to 240° F. a bit of syrup dropped from a spoon into cold water will form a soft ball.

At 246° to 248° F., a firm ball.

At 265° to 270° F., a hard ball.

At 295° F. the hardened syrup will bend, then crack.

At 300° F. it has the consistency of peanut brittle.

At 310° F., the consistency of rock candy.

Electric beaters are great time and energy savers, so you should use one whenever possible for mixing batters (which do not have specific requirements), or beating egg yolk or egg-sugar combinations. Rotary hand-beaters, however, are preferable for beating egg whites; and wire whisks which take more time and labor are best of all. This is true also where whipped cream is concerned. Whipped cream should not be thought of simply as cream whipped stiff in any off-hand manner; it has special qualities which are brought out by special beating. It may be very soft and just barely whipped to hold a shape or it may be stiff enough to stand in straight high peaks. But it should always be smooth and of a silky texture. Over-beating or too fast or too hard beating will make it pebbly. If taken beyond a certain stage of stiffness it assumes a buttery taste and texture. And beyond that, of course, it becomes butter in fact.

Cream, to whip properly, should be refrigerator-cold and the bowl used for whipping should be cold as well. Egg whites, on the other hand, should be at room temperature.

When whipped cream is incorporated in any mixture, the mixture must be cold when the cream is added if it is to remain whipped. If whipped cream is added to a warm mixture, it gradually weeps away.

Once whipped, cream will stay whipped for several hours under refrigeration. Actually, if turned into a fine-mesh sieve (which should in turn be set over a bowl of some sort), the whipped cream will improve under refrigeration for its watery content will drain away, leaving a firmer cream than otherwise.

Unlike whipped cream, beaten egg whites may be folded into *either* warm or cold mixtures. Their light, fluffy quality will not be affected. If you wish them to have added gloss and stiffness when combining them with a cream custard, whip in a small amount of sugar after they form soft peaks.

When creaming butter, start the process by hand if the butter is cold and hard. If you use an electric beater on hard butter (unless it is fitted with a pastry blending attachment), you will simply clog the blades.

In many of the following recipes we have specified use of a double boiler not because the double boiler is essential to the cooking process in question but simply because it obviates many difficulties and hazards—especially where chocolate and/or eggs or egg yolks are concerned. If you lack a large enough or small enough double boiler for any particular operation, use a saucepan of the required size for the top and set this over and in a larger saucepan with an inch or two of hot water. The water in most cases should be below the under surface of the upper pot; and it should be kept at whatever temperature is indicated by the recipe—sometimes merely hot, sometimes at a full boil.

For grinding nuts the best utensil to use is a nut grinder, of course, which is specially made for the purpose and grinds the nuts to a fine powder without having them oil, a matter of the nutmeat and oil separating. Lacking such a grinder, an electric blender is the best substitute. Use ½ cup nutmeats at a time and flick the blender on at high speed for only 30 seconds. Meat grinders, unless their blades are very sharp, are apt to mash the nuts to a paste.

So that you may roughly estimate the quantity of nuts you need to buy for any recipe, let us say that 1 cup whole blanched almonds or pecan or walnut halves weighs approximately 5½ ounces; 1 pound nuts in the shell equals approximately ½ pound shelled; and ½ pound shelled equals approximately 1½ cups.

And to refresh your memory on other data:

2 cups equal	1 pint
2 pints	1 quart
16 ounces	1 pound
4 cups flour	1 pound
2 cups granulated sugar	1 pound
3½ cups powdered sugar	1 pound

Chocolate—
The Drink

The natural place to start a group of chocolate recipes is with the use of chocolate as a beverage, for it was as a drink that chocolate first became known to the Spaniards in Mexico and hence to the world at large. The chocolate of which Montezuma drank his fifty "pitchers" a day was a cold, bitter potion, however; and though it was often thickened with *atolle* (a "kind of pap of Indian meal") or with a flour made from ground nuts, it was essentially thin. The ground chocolate and spices and other ingredients had a tendency to separate, leaving the drink watery. Constant stirring was needed to give it the proper consistency. And for this a kind of swizzle stick was used, much like the *molinillo* found in Mexico today.

Mexican chocolate (and other drinks of Latin America patterned on it) is perhaps the only chocolate served today that stems directly from that which the Aztecs drank so avidly. In present-day Mexico, one finds *pastillas de chocolate* (round chocolate cakes) and *tabillas de chocolate* (chocolate bars) made of roasted cacao beans, ground nuts, spices and sugar. These, when melted with water, are whipped to a foam with *molinillos*. In the eighteenth century, the Spanish author Marchena wrote that Mexican chocolate was made of 2 pounds sugar, 2 ounces cinnamon, 14 grains of pepper and ½ ounce cloves for each 10 pounds cacao. Occasionally anise seed was added in small quantity. And almost invariably the mixture was bound by some nut flour. This formula based on the original Aztec chocolate produces a drink much like the present-day *pinillo* of Nicaragua, and differs from the Mexican *champurrado* only in that the latter uses milk and cornstarch.

For a typical Mexican chocolate of today, try the following:

MEXICAN CHOCOLATE

4½ ounces Mexican cinnamon
   chocolate (See NOTE below)
2 ounces bitter chocolate

3½ cups scalded milk
1½ inch cinnamon stick

In the top of a double boiler over hot (not boiling) water melt the Mexican chocolate (which is sweetened) with the bitter chocolate. When smooth, add the scalded milk and cinnamon stick. Blend thoroughly. Add extra sugar to taste if desired. Pour into an earthenware pitcher (called a *jarro* in Mexico) and insert an over-size swizzle stick (the *molinillo*). In this country, a long-handled, spoon-tipped martini-stirrer will answer the same purpose. Twirl the handle between the palms of your hands until the liquid is foamy; this also serves to prevent a skin from forming over the hot milk. Serve and drink immediately. Serves 4 to 6.

NOTE: If Mexican chocolate is not available, use 4½ ounces plain semisweet or sweet chocolate (as desired) with two teaspoons ground cinnamon.

In France in the eighteenth century, when chocolate-drinking had become virtually a court ritual, the great ladies of the court each had her own special chocolate recipe which, in many respects, was regarded as a magic formula. Chocolate in those days was thought of not only as a marvelous drink for its own rich sake but as a potion filled with all the rare qualities that had endeared it to the Aztec kings. The flavorings and spices that went into it—sometimes along with secret powders—were supposed to add not only to its flavor but to its effectiveness as well. Mme. du Barry served her special chocolate to the aging Louis and attributed no small part of her success with the monarch to its spicey virtues. Vanilla was invariably added; and often cinnamon or ginger or both gave an extra fillip, while a pinch of pepper provided an actual (but pleasant) bite.

Then, too, great importance was attached to the way in which the chocolate was poured, and to the cups from which it was sipped. The method of pouring was the same as that which is used in France today for *café au lait*. The thick, rich chocolate was served in one pot with hot milk or cream or a mixture of the two in another, and these were poured simultaneously into little porcelain cups so that with more or less of one or the other the resulting beverage would attain the desired consistency—and, of course, its proper power.

Brillat-Savarin, in the nineteenth century, reflected the French national view of chocolate when he wrote: "Chocolate is one of the most effective restoratives. All those who have to work when they might be sleeping, men of wit who feel temporarily deprived of their intellectual powers, those who find the weather oppressive, time dragging, the atmosphere depressing; those who are tormented by some preoccupation which deprives them of the liberty of thought; let all such men imbibe a half litre of *chocolat ambré* . . . and they will be amazed." *Chocolat ambré,* as Brillat-Savarin made it, had a "knob of ambergris the size of a bean, pounded with sugar [added] to a strong cup of chocolate." But for plain hot chocolate (to which he attributed very nearly the same virtues) he followed the strictures laid down by Mme. d'Arestel, Mother Superior of the Convent of the Visitation at Belley. Never boil, said Mme. d'Arestel. Cook gently, let stand and then reheat. And these directions still hold true no matter what chocolate you use, or how it is flavored or seasoned. Unlike coffee and tea, chocolate and cocoa improve on standing. They mellow. Like stew, they improve on being gently reheated. Vanilla is still the best flavoring for chocolate (though orange is delicious, too, as are many kinds of spirits and liqueurs), and both cinnamon and ginger still both add pleasant touches (as does allspice); and a tiny pinch of pepper gives a delightful and hard-to-identify bite.

Here with both vanilla and liqueur is a Superb Hot Chocolate to begin with.

SUPERB HOT CHOCOLATE

6 ounces semisweet chocolate bits	1 tablespoon Grand Marnier
	¼ cup heavy cream
1 pint cream	½ teaspoon vanilla

Melt chocolate in top of double boiler over hot (not boiling) water. Add cream and blend thoroughly. Stir in Grand Marnier. Remove from heat and let stand over hot water. Whip cream until just stiff and add vanilla. Pour chocolate into cups. Top with whipped cream and serve immediately. Serves 4.

This same chocolate may be made using 1 teaspoon vanilla instead of the Grand Marnier. If vanilla is used, the chocolate may be varied with a thin chocolate mint placed in each cup before the hot chocolate is added. This will slowly melt into the chocolate, gradually increasing its minty flavor.

The quality of chocolate cups is still as important to the seeming quality of the beverage as it was two centuries ago in France. They should be rather small as a rule (of about the same capacity as tea cups); and the thinner, finer and costlier the china or porcelain the better they will fulfill their purpose. Your enjoyment of chocolate will be increased immeasurably by the very best cups your budget will afford. Victorian chocolate services occasionally turn up in antique shops and their tall, narrow, straight-sided cups are still the best chocolate cups that have ever been designed. They will make even the plainest of hot chocolate taste like an extravagant luxury—this one, for instance.

PLAIN HOT CHOCOLATE

4½ ounces bitter chocolate
⅓ cup sugar
⅛ teaspoon salt
1½ cups boiling water

4½ cups scalded milk
1 teaspoon vanilla
Whipped cream

Melt chocolate in the top of a double boiler over hot (not boiling) water. Add sugar and salt. Blend. Slowly add the boiling water, stirring as you do so. Then add the scalded milk. Cook over low heat 3 to 4 minutes. Remove from heat and beat with a wire whisk until frothy. Add vanilla. Pour into heated chocolate pot or directly into cups. Pass whipped cream in a bowl. Serves 6 to 8.

For Mocha Chocolate, substitute strong black coffee for the boiling water.

A length of cinnamon stick previously boiled in the water will give a cinnamon flavor if desired.

Several strips of the outer orange-colored part of orange peel may also be boiled in the water for an orange flavor. Do not use the white under-part of the peel; this gives an unpleasant bitter taste.

A small amount of cornstarch added to a hot chocolate or cocoa will give it a richer-seeming, thicker consistency without altering its taste noticeably. The amount used, however, must be small. The thickness should be no more than that of heavy cream. Use ½ teaspoon cornstarch for each cup milk or light cream. Moisten it to paste consistency with a little cold water or milk or cream before stirring it into the heated liquid. Then cook it thoroughly over gentle flame, stirring as you do so, until its full thickening capacity has been reached. Arrowroot may be used instead of cornstarch if desired but as its thickening powers are stronger than those of corn flour, use less of it. One-third teaspoon arrowroot to each cup liquid should be sufficient.

Cocoa contains less cocoa butter than chocolate, and so makes a less rich beverage. Cocoa, the brew, often makes up for the difference with the added richness of cream; and then, too, sugar adds its richness as well. The following Hot Cocoa is certainly not a *lean* drink no matter how it stands in comparison to chocolate.

HOT COCOA

⅓ cup cocoa
¾ cup sugar
¼ teaspoon salt
½ cup water

6 cups milk, scalded
½ teaspoon vanilla
1 pinch cinnamon (optional)
½ cup heavy cream

Combine cocoa, sugar, salt and water in the top of a double boiler. Cook over hot (not boiling) water, stirring constantly, until the sugar is melted. Remove from heat and add scalded milk. Beat with rotary beater until foamy. Return to heat and cook over moderate heat 4 to 5 minutes, stirring frequently. Remove from heat and add vanilla. Add cinnamon also, if desired. Whip cream until stiff and pass separately or add a dollop to each cup of cocoa. Serves 6 to 8.

Cold chocolate and cocoa drinks are quite as delicious as hot ones. Some are rich, some are plain; some are comparatively complex, others are simplicity itself. Here is a cold coffee with chocolate flavor.

COFFEE À LA RUSSE WITH CHOCOLATE

1 ounce semisweet chocolate
¼ cup sugar
⅛ teaspoon salt
1¾ cups boiling water

½ cup milk
½ cup cream (or omit milk and use 1 cup cream)
1 teaspoon vanilla
2 cups strong black coffee

Melt chocolate in the top of a double boiler over hot (not boiling) water. Add sugar, salt and boiling water. Blend. Simmer 5 minutes, stirring frequently. Add milk and cream (or all cream). Cook gently until the mixture comes just barely to a boil. Remove from heat and stir in vanilla and coffee. Beat thoroughly. Chill. Beat again before serving. Serves 4.

Very good and very easy is this Cocoa Sherry Frosted.

COCOA SHERRY FROSTED

1 cup rich milk
¼ cup cocoa

½ cup dry sherry (the best
    available)
½ cup vanilla ice cream

Combine all the ingredients in an electric blender or beat with a rotary beater until thoroughly mixed. Pour into tall, thin, chilled glasses or into goblets. Serves 2 to 3.

The majority of cold chocolate drinks are made with chocolate syrup, and this, of course, is available canned in most markets—and of excellent quality, too. But homemade chocolate syrup can give drinks an individual touch that commercial syrups fall short of. Here are several syrups you can make and keep on hand to use when needed.

BITTERSWEET CHOCOLATE SYRUP

8 ounces bitter chocolate
1¾ cups sugar
¼ teaspoon salt

1⅓ cups boiling water
2 egg yolks
1 teaspoon vanilla

Melt chocolate in the top of a double boiler over hot (not boiling) water. Add sugar and salt; blend. Slowly pour in the boiling water, stirring as you do so. Cook until sugar is completely dissolved. Beat egg yolks until light. Pour some of the hot liquid into yolks, then pour yolk mixture slowly into chocolate, still stirring. Cook 1 minute. Remove from heat. Add vanilla. Store covered in the refrigerator to use as needed. Will keep 1 week. Add to milk or cream—hot or cold—for drinks of all kinds. 3 to 4 teaspoons syrup to 1 cup milk for average taste. Makes 1 pint.

COCOA SYRUP

1½ teaspoons cornstarch
2 tablespoons cold water
1 cup boiling water
1 cup sugar

½ cup plus 1 tablespoon cocoa
½ teaspoon vanilla
1 pinch salt

Moisten cornstarch with the cold water. Combine boiling water and sugar in saucepan and cook 3 to 4 minutes at a full boil. Reduce heat. Blend cocoa with cornstarch mixture and stir into hot syrup. Cook gently about 8 minutes, stirring constantly. Remove from heat and stir in vanilla and salt. Cool. Store covered in the refrigerator to use as needed. Keeps indefinitely. Makes 1 pint plus.

Here is a syrup that offers a somewhat more chocolate flavor than the Cocoa Syrup, is less rich than the Bittersweet Syrup, and keeps indefinitely.

DRINK SYRUP

2¼ cups sugar
1¼ cups water
1¼ tablespoons cornstarch
 2 tablespoons cold water

2½ ounces bitter chocolate, grated
1¼ teaspoons vanilla
1 pinch salt

Combine sugar and water in a saucepan and cook over moderate heat until sugar is melted. Moisten cornstarch with cold water. Stir into hot syrup; blend. Add grated chocolate and cook gently 5 to 10 minutes, stirring constantly. Remove from heat and stir in vanilla and salt. Cool. Store covered in the refrigerator to use as needed. Makes about 3 cups.

Chocolate syrups are particularly useful in making the cold chocolate drinks that are particularly desirable in households with children and teenagers.

CHOCOLATE SODA

For each soda you will need:

2 scoops chocolate ice cream
2 tablespoons whipped cream
 (heaping)

4 tablespoons (¼ cup) Bittersweet Chocolate Syrup (or one of the others)
Club soda
Extra whipped cream
Maraschino cherry and juice

Put 2 scoops of ice cream in the bottom of a tall glass. Add the 2 tablespoons whipped cream, then gently pour on the chocolate syrup. Fill glass half-way with soda. Stir with a long spoon to mix the syrup, cream and ice cream. Fill glass to top slowly with additional soda. Top with extra whipped cream and garnish this with a maraschino cherry. Dribble 1 tablespoon of maraschino cherry juice over the cream so that it runs down into the soda.

A chocolate soda for grownups may be made in the same way as the soda above but with a portion of rum added; or coffee may be used instead of the initial *dosage* of soda (with rum and coffee being added together); or the quantity of chocolate syrup may be reduced to 2 tablespoons and the difference made up with crème de cacao or Grand Marnier.

Chocolate Frosteds are best when made in a blender. This one may be varied in any of the ways suggested above for the soda.

CHOCOLATE FROSTED

For each frosted you will need:

2 scoops chocolate ice cream   4 tablespoons chocolate syrup
½ cup milk   (¼ cup)
                                      Flavoring as desired

Combine all ingredients in blender and whirl until ice cream has been beaten smooth with the milk and syrup. For additional flavoring you may use either coffee, rum, vanilla or any orange liqueur or syrup. Several spoonfuls of rather soft strawberry jam stirred into the frosted after blending makes for a delectable drink indeed. Fattening but fun.

Another favorite among children (and grownups on the sly) is chocolate malted milk, a tall glassful of which is just about equivalent to a full day's needed nourishment.

CHOCOLATE MALTED MILK

½ cup chocolate syrup (Her-   ¼ cup malted milk powder *
shey's or home-made . . . see   ½ cup cream
pages 20–21)   3½ cups ice-cold milk

Combine all ingredients and beat with a rotary beater or in a blender until thoroughly mixed. Serve immediately. Serves 3 to 4.

Crème de cacao is one of the most delicious of all liqueurs. And although it has come to be thought of, through the years, as a lady's drink, you will find that there are many men who will take it without

---

* Malted milk powder is obtainable either plain or chocolate flavored. If the latter is used, reduce the amount of syrup as desired.

too much arm-twisting. One of the most delectable ways of serving it is in combination with coffee. When presented in the following manner, this combination can more than satisfactorily replace a dessert at the close of a rich dinner.

CAFÉ AU CACAO

Half fill a cocktail shaker with finely cracked or shaved ice. Add equal parts lightly sweetened, chilled black coffee (very strong) and crème de cacao. Shake vigorously and quickly. Pour immediately into champagne coupes and serve with short straws. A 1 quart cocktail shakerful will serve 6.

Chocolate Sauces

Chocolate sauce in its simplest form is merely melted chocolate. Melt any chocolate over hot water and, by force of circumstance, there is a sauce. It may be thinned by water or other liquid, enriched by butter or cream or both, sweetened by sugar or syrup and made fluffy with whipped cream or egg white. It may be flavored by any of an almost infinite variety of ingredients. You can, in short—and at no great expense or effort—make melted chocolate into a host of sauces, rich or plain, simple or complex.

The simplest chocolate sauce, of course, is nothing more than chocolate and water, its sweetness governed by the kind of chocolate used—sweet, semisweet or bitter. Here is a good one.

SIMPLE CHOCOLATE SAUCE

6 ounces sweet chocolate *or* 1 6-ounce package semisweet chocolate bits

¾ cup water
1 pinch salt

Combine chocolate with water in top of double boiler and melt over hot water. Stir until smooth. Add pinch of salt. Store in covered jar in refrigerator until needed. Makes about 1½ cups.

If dining were entirely a matter of logic, you would expect that a rich dessert, cake, pudding or cream would take a less rich sauce; but this is not always the case. Richness, for some odd reason, often demands more richness by way of embellishment, and fudge sauce is frequently the very thing that fills the need. Here is a quick and easy one.

CREAMY FUDGE SAUCE

4 ounces German sweet choco-
    late

2 tablespoons water
3 tablespoons cream
1 pinch salt

Combine chocolate and water in a saucepan over very low heat (or hot water) and stir until melted. Remove from heat and stir in cream and salt. Continue to stir until smooth. Serve warm or cold. Makes ¾ cup.

Hot Chocolate Sauce flavored with sherry is also delectable and seems to be especially well suited to puddings of various kinds, as well as plain cakes, of course.

HOT CHOCOLATE SHERRY SAUCE

1½ cups sugar
3 tablespoons butter
4 ounces bitter chocolate,
    grated or chopped

1 cup cream
1 pinch salt
¼ cup sherry
1 teaspoon vanilla

Combine all ingredients except sherry and vanilla in a saucepan. Cook over moderate heat, stirring constantly, until sugar is dissolved. Let come to an easy boil and cook without stirring 7 minutes. Remove from heat and add sherry and vanilla. Keep hot or warm over hot water until needed. Makes about 2 cups.

For an altogether different chocolate sauce try the following sweetened and flavored with honey.

CHOCOLATE HONEY SAUCE WITH ALMONDS (OR WALNUTS)

4 ounces bitter chocolate
⅝ cup strained honey
1 pinch salt

⅓ cup slivered, blanched,
    toasted almonds

Melt chocolate in the top of a double boiler over hot (not boiling) water. Add honey and blend. Cook over low heat until the sauce is smooth. Add a pinch of salt and the almonds. Remove from heat and let stand 15 minutes before serving, stirring from time to time.

Confectioners' sugar gives its own special consistency to sauces, as you will discover with this delectable Confectioners' Chocolate Sauce.

CONFECTIONERS' CHOCOLATE SAUCE

½ cup (¼ pound) butter
2⅓ cups sifted confectioners' sugar

6 ounces bitter chocolate, grated
⅔ cup evaporated milk
1 pinch salt

Combine butter and sugar in the top of a double boiler and cook over hot water, stirring constantly, until sugar is melted. Add chocolate, milk and salt and cook without stirring over moderately low heat 30 minutes. Remove from heat and beat until cool. This may be stored in the refrigerator and reheated over hot water as often as desired. To thin the sauce add the least bit of cream. Makes 3 cups.

Using 1 cup of the above sauce you can make a delectable Orange Chocolate Sauce as follows:

ORANGE CHOCOLATE SAUCE

1 cup Confectioners' Chocolate Sauce
¼ cup strained orange juice

2 tablespoons grated orange rind
2 tablespoons curaçao or Grand Marnier

Combine in top of double boiler and blend over hot water. Serve hot or warm over vanilla—*real* vanilla—ice cream or angel food cake.

And using ½ cup of the Confectioners' Chocolate Sauce you can make a Foamy Rum Sauce.

FOAMY RUM SAUCE

½ cup Confectioners' Chocolate Sauce

½ cup dark rum
1 cup heavy cream, whipped

Combine sauce and rum in the top of a double boiler and heat together over hot water. When thoroughly blended, remove from heat and cool. When cold, fold in the whipped cream.

Egg yolks give the added richness to this delicious Chocolate Ice Cream Sauce.

CHOCOLATE ICE CREAM SAUCE

2 cups milk	1 cup sugar
2½ ounces bitter chocolate	1 pinch salt
4 egg yolks	¾ teaspoon vanilla

Melt chocolate with milk in top of double boiler over hot (not boiling) water. Stir until chocolate is thoroughly blended. Beat egg yolks with sugar and salt until smooth. Add chocolate mixture to beaten eggs and blend; return to top of double boiler and cook, stirring constantly, 5 minutes. Remove from heat and cool. Add vanilla. Serve hot or cold as desired. Makes 2½ cups.

Brown Sugar Sauce has a special flavor all its own and is particularly good over orange sherbet.

BROWN SUGAR SAUCE

8 ounces bitter chocolate	1 pinch salt
2 cups light brown sugar, packed	½ teaspoon vanilla or other flavor
1 cup cream	

Melt chocolate in double boiler over hot (not boiling) water. Add sugar, cream and pinch of salt. Cook, stirring constantly, until sugar is completely dissolved. Continue cooking with frequent stirring until sauce is of desired consistency. Remove from heat and add vanilla. Makes 2 cups.

Sour Cream Chocolate Sauce is another with a distinctive flavor.

SOUR CREAM CHOCOLATE SAUCE

3½ ounces bitter chocolate	1 pinch salt
1¼ cups sugar	1½ cups sour cream

Melt chocolate in double boiler over hot (not boiling) water. Add sugar, salt and cream. Stir once to blend. Increase heat so that water is boiling. Bring mixture in double boiler just to boiling point, and cook without stirring 8 to 10 minutes. Remove from heat and serve sauce warm over puddings, cake or ice cream. Makes about 2¼ cups.

Corn syrup gives this delicious sauce its velvet consistency. Its flavoring is a matter of personal taste. We opt for the Grand Marnier.

FUDGE SAUCE DIVAN

2 ounces bitter chocolate
1 tablespoon butter
⅛ cup boiling water
1 cup sugar

2 tablespoons light corn syrup
1 pinch salt
2 teaspoons vanilla, rum, curaçao
   or Grand Marnier

Melt chocolate with butter in the top of a double boiler over hot (not boiling) water. Blend. Add water, then sugar and corn syrup. Stir until well blended. Place pot over direct heat and bring to a boil. Cook without stirring 5 to 8 minutes. Remove from heat and add pinch of salt. Cool slightly and add the flavoring of your choice. If you like a sauce that hardens when poured on ice cream, cook this the full time. If you wish it to stay soft and runny, cook only 5 minutes. Always serve hot. If made ahead of time, sauce may be reheated over hot water. It may also be stored indefinitely (covered) in the refrigerator. Makes about 1¼ cups.

Some Desserts
with Chocolate Sauce

There are many desserts that people think of as chocolate because they are served with chocolate sauce, or chocolate glaze, or have enough chocolate in some way—grated, shaved, curled—to give the impression of chocolate. A classic is *Poires Hélène*—pears poached in vanilla syrup, then served with vanilla ice cream and chocolate sauce.

POIRES

3 firm ripe pears
2 cups water
⅔ cup sugar

1 teaspoon vanilla
1 quart vanilla ice cream
Fudge Sauce (see below)

Peel, halve and core the pears. Combine water and sugar in a saucepan and bring to a boil. Add pears; reduce the heat to low. Simmer covered about 5 minutes or until the pears are just tender. Turn them gently once. Do not overcook them. Remove from heat and add vanilla. Let pears cool in the syrup.

To serve, divide the ice cream equally on six chilled dessert plates, mounding it neatly. Place half a pear, round-side up, on each portion of cream. Top with the Creamy Fudge Sauce (page 25) or pass it separately. Candied violets are often added by way of embellishment and these may usually be found at food specialty stores. If desired, canned pears may be used instead of fresh. If so, drain them and reduce the syrup over high heat until thick, adding a bit more sugar if needed. Cool and add vanilla to taste. Return the pears to the syrup and let them stand in it an hour or more until serving time. They are even better chilled and make a delicious contrast to hot Fudge Sauce Divan (see page 28). Serves 6.

Raspberries Chantilly with Chocolate Sauce (a fine dessert for a large party) is as easy to make as it is delectable. Here is the recipe for 20 to 24 with proportions that may be reduced for family dining.

RASPBERRIES CHANTILLY WITH CHOCOLATE SAUCE

8 cups fresh ripe rinsed and drained raspberries
1 quart heaviest cream

3 tablespoons powdered sugar, or to taste
Raspberry liqueur (framboise) to taste
Chocolate Sauce (see below)

Rinse, drain and pick over the berries. Whip the cream until just stiff, then whip in the sugar and the liqueur to taste. Chill the cream several hours before serving.

To serve, fold berries and cream together gently and spoon into tall, stemmed glasses. Pass the chocolate sauce (cooled in this case) on the side, and because the cream is itself so light and delicate, the sauce should be relatively light as well (which does not mean skimpy).

A LIGHT SWEET CHOCOLATE SAUCE FOR 24

2 cups water

1½ pounds dark, sweet chocolate, grated or chopped
Honey to taste
Vanilla to taste

Combine water and chocolate in a double boiler and cook over hot (not boiling) water until chocolate is melted. Stir until smooth. Remove from heat and add honey and vanilla to taste. Blend. Stir several times as the sauce cools. Serve at room temperature.

A plain loaf cake of the poundcake sort may be made into a splendid dessert that is a cross between pudding and cake by the use of a rich filling, chopped nuts and a chocolate sauce. In one of Uruguay's leading hotels, just such a dessert is often featured on the menu.

COPA EL GALEON

1 loaf poundcake
1 quart rich Cream Filling (see index)

2 cups chopped filberts
3 cups hot Fudge Sauce (page 28)

Slice a poundcake into 4 or 5 horizontal layers of equal thickness. If the cake has 5 layers, spread four of them with a generous layer of the Cream Filling. Sprinkle the Cream Filling with all but ⅓ cup of the chopped filberts. Put the cake together layer-cake fashion. Chill for 2 hours, the longer the better. When the cake is ice cold, pour the hot fudge sauce over it, coating it completely. Sprinkle top with remaining filberts and serve immediately. Serves 8-10.

Chocolate Pineapple Fondue is a Hirsch creation. Nothing is better by way of dessert for an informal buffet where people are wandering about and may wish to take their sweet in bits and pieces. It may also be served at an informal seated dinner if the table is small enough so that guests can reach the center of attraction. Or it may be served in the living room after dinner along with the coffee. Its essentials are only pineapple chunks, toothpicks, chocolate sauce and a chafing dish or candle warmer.

CHOCOLATE PINEAPPLE FONDUE

40 to 50 drained pineapple chunks, fresh, canned or frozen

12 ounces Maillard's Eagle sweet chocolate (see note below)
⅔ cup butter

Place a toothpick in each of the drained pineapple chunks and arrange them on a sheet of foil or cookie sheet separated from one another. Freeze. Combine chocolate and butter in top of double boiler and cook until the chocolate is completely melted. Blend thoroughly. Keep warm until needed. To serve, place the chocolate sauce in the pan of a chafing dish over hot water (or in the same way on a candle burner); it must be kept hot but not cooking. Around it, arrange the frozen pineapple chunks in a circle. Let each diner dip a pineapple chunk into the hot chocolate sauce. The hot sauce hardens immediately (though it will still have a somewhat creamy consistency), and the heat of the sauce will at the same time thaw the pineapple. Serves 10 to 12. Candied fruits of all kinds, if made ice cold in the freezer, may be used in this same way. Cherries are especially good!

NOTE: Maillard's chocolate, of which there are many different kinds, is usually found in food specialty stores and a search for it will always prove to have been well worth any trouble. Its flavor and quality are superb. In New York it may be found at Verdi's Original Market, 534

Third Avenue, and at Bloomingdale's, Lexington Avenue at 59th Street. It may be purchased from the latter by mail order.

Profiteroles are little cream-filled puff pastries with a chocolate sauce.

PROFITEROLES

For the puffs:

2 tablespoons butter
1 cup water
1 pinch salt

1¼ cups flour, sifted
5 eggs

Combine butter and water in a heavy saucepan and bring to a boil; add salt and the sifted flour all at once. Remove from fire and stir until the mixture leaves the sides of the pan. One by one, beat in 4 of the eggs. Place dough in refrigerator for 1 hour. Beat the remaining egg and set aside.

Butter a cookie sheet and put small balls of the dough (using a teaspoonful of dough for each) on the sheet an inch apart. Brush the tops with the beaten egg and bake about 25 minutes at 325° F. (*or* 20 minutes at 375° F. and 5 minutes at 300° F.). The puffs should be firm when done and a golden brown. Remove to a rack and cut a small gash in the bottom of each for the steam to escape.

For the filling:

1 cup heavy cream
2 tablespoons powdered sugar
½ to 1 teaspoon vanilla or Grand Marnier, curaçao, framboise or Kahlua

Whip cream until just stiff, then beat in sugar and flavoring. When puffs are cold, fill with whipped cream through slit in bottom. Do not remove pastry at slit but leave it so it is hinged, as it were, to close on the cream like a door. Pile puffs in a serving dish and sprinkle with powdered sugar. Serve with a hot fudge sauce passed separately or, for a change, the Orange Chocolate Sauce (page 26). Serves 6-8.

Soufflés are marvelous desserts all by themselves but many are made the more so by the addition of a rich sauce.

COCONUT SOUFFLÉ WITH CHOCOLATE SAUCE

4 eggs, separated
½ cup sugar
1 teaspoon vanilla
3 tablespoons butter
¼ cup sifted flour

1 cup milk
¼ teaspoon salt
1 cup shredded coconut
¼ cup additional shredded
   coconut

Beat the egg yolks until very light and then beat with the sugar until thick and lemon colored. Add the vanilla and set aside. In a double boiler over hot water, melt butter and add the flour; blend. Stir in the milk and salt and cook, stirring constantly, until thickened. Slowly stir in the egg yolk mixture and blend. Cool by setting the pan in a bowl of cold water.

Now beat the egg whites until stiff and fold in 1 cup coconut. Fold this mixture gently into the yolk mixture. Pour into a buttered 1-quart soufflé dish. Sprinkle the top with the additional coconut and bake at 350° F. for 30 minutes. Serve immediately with a chocolate sauce—the Confectioners' Chocolate Sauce (page 26) flavored with vanilla or the Fudge Sauce Divan (page 28) cooked for only 5 minutes. Serves 6-8.

Ice Cream and
Other Frozen Desserts

Despite the fact that there is more vanilla ice cream sold annually in this country than any other kind, it is still safe to assume that chocolate is the favorite flavor. Vanilla, as a rule, is sought not so much for its own sake as for the way it blends with other flavors, the way it takes to different sauces. Chocolate ice cream, on the other hand, is often served just as it comes from the freezer. It is enjoyed because it is chocolate. And this has been the way of it for the past hundred and fifty years, perhaps a bit longer.

George Washington, so it is claimed, owned the first ice cream freezer in this country, but Thomas Jefferson reputedly brought the first ice cream recipe to this country from France. His was a recipe for a vanilla ice cream made in the French fashion with many egg yolks and vanilla bean, a delicious concoction. And it was not until some years later that chocolate ice cream appeared on the scene. But by mid-nineteenth century, the popularity of chocolate ice cream as a special dish for special occasions had surpassed that of vanilla. It is odd that people in this country, where ice cream sells annually by the millions of quarts and even gallons, have not discovered (as they have in Europe) that chocolate ice cream takes as well to sauces of different kinds as vanilla. It is perhaps from lack of culinary daring, or possibly from lack of culinary imagination, that they have missed such treats as chocolate ice cream with maraschino cherries, for instance, or chocolate ice cream with raspberry syrup or chocolate ice cream (as in Italy) with fresh ripe strawberries that have been soaked in Aurum. Surely it is not from any lack of good chocolate ice cream itself, as the following recipes should prove conclusively.

SOME GENERAL RULES FOR ICE CREAM

When making ice cream in a hand-operated freezer, scald, drain, dry and chill the can, cover and dasher before using. Place can in freezer, fill ¾ way to brim with cold or chilled ice cream mixture, adjust dasher and cover securely. Pack with a mixture of 3 parts cracked ice to 1 part rock salt.

For first 5 minutes, turn crank slowly, or until the mixture begins to stiffen noticeably. Then turn as quickly as possible until it is almost impossible to turn any more. Add more ice and salt in the same proportion as above if and when needed. Drain off salt water as the ice melts.

To pack and hold until needed, scoop ice and salt from freezer to about 1 inch below rim of can. Wipe top and rim of can with a clean cloth. Uncover, remove dasher. Scrape ice cream from dasher back into can. Cover cream with lightly oiled paper. Replace cover on can and put stopper of some sort in hole left by removal of dasher. Repack freezer with ice and salt to edge of can cover. Spread ice alone over top of can. Place newspaper or heavy sacking over entire freezer and let stand several hours so that the flavor will have a chance to ripen.

When making ice cream in an electric freezer, follow the manufacturer's direction for your particular model.

When making ice cream in refrigerator trays, unless otherwise specifically directed, it is best to start with a base thickened at least slightly with either flour, cornstarch, eggs or gelatin. The mixture is first frozen to a mush (with the freezer unit set very low), then turned out into a chilled bowl and beaten until light. At this juncture whipped cream is often added for additional richness and better texture. The mixture is then poured back into freezer trays and frozen until firm.

To freeze ice cream in a mold, as for a frozen mousse (see index), pour the mixture, made with heavy cream whipped just until it holds soft peaks, into a mold very lightly greased with a tasteless vegetable oil. Cover tightly either with the mold's own cover or several thicknesses of aluminum foil tied securely in place. Then pack mold (and cover it as well) with a mixture of 4 parts cracked ice to 1 part rock salt. A 6-cup mold will freeze in about 4 hours.

To start with, let's have French Chocolate Ice Cream made with egg yolks and both sweet and bitter chocolate:

FRENCH CHOCOLATE ICE CREAM

6 ounces sweet chocolate
½ ounce bitter chocolate
½ cup sugar
¼ cup water
3 egg yolks, beaten

¼ teaspoon vanilla
1 pinch salt
3½ cups heavy cream, lightly whipped

Melt the two chocolates together in the top of a double boiler over hot (not boiling) water; cool. Combine sugar and water in a small saucepan and boil until the syrup spins a thread. Pour the syrup very slowly over the beaten egg yolks, beating constantly as you do so. Beat until quite stiff. Add the chocolate, vanilla and salt, and blend. Add the lightly whipped cream and blend. Pour into ice cream freezer and freeze. Makes about 1 quart.

This chocolate ice cream is excellent for making the Italian *Tartufo di Cioccolata*, chocolate ice cream balls with chopped cherries which have a coating of either grated or shaved chocolate. Delicious!

TARTUFO DI CIOCCOLATA

1 pint French Chocolate Ice Cream (see above)
2 tablespoons chopped candied cherries

⅓ cup grated semisweet chocolate

Soften the ice cream slightly and blend with the chopped cherries. Form into four balls of equal size. Roll these in grated chocolate to coat them evenly, place on foil or a tin dish, keeping them separate from one another and freeze until needed. Serve with a topping of whipped cream lightly sweetened and flavored as desired (use vanilla, rum, liqueur or orange).

This Plain Chocolate Ice Cream is *plain* only in that it lacks the egg yolks and hence some of the richness of the ice cream above. It is not plain in the sense of being inferior. It is, in fact, very good indeed.

PLAIN CHOCOLATE ICE CREAM

2½ ounces bitter chocolate
2 cups milk
1¼ cups sugar
1 pinch salt

1¾ teaspoons vanilla
2 cups heavy cream, whipped stiff

Combine chocolate and milk in top of double boiler and cook over hot (not boiling) water until chocolate is melted. Add sugar and salt. Stir until sugar is dissolved. Remove from heat and beat with a whisk until frothy and cool. Add vanilla and fold in whipped cream. Pour into freezer and freeze. Makes about 2 quarts.

Many ice creams are made with a custard base, using eggs and milk or cream, of course, and either flour or cornstarch.

CHOCOLATE CUSTARD ICE CREAM

2 ounces bitter chocolate	2 eggs, separated
1 cup milk	2 cups light cream
¾ cup sugar	1 pinch salt
2 tablespoons cornstarch	2 teaspoons vanilla

In the top of a double boiler melt the chocolate over hot (not boiling) water; cool. Scald the milk. Combine sugar and cornstarch. Pour the hot milk over the sugar-cornstarch mixture and blend. Pour into top of double boiler and cook about 20 minutes, or until smooth and thickened, stirring frequently. Beat egg yolks until lemon colored and slowly stir them into the milk. Add chocolate and blend. Cook about 5 minutes, stirring from time to time. Remove from heat and cool. Add cream and blend. Strain into a freezer tray and freeze to a mush. Meanwhile, beat the egg whites with the pinch of salt until stiff. Turn the cream from the tray into a mixing bowl. Add vanilla and beat until creamy with a rotary beater. Fold in the beaten egg whites. Return to freezer tray and finish freezing. Serves 6 to 8.

Frozen mousses are ice creams frozen in molds or refrigerator trays without the constant churning action of a dasher of some kind, which is the very thing that gives regular ice creams their velvet smoothness. Most frozen mousses use whipped cream alone in lieu of liquid, but some use both whipped cream and beaten egg whites. Many gain added richness from a custard base. The one that follows, Molasses Chip Mousse, uses chocolate syrup and heavy cream.

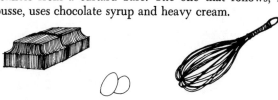

MOLASSES CHIP MOUSSE

4 cups heavy cream
5½ ounces chocolate syrup
(Hershey's or homemade)

1 pound chocolate molasses
chip candy, crushed

Whip the cream until it holds its shape. Do not over-whip. Gradually beat in the syrup. Fold in the crushed candy, which should be of a rather irregular consistency. Pour into 2 6-cup molds (or 1 large one or refrigerator trays) and freeze. Makes 2½ quarts plus.

New Orleans Delight is the name of this ice cream and it has just about everything in its favor—egg yolks for richness, marshmallows for velvet consistency and coffee for added flavor. Delectable!

NEW ORLEANS DELIGHT

8 ounces dark sweet chocolate
1 5-ounce package miniature
marshmallows
4 cups heavy cream

½ cup sugar
1¼ cups strong black coffee
6 egg yolks
1 pinch salt

Combine chocolate, marshmallows and ½ cup of the cream in the top of a double boiler and cook over hot (not boiling) water until the chocolate is melted, stirring frequently. Add sugar and coffee and stir until the sugar is dissolved. Beat the egg yolks with the pinch of salt and ½ cup of the cream until light. Pour this slowly into the chocolate mixture and blend. Cook until thick over low heat, stirring constantly, about 10 minutes. Remove from heat and cool. Add remaining cream, blend, pour into freezer and freeze. Serve with the Fudge Sauce Divan (page 28), cooked for 8 minutes. Makes about 1½ quarts.

Five Minute Ice Cream actually takes a bit less than five minutes from the time you start making it to the time it goes into the freezer.

FIVE MINUTE ICE CREAM

2 cups whipping cream
1 teaspoon vanilla
4 egg whites
1 pinch salt

1 16-ounce can Hershey's chocolate syrup or homemade (see index)
½ cup chopped pecans

Whip cream just until it holds its shape; add vanilla and beat in lightly. Whip egg whites with pinch of salt until stiff. Fold egg whites and cream together. Combine with chocolate syrup. Fold in nuts. Pour into refrigerator tray and freeze. Serves 6 to 8.

One of the most beautiful of all French desserts is the so-called *soufflé glacé*, which is actually a mousse (see index). And of its many variations the most glamorous (to our way of thinking) is the *soufflé glacé au chocolat*, Frozen Chocolate Soufflé.

FROZEN CHOCOLATE SOUFFLÉ

6 ounces semisweet chocolate	4 egg yolks
1½ cups sugar	2 cups heavy cream, whipped
⅔ cup water	

Melt chocolate in a double boiler over hot (not boiling) water; cool. Combine sugar and water in a saucepan and boil until it spins a thread or registers 230° F. on your candy thermometer. Beat the egg yolks until very thick and lemon colored, and continue beating as you pour the hot syrup slowly over them. Beat in the melted chocolate. Continue whipping as the mixture cools and increases in volume. When very light and fluffy, fold in the whipped cream. Lightly butter a strip of wax paper about three inches wide and about 2 inches longer than the perimeter of a 1½-quart soufflé dish. Gently pour the soufflé mixture into the dish until just level with the top of the dish. Form a circle of the oiled paper to fit precisely inside the rim of the soufflé dish. Slide this down about ½ inch into the dish between the soufflé mixture and the porcelain. If it does not stand erect at the joint, make a small fold to hold it together. Pour in the remaining soufflé mixture. Tie a thread around the collar if necessary. Cover with additional wax paper and freeze 4 hours. Before serving, remove top sheet of paper and collar. If the collar is reluctant to leave the dish, hold a warm towel around the rim for 1 minute. Decorate soufflé with whipped cream, if desired, and candied cherries for good measure and some curls of semisweet chocolate. Serves 8 to 10.

A velvet, as its name implies, is a dessert of great richness. Here is a Chocolate Egg Yolk Velvet, a frozen cream of marvelous flavor and consistency.

CHOCOLATE EGG YOLK VELVET

⅔ cup cocoa
2 cups sugar
½ cup water
8 egg yolks

1 generous pinch salt
½ teaspoon vanilla
⅛ cup brandy
6 cups heavy cream, whipped

Combine cocoa, sugar and water in a saucepan; bring to a boil and cook until your candy thermometer registers 238° F. (the soft-ball stage).

Beat the egg yolks with the pinch of salt until very thick, then slowly pour the hot syrup over them, beating constantly (an electric beater is best for this) and continue to beat until the mixture forms peaks. Beat in vanilla and brandy. Fold in the whipped cream. Turn into a large mold or small individual ones. Freeze. Makes about 2½ quarts.

For a Mocha Velvet blend 1 tablespoon powdered coffee into the syrup just before pouring it over the egg yolks.

The parfait in France and the parfait in America are two very different desserts. Ours is made of ice cream with fruits and sauces layered and arranged in special tall glasses, which come to the table with a topping of whipped cream and additional fruit for decoration. The French parfait is a frozen mold such as this Chocolate-Peppermint Parfait.

CHOCOLATE-PEPPERMINT PARFAIT

8 to 10 thin chocolate-covered
   peppermints
⅔ cup sugar
¼ cup water

2 egg whites
1½ cups whipping cream
1 teaspoon vanilla

Melt chocolate peppermints in the top of a double boiler over hot (not boiling) water; cool. Combine sugar and water in a saucepan and boil until the syrup spins a thread (230° F. on your candy thermometer). Beat egg whites until they hold peaks. Slowly pour the hot syrup over the beaten whites, beating as you do so. Continue beating vigorously until the mixture is thick and creamy. Mix ½ cup of the cream with the vanilla and melted chocolate peppermints. Fold this gently but thoroughly into the egg white mixture. Beat the remaining cream until stiff and fold into the mixture also. Turn into a mold or glass bowl and freeze until firm. If frozen in a mold, turn out on a chilled dish before serving. Serves 4 to 6.

Another delicious cream frozen in a mold is the Sicilian *Cassata*. This, of course, is not usually a chocolate dessert but this particular version not only has a chocolate flavor imparted by a chocolate liqueur, but bits of sweet chocolate scattered through it.

CASSATA ALLA SICILIANA

Sliced sponge cake to line and cover a 9½ × 5¼ × 2¾-inch loaf pan
1¼ pounds ricotta cheese
2 cups sugar

1 teaspoon vanilla
¼ cup crème de cacao
¼ cup sweet chocolate bits
¼ cup mixed candied fruits, cut in small pieces

Line bottom and sides of loaf pan with slices of cake cut not more than ½-inch thick. Fit the slices together as closely as possible. In a mixing bowl, combine cheese, sugar, vanilla and liqueur. Beat with an electric beater until creamy. Fold in chocolate bits and candied fruits. Pour into cake-lined tin. Top with another layer of cake, also closely fitted together. Press cake down slightly. Cover tightly with foil. Freeze at least 4 hours. To serve, turn out on a cold serving plate. Sprinkle top of *Cassata* with powdered sugar and cocoa in equal parts. Decorate if desired with lightly sweetened whipped cream. Serves 8 to 10.

And still another delectable frozen mold is this Chocolate Macaroon Fruit Cream.

CHOCOLATE MACAROON FRUIT CREAM

½ cup sugar
½ cup hot water
4 ounces dark sweet chocolate, grated
6 eggs, separated
2 cups heavy cream, whipped

12 dry almond macaroons, crumbled
¼ pound candied cherries, halved
1 tablespoon brandy

Combine sugar and water in a saucepan and boil 5 minutes. Add the chocolate and stir until dissolved. Beat the egg yolks until thick and lemon colored. Slowly pour the hot chocolate syrup over the egg yolks, beating constantly. Continue beating as the mixture cools. Beat the egg whites until stiff. Fold into the yolk mixture. Beat the cream until stiff and fold this into the mixture also. Fold in macaroon crumbs, bit by bit, and the cherries and brandy. Pour into a 2-quart mold and freeze until just firm. Turn out on a cold dish before serving. Decorate with additional candied cherries and shaved chocolate.

Chocolate ices are a rarity in this country but before going on to the unfrozen creams we should give at least one just to prove how good they can be.

CHOCOLATE ORANGE ICE

4 ounces bitter chocolate
2 teaspoons gelatin
3½ cups plus 2 tablespoons water
    Grated rind of 1 orange

2 cups sugar
½ teaspoon grated lemon rind
1 teaspoon vanilla
½ cup strained fresh orange
    juice

Melt chocolate over hot (not boiling) water; cool. Soften gelatin in 2 tablespoons cold water; set aside. Combine 3 cups water with sugar in small saucepan and heat gently until sugar is dissolved. Increase heat and boil syrup rapidly 5 minutes without stirring. Remove from heat and add orange and lemon rind. Add gelatin and stir until dissolved. Cool to lukewarm.

Now gradually pour the warm gelatin mixture into the chocolate, beating with a rotary beater as you do so. Add vanilla and orange juice and blend. Pour into refrigerator tray, cover with foil and freeze until the edges are hard but the middle is still mushy. Turn into bowl again and beat until smooth. Return to freezer tray, cover again with foil and freeze until hard. Remove from refrigerator about 15 minutes before serving. Makes 1 quart.

Creams, Custards,
Puddings, and
Molded Desserts

The arrangement of a cookbook would be a simple enough matter if dishes were themselves neatly and precisely of this or that category, or if the names of different categories were applicable only to specific kinds of dishes. When you say "pudding," the word connotes to most people some special kind of dish, of course; and in most cases this is a contained dish, served probably from its cooking vessel—such as rice pudding, or an Indian pudding. To others, the word may bring something altogether different to mind. And to still others, it may evoke images of several different kinds of dishes. A chocolate pudding, for example, may be a baked custard or it may be of a bread- or cake-like consistency (baked or steamed) or it may have no form whatever and be more on the order of a boiled custard (as is the way with chocolate puddings made from commercial mixes). Or it may be a combination of custard-like cream and cake. As beauty is said to be in the eye of the beholder, so puddings are puddings in the eye of the beholder. One man's pudding may well be another man's pie or icebox cake or even conceivably something as elegant as a *charlotte Malakoff* traveling incognito. So if the progression that we have followed in the following recipes seems arbitrary and capricious to some, it will, we hope, seem logical to others.

Custards may be either boiled (though never *really* boiled at all) or baked; and while the former if sufficiently rich in egg yolks and cream will become firm when chilled (and so become puddings), the latter invariably have a firmness. Boiled custards may be made of such a consistency, however, that whether chilled or not they will remain creamy. In French culinary parlance, a custard is a cream, *crème*. The *crème anglaise* of the French is a light "boiled" custard sauce; the *crème pâtissière* is a rich custard filling thickened with cornstarch or flour. All custards, of course, are made with eggs and milk or cream or both, and sugar, and flavorings. As a security measure to prevent curdling, boiled custards, even the thinner, lighter sort, may have a small admixture of flour or cornstarch (1 teaspoon cornstarch, for instance, for a mixture of, say, 4 egg yolks and 2 cups milk). But boiled custards by nature, unlike the baked variety, lend themselves to variations which depend chiefly on how the eggs are combined with the other ingredients—whether they are separated or not, whether their whites are beaten stiff before addition, whether the yolks are fully cooked or partially cooked by being beaten with hot liquid—and whether the cream (if used) is plain or whipped, and when it is added (*whipped cream,* bear in mind, must always be added to a *cold* mixture if you want it to stay whipped; beaten egg whites, on the other hand, may go into a warm mixture). Soft custards are points of departure for a multitude of desserts which, when done, bear little relation to the custard they began with and even less to each other. The experienced cook with a gifted imagination can evolve a variety of delectable desserts for herself without any recipes at all by blending and folding and flavoring the basic ingredients in different ways and adding to them, as desired, chopped candied fruits, crushed fresh fruits, chopped nuts, macaroon crumbs, ladyfingers or cubes or slices of cake. And the inexperienced cook with recipes to follow should discover soon enough that even the elaborate desserts that start with a custard of some sort are easy enough to make provided they are given the requisite attention. This at most is a matter of minutes.

Perhaps the best-known of all custard desserts is the floating island, usually made with a vanilla-flavored custard. Made with a chocolate custard, however, it is popular in France, with its name changed to *Boules Sur Chocolat.* Or if you like, using the vanilla custard, you can have chocolate instead of gleaming white meringue islands.

BOULES SUR CHOCOLAT

4½ cups milk	8 eggs, separated
2 teaspoons vanilla *	⅔ cup regular granulated sugar
2¼ cups superfine granulated sugar	⅔ cup cocoa
	1 pinch salt

Combine milk, vanilla and 1 cup fine sugar in a large heavy skillet.

* A 3 to 4 inch length of vanilla bean gives immeasurably better flavor than the extract. Use it by all means if you can and remove from the milk after the meringues have been poached.

Over lowest possible heat, bring just to a simmer. Stir until sugar is dissolved. Beat the egg whites (at room temperature) until they hold soft peaks, then bit by bit beat in the remaining 1¼ cups fine sugar. Beat until stiff and satiny. Remove the hot milk from heat for a minute. Using 2 tablespoons, mold the meringue into balls and drop them gently into the hot milk so that they do not touch. Return pan to lowest heat and barely simmer 4 minutes, turning the meringues carefully after 2 minutes. Remove from milk with a slotted spoon and let drain on a clean towel until needed. Reserve the milk.

Now in a 6-cup double boiler (or larger) combine the granulated sugar, cocoa, salt and egg yolks. Blend. Slowly pour the hot milk from the skillet into the yolk mixture, stirring as you do so. Place over hot water and cook gently, stirring constantly, until the custard is thick enough to coat the spoon. This does not mean *to stick* to the spoon as a mayonnaise might stick, but to coat it with a heavy film when the spoon is withdrawn from the mixture. Remove from heat and cool. Stir several times in the process. When cold, pour into a glass serving dish. Arrange the meringues on top and chill at least 1 hour.

If you wish to make chocolate meringues, add ¼ cup cocoa to the egg whites while you are beating in the sugar, or more if desired. The chocolate meringues are very good indeed if the vanilla custard on which they float is also flavored with rum or any one of the orange liqueurs.

With no great change of method and virtually no change of ingredients, Simple Chocolate Custard (next recipe) can be made into a dessert that gives a lavish effect. The whipped cream, in this instance, is folded into the custard instead of being heaped on it just before serving. And a flavoring of good brandy can work wonders with any dessert.

In Brazil little individual molds of custard called *Copinhos Delicia* are made of vanilla and chocolate custard, half and half, the one very carefully poured on top of the other before chilling. Before serving, these molds are sprinkled with cinnamon, then topped with the sweetened whipped cream. Chocolate and orange custards are excellent together in this way, or chocolate and a custard flavored with liqueur.

A word must be said here about the custard-like desserts that may be made from the packaged pudding mixes to be found in virtually all markets today. These mixes, on the whole, are excellent indeed; and certainly they are easy to use. Some require nothing but the addition of cold milk. To achieve any kind of distinction with them, however, they must be doctored. And if you are going to doctor packaged mixes, you might as well make homemade desserts start to finish. The cooking in most cases is a matter of minutes. You may save pot and pan-washing by use of the packaged mix. But the cost of the added ingredients you need to achieve distinction with a mix may be high. For where good basic ingredients and careful preparation can make a homemade dessert a mouth-watering affair, only the very best embellishments will offset the packaged taste and consistency of the mix. And to add them with telling effect requires the time, effort and dish-washing that was sidestepped by use of the mix in the first place. Also homemade desserts using the costliest ingredients in profusion will cost less in the long run than those made from packaged mixes.

Of the molded custards, one of the simplest is the following:

SIMPLE CHOCOLATE CUSTARD

4 tablespoons sugar
1 tablespoon hot water
2 tablespoons grated bitter
  chocolate
2 cups milk, scalded

3 egg yolks
1 teaspoon vanilla
1 cup heavy cream, whipped
2 tablespoons powdered sugar

Combine 1 tablespoon sugar with the hot water and chocolate in the top of a double boiler over hot water and cook until the chocolate is melted, stirring frequently. Scald the milk; pour into the chocolate mixture and blend. Beat the egg yolks with the remaining 3 tablespoons sugar until light. Slowly pour the hot chocolate mixture into the yolks, beating constantly. Return all to double boiler and cook, stirring constantly, until thick. Remove from heat and cool, stirring several times in the process. Add vanilla. Pour into individual molds that have been rinsed in cold water. Chill several hours. Turn out on cold dessert plates before serving and top with whipped cream sweetened with powdered sugar.

Zabaione or *Zabaglione* or *Sabayon* is an Italian custard which may be served by itself, warm or cold, or may be used as a sauce over cake or other dessert. When chilled, like any other custard, it tends to thicken. And if whipped cream is folded into it, it becomes a mousse. Generally its only flavor is the Marsala with which, in conjunction with egg yolks and sugar, it is made. With chocolate added it becomes a different dessert altogether, though still called by one of its European names.

A SIMPLE CHOCOLATE ZABAIONE

6 egg yolks	2 ounces grated dark sweet
1 pinch salt	chocolate
6 tablespoons sugar	⅔ cup Marsala

In the top of a double boiler, beat the egg yolks with salt and half the sugar; add chocolate and blend. Using a wire whisk, beat in the remaining sugar and the wine. Place the mixture over boiling water and, beating continuously with the whisk, cook as the mixture foams up in the pot and begins to thicken. Keep beating until chocolate is melted. Do not overcook. Pour into sherbet glasses and serve warm, cool or chilled. Or, serve as a sauce if you desire. Serves 4 as dessert.

Pots de crème are rich little custards served in individual cups with handles, made especially for this purpose. These custards may, of course, be served in plain custard cups (pottery or Pyrex) but somehow, the special dishes seem to give a special richness, which is a very great richness indeed in the following:

CHOCOLATE POTS DE CRÈME

1 cup each milk and cream	6 egg yolks, well-beaten
1 pound Maillard's sweet choco-	
late (see note page 31)	

Scald the milk and cream; add the chocolate and cook, stirring constantly, over moderate heat until the chocolate is melted. Bring just to the boiling point. Remove from heat. Pour over beaten egg yolks slowly, beating as you do so. Strain through a fine sieve into small cups and cool, then chill thoroughly. Serves 8.

For a somewhat less rich dessert, use ½ pound of any sweet chocolate other than the Maillard's, and cook and chill as above.

A good chocolate mousse is about on a par with *pots de crème* for richness, but its consistency is (or should be) somewhat lighter due to the fact that it contains beaten egg white and more often than not whipped cream. One of the best is this Mocha Mousse.

MOCHA MOUSSE

2 tablespoons very strong black coffee
3 ounces Mallard's sweet choc-olate (see note page 31)

4 eggs, separated
½ cup sugar
1 pinch salt
1½ cups heavy cream, whipped

Melt chocolate with coffee in the top of a double boiler over hot (not boiling) water. Stir until smooth, then set aside. Beat the egg yolks with the sugar and salt until thick and lemon colored. Add the cooled chocolate and beat until thoroughly blended. Beat the egg whites until stiff but not dry and fold into the mixture. Fold in the whipped cream. Pour into a dry 2-quart mold or individual molds and chill thoroughly. To serve, turn out on a cold serving dish or dessert plates and, if desired, decorate with additional lightly sweetened whipped cream.

The best plain chocolate mousse (if it can be called such) is this one from Paris.

FRENCH CHOCOLATE MOUSSE

8 ounces semisweet chocolate
3 tablespoons boiling water
½ cup plus 2 tablespoons butter

6 eggs, separated
½ cup heavy cream, whipped
5 tablespoons sugar

Melt chocolate with boiling water in the top of a double boiler over hot water; stir until smooth, add butter and blend. Beat the egg yolks until thick and lemon colored, add the chocolate mixture and beat again. Cool. Whip the cream and add the sugar, then whip again. Beat the egg whites until stiff. Fold cream and whites gently into the chocolate mixture, blending thoroughly. Pour into a mold or glass bowl or individual molds and chill. Serves 6 to 8.

Occasionally you will find a chocolate mousse that is made without cream. On the face of it, this would seem to be a simpler, plainer dessert but the lack of cream is often made up for by the addition of butter. And in the following recipe, the flavor of Grand Marnier adds a richness all its own.

CHOCOLATE MOUSSE WITH GRAND MARNIER

4 ounces semisweet chocolate
4 eggs, separated
2 tablespoons softened butter
3 tablespoons Grand Marnier

¼ cup very finely diced pre-
   served orange peel
1 pinch salt

Melt chocolate in the top of a double boiler over hot (not boiling) water; set aside to cool. Beat the egg yolks until thick and lemon colored, add the cooled chocolate and butter and beat again. Stir in the Grand Marnier and diced peel. Beat the egg whites with a pinch of salt until stiff. Beat about ⅓ of them into the chocolate mixture; gently fold in the remaining whites. Turn into a glass bowl or mold or 6 individual molds and chill. Serves 6.

Crème Duchesse is much the same as the creamless mousse in theory, but in actuality it is one of the richest desserts imaginable—and well worth every calorie:

CRÈME DUCHESSE

8 ounces dark, sweet chocolate
4 eggs, separated
½ cup sugar

½ cup (¼ pound) butter,
   softened
Whipped cream, lightly sweet-
   ened and flavored with brandy

Melt the chocolate in the top of a double boiler over hot (not boiling) water; cool. Beat the egg yolks until frothy, add the sugar and continue beating until thick and lemon colored. Add the chocolate and beat again; add the softened butter and beat until the mixture is thick and creamy. Whip the egg whites until stiff and fold in gently. Pour into a 6-cup oiled ring mold and chill until set. Before serving, turn out on a cold dish and fill center with sweetened whipped cream flavored with brandy. Serves 4 to 6.

Evaporated milk as it comes from the can has a taste that many find unpleasant. If the milk is chilled and whipped and added to a dessert like whipped cream, this seems to disappear. And not only does it disappear when the milk is cooked, but the milk itself gives to any dish a very special richness. Such is the way in this Chocolate Mold.

CHOCOLATE MOLD

8 ounces sweet chocolate
2 tablespoons butter
½ cup evaporated milk
4 eggs, separated
1 teaspoon gelatin

2 tablespoons cold water
2 tablespoons boiling water
1 cup heavy cream
1 tablespoon powdered sugar
1 tablespoon curaçao

Combine chocolate, butter and milk in the top of a double boiler and cook over hot water until the chocolate is melted, stirring constantly. Beat egg yolks and pour the hot chocolate mixture over them slowly, beating as you do so. Return to double boiler and cook 1 minute. Moisten gelatin with cold water; add boiling water and stir until dissolved. Add to egg yolk mixture and blend. Beat egg whites until stiff and fold into chocolate mixture gently but thoroughly. Pour into a mold rinsed in cold water and chill several hours. Whip cream with powdered sugar, then add the curaçao. Before serving, turn the mold out on a cold dish and mask with the whipped cream. Sprinkle with shaved bitter chocolate if desired. Serves 6.

Marshmallows melted in milk, then chilled, give a consistency much like that of cream or custard. And when whipped cream is folded in, the effect is for all the world like that of a mousse.

CHOCOLATE MARSHMALLOW MOLD

2 ounces bitter chocolate
1 cup milk
¼ pound marshmallows (about 20)

¾ teaspoon vanilla
1 pinch salt
1 cup heavy cream

Combine chocolate, milk and marshmallows in the top of a double boiler and cook over hot water, stirring frequently, until the chocolate and marshmallows are melted. Remove from heat. Stir in vanilla and salt. Cool. Whip cream until it just holds a shape. Fold this into the marshmallow mixture. Pour into a lightly oiled mold or refrigerator tray and chill until firm. Serve with additional whipped cream if desired or an orange sauce. Serves 4 to 6.

Blancmange in the old days was a popular family dessert both in this country and abroad. It was (and still is or should be) a cornstarch pudding, and while its consistency had (and should have today) a certain solidity—enough so that it would hold various fanciful shapes —it was not in the least rubbery with gelatin and, in fact, often had no gelatin at all. The increasing use of gelatin through the years was probably the cause of its downfall, for with gelatin virtually any kind of milk-flour mixture could be molded as *blancmange,* although it had nothing but its shape to recommend it.

CHOCOLATE BLANCMANGE

3 ounces bitter chocolate, grated	½ cup sugar
2½ cups milk	4 tablespoons plus 1 teaspoon cornstarch
1 teaspoon grated orange rind	⅛ teaspoon salt
¼ teaspoon cinnamon	1 teaspoon vanilla

Combine chocolate with 2 cups of the milk, orange rind and cinnamon in a saucepan and cook over low heat until the chocolate is melted, stirring frequently. Combine sugar, cornstarch and salt with remaining ½ cup milk and blend thoroughly. Slowly pour into the chocolate mixture. Stir constantly until thickened. Place pan over hot water, cover and cook over very low heat 10 minutes. Remove from heat, and stir in vanilla. Pour through a fine sieve into a lightly oiled 1-quart mold. Cool, then chill several hours. To serve, unmold on cold dish and top with whipped cream if desired. Serves 4 to 6.

Chocolate Blancmange, is of course, the ancestor of what we today generally call chocolate pudding. More or less cornstarch makes it stiffer or creamier. As *Blancmange,* it invariably has a stiffness; as pudding, on the other hand, it may have almost any consistency.

One of the most beautiful of all desserts is Bavarian cream. It is lovely to look at, delicious to taste and, all things considered, very easy to make. It's a dessert for family and festivities alike, and particularly good when made with chocolate.

CHOCOLATE BAVARIAN CREAM

2½ ounces bitter chocolate	1½ teaspoons vanilla
1 tablespoon gelatin	1 tablespoon rum
¼ cup strong, cold, black coffee	1 pinch salt
5 eggs, separated	2 cups heavy cream
⅓ cup sugar	¼ cup sugar, additional

Melt chocolate in top of double boiler over hot (not boiling) water; cool. Moisten gelatin with cold coffee; set over hot water and stir until completely dissolved. Beat egg yolks with ⅓ cup sugar until very thick and lemon colored; they should nearly double in volume. Add chocolate and gelatin; stir in vanilla and rum. Beat the egg whites with pinch of salt until stiff but not dry. Fold into the chocolate mixture gently but thoroughly. Beat the cream until just barely stiff with the additional sugar. Blend this gently into the chocolate mixture also. Turn into a large mold that has been rinsed in cold water, cover with wax paper and chill several hours. Unmold on a cold dish before serving and garnish with whipped cream if desired—very lightly sweetened and itself garnished with shavings or curls of bittersweet chocolate. Serves 8 to 10.

A Bavarian cream, if desired, may be made in a soufflé dish with a collar to give it height in precisely the same way as the Soufflé Glacé (page 39).

Many of the best French desserts combine a cream of one sort or another with cake; and of these perhaps the best known are the ones that combine the cream with either macaroons or ladyfingers, or sometimes both. Some are made in a mold, the various *charlottes*, for instance; others, such as the *pavé au chocolat*, are composed in such a way that they *seem* to have been made in molds. Both kinds, ideologically, are probably ancestors of what we in this country have long called icebox cakes.

A word should be said at this point about the ladyfingers available in most stores. These are usually not like real ladyfingers at all. The real ladyfinger is a wispy light nothing of crispness that seems to dissolve in much the same way that a well-made meringue turns into nothing on the tongue. Commercially packaged ladyfingers, on the other hand, have a soft, rather cake-like interior and may even be soft and cake-like on the exterior as well. These may provide a very good dessert, but they may give something altogether different from what the recipe intended. If possible, buy ladyfingers from a baker who knows how to make them. Or bake them yourself. They are not difficult. If you do buy commercially packaged ladyfingers, however, they will be improved for further culinary use by a brief toasting or crisping in a slow oven.

Ladyfingers give the characteristic touch to most dessert *charlottes*. Usually moistened with some liqueur or brandy, they are used to line a mold (and sometimes form a top for it), thus making a fragile wall of cake to contain the cream filling, which may be plain whipped cream stiffened with gelatin, or a rich custard with whipped cream folded into it or the buttery almond cream flavored with kirsch that is the hallmark of a *charlotte Malakoff*. The cream for a *charlotte russe*, more often than not, is plain, but this may be made very fancy indeed, as is the case in this Chocolate *Charlotte*.

CHOCOLATE CHARLOTTE RUSSE

The mold specially made for *charlottes* is a round, flat-bottomed metal affair with vertical sides 3 to 4 inches high. Use one if possible for it will give the *charlotte* a distinctive shape that somehow seems to make the flavor and consistency of the filling richer and more luscious. If you lack such a mold, a soufflé dish will give approximately the same effect.

5 envelopes unflavored gelatin	½ cup plus 1 tablespoon hot
½ cup strong black coffee	water
1¼ cups milk, scalded	¼ teaspoon salt
6 ounces bitter chocolate	2 teaspoons vanilla
2 cups sugar	2 cups heavy cream
	12 ladyfingers, split

Moisten the gelatin with cold coffee; pour on the hot milk and stir until the gelatin is dissolved. In the top of a double boiler over hot (not boiling) water, melt the chocolate. Add 1 cup of the sugar and the hot water. Stir until the sugar is melted. Add the gelatin mixture, the remaining cup of sugar, the salt and vanilla. Blend. Refrigerate until very thick but not quite set. Beat with a wire whisk until light and fluffy. Whip cream until just stiff and fold into the chocolate mixture. Grease a mold lightly and line it with the ladyfingers set vertically edge to edge and flat-side out. In the bottom arrange the remaining ladyfingers flat-side down like the spokes of a wheel (or in any pattern you desire). Gently pour on the prepared chocolate cream. Refrigerate (lightly covered) about 4 hours. Unmold onto a chilled serving plate and garnish with additional whipped cream, sweetened or not as desired. Serves 8.

The *charlotte Malakoff* is one of the great desserts of the French classic tradition and like so many French dishes, it gives an impression, by means of its luscious taste and texture, of great effort expended in its making. It is, actually, a rather easy dessert, but its basic requirements must be followed to the letter: the *charlotte* mold, for instance, must be completely covered with ladyfingers—bottom and sides alike—which have been moistened with a liqueur, and the cream filling must in turn be topped with ladyfingers. To make the ladyfingers fit the mold, it is necessary to trim some of them to pointed wedges so that they will fan out on the bottom and top of the mold with their sharp pointed ends at the center. The filling for a *charlotte Malakoff* is an almond cream which is often combined with strawberries or raspberries; or it may be flavored with chocolate in which case the fruit is omitted.

CHARLOTTE MALAKOFF WITH CHOCOLATE

24 ladyfingers, split
⅓ cup curaçao or other orange liqueur
⅓ cup water
4 ounces semisweet chocolate
¼ cup strong black coffee
1 cup (½ pound) sweet butter
1 cup finest granulated sugar
¼ cup additional orange liqueur
¼ teaspoon almond extract
1¼ cups very finely ground almonds (about 7 ounces whole, blanched)
2 cups heavy cream

Place the split ladyfingers close together on a cake rack. Combine ⅓ cup curaçao with water and sprinkle this over the ladyfingers. Turn them and sprinkle the other side. They should be moist but not wet. Let them stand while you prepare the filling.

Melt chocolate with coffee in the top of a double boiler over hot (not boiling water); blend and set aside. Cream the butter and sugar until very light and fluffy. Beat in the additional curaçao and almond extract. Add the chocolate and blend thoroughly. Stir in the ground almonds. Whip the cream.

Cover bottom of the *charlotte* mold with lightly oiled wax paper. Cover this with the trimmed ladyfingers (see above) fanning out from the center. Stand split ladyfingers, flat-side out, edge to edge around the sides of the mold.

Fold whipped cream into the almond mixture. Blend gently but thoroughly. Pour ⅓ of the cream filling into the mold, cover this with a layer of ladyfinger halves; add another ⅓ of the cream, another layer of ladyfingers and then repeat layers a third time. Level top with spatula. Now you may either cover the mold with a sheet of lightly oiled wax paper or you may add a final layer of ladyfingers (which you then cover with wax paper). Chill 6 to 8 hours or overnight. To unmold, remove paper and loosen sides of mold by running a knife blade carefully around the edge. Invert onto a chilled serving plate. Garnish with very lightly sweetened whipped cream. Do *not* let this stand too long at room temperature. Serve 6 to 8.

The *Pavé au Chocolat* is another delectable dessert that requires ladyfingers and a cream. And though it may be flavored with either rum or good brandy, it is best made with kirsch or one of the orange-flavored liqueurs or Cointreau. Unlike the *charlotte,* this dessert is not molded but, in a sense, is built.

PAVÉ AU CHOCOLAT

4 ounces bitter chocolate	¼ cup kirsch
½ cup (¼ pound) butter	½ cup water
¾ cup powdered sugar	18 to 24 ladyfingers
4 egg yolks	

Melt chocolate in the top of a double boiler over hot (not boiling) water; cool. Cream butter and sugar together until light and fluffy. Beat in the egg yolks one by one, beating well after each addition; beat in the chocolate. Combine kirsch with water. Lay ladyfingers on a rack and sprinkle them with the liqueur mixture. Turn and sprinkle the other side. They should be moist but not wet. Let them stand a few minutes. Now arrange ⅓ of the ladyfingers side by side and just touching on a platter. Coat with some of the chocolate mixture. Arrange a second layer of ladyfingers on top of the first. Add a second layer of chocolate. Repeat for a third layer, ending with chocolate on top. Whip the remaining chocolate vigorously until it is thick and creamy. Spread it evenly over the entire cake. Chill at least 3 hours. Garnish with whipped cream before serving, if desired, or sprinkle the top of the *Pavé au Chocolat* with chopped pistachio nuts. Serves 6 to 8.

When a dessert like the *Pavé au Chocolat* is weighted while it chills, the result is altogether different. Here is a dessert from Italy called a Chocolate *Torta* which when chilled overnight under a weight gives an impression of almost unbelievable richness.

CHOCOLATE TORTA

6 ounces butter, softened
1 cup confectioners' sugar
4 egg yolks
1 cup chocolate syrup . . .
   homemade (page 20) or
   commercially canned

2 tablespoons instant coffee
18 to 24 ladyfingers
½ cup Cointreau

Cream butter and sugar until light and fluffy, then beat in the egg yolks, one by one, beating well after each addition. Add chocolate syrup and coffee. Blend thoroughly. Line an 8-inch square cake pan with wax paper, lightly oiled. Split the ladyfingers and sprinkle them on both sides with Cointreau. Use more than the half cup if necessary but the ladyfingers should be moist, not wet. Now arrange a layer of ladyfingers side by side and just touching, flat-side down, in the bottom of the pan. Add half of the chocolate mixture, repeat with second layer of ladyfingers; add remaining chocolate and top with the remaining ladyfingers. Cover with another sheet of oiled wax paper. Put a second square cake pan over the *torta* and in it put a weight just heavy enough to press the cake down gently but not mash it. Chill overnight. To unmold, remove weight, pan and top paper. Invert *torta* on a chilled plate. Remove paper from sides and bottom. One hour before serving frost with lightly sweetened whipped cream flavored with additional Cointreau, or just before serving sprinkle with powdered sugar. Serves 8.

A chocolate crown (which also calls for ladyfingers) is made in a 9-inch springform pan. Its creamy texture comes from cream cheese instead of butter, and its special flavor comes from brown sugar instead of white.

CHOCOLATE CROWN

18 ladyfingers, split
½ cup strained fresh orange
   juice
6 ounces semisweet chocolate
   bits
½ pound cream cheese

⅛ teaspoon salt
1 cup brown sugar, packed
3 eggs, separated
1½ teaspoons vanilla
1½ cups heavy cream

Lay split ladyfingers flat-side down on a cookie sheet and toast them in the oven at 375° F. for 5 minutes. Let cool 10 minutes, then sprinkle on both sides with orange juice. Line bottom and sides of a lightly oiled 9-inch springform pan with them, touching edge to edge and flat-side out.

In the top of a double boiler melt the chocolate over hot (not boiling) water. Cool for 10 minutes. Cream the cheese with salt and ½ cup of the sugar. When light and fluffy, beat in the egg yolks, one by one, beating well after each addition. Add chocolate and blend. Beat the egg whites until they hold soft peaks, then beat in the remaining sugar and vanilla. Continue beating until they are stiff and glossy. Fold these into the chocolate mixture. Whip the cream until stiff and fold that in also. Pour into the prepared springform pan, cover with oiled wax paper and chill overnight. Remove rim of pan before serving and garnish the top of the crown, if desired, with additional whipped cream. Serves 8 to 10.

Sometimes desserts are made with ladyfingers and macaroons in combination. One of the best of these is this Chocolate-Almond Mold which, when unmolded, has a surface consistency much like candy.

CHOCOLATE-ALMOND MOLD

10 ladyfingers, split	¼ cup curaçao
30 macaroons, quite dry	½ pound blanched almonds,
3 ounces semisweet chocolate	ground
1 cup sweet butter (½ pound)	1½ cups heavy cream
softened	2 tablespoons powdered sugar
1½ cups fine sugar	1 tablespoon rum, or to taste
5 eggs, 2 whole and 3 separated	

Lightly oil a straight-sided 2-quart mold and line the sides with ladyfingers arranged flat-side out and touching one another. Line the bottom of the mold with macaroons, flat-side down, and fill the open spaces with broken bits of ladyfingers.

Melt chocolate in the top of a double boiler over hot (not boiling) water, then cool. Cream butter and sugar until light and fluffy. One by one beat the whole eggs into the butter mixture, then beat in the 3 egg yolks. Add the chocolate and blend. Add curaçao and almonds. Blend thoroughly. Beat the egg whites until stiff and fold them gently into the chocolate-almond mixture. Pour half of this over the layer of macaroons. Add another layer of macaroons and fill the open spaces with broken bits of macaroon or ladyfinger or both. Add the remaining chocolate mixture and top with another layer of macaroons. Fill the open spaces in the same way as before. Cover with lightly oiled wax paper and refrigerate for 36 hours. Remove paper and unmold on a cold serving dish. Whip cream until it just holds a shape, whip in sugar, and then the rum, adding more rum to taste if desired. Pile the whipped cream on the mold and chill one more hour before serving. Serves 8.

Icebox Cakes

The term icebox cake includes just about anything in the way of cake and cream in combination that gains a wanted consistency by chilling. Some European desserts would undoubtedly have been called icebox cakes had they been created in America. But their foreign names give them a panache that so-called icebox cakes rarely if ever attain.

GÂTEAU SUISSE

1 pound white potatoes	1 teaspoon vanilla
5 ounces bitter chocolate	1 tablespoon rum
¾ cup (1½ sticks) butter	2 egg yolks
1½ cups fine granulated sugar	

Boil the potatoes in their jackets until tender. Peel, then put through a fine sieve or ricer. Keep warm until needed. Melt chocolate in the top of a double boiler over hot (not boiling) water. Cool. Cream butter until light and then gradually work in the sugar. Add vanilla, rum and egg yolks. Beat thoroughly. If you have an electric beater, use it by all means. Add chocolate. Beat again. Add the sieved potatoes. Beat until smooth. Pour into a buttered oblong 1-quart loaf pan. Cover with foil and refrigerate 4 to 5 hours or overnight. To serve, dip a knife in hot water and run the blade around the edge of the cake. Place bottom of pan in hot water for about 30 seconds. Invert on cold serving plate. Return cake to refrigerator immediately and leave until the surface is firm again. Sprinkle with powdered sugar just before serving. Serves 6 to 8.

Much on this same order is an Italian "cake" known for some reason as Milady's Secret.

MILADY'S SECRET

1 egg
¾ cup fine granulated sugar
¾ cup cocoa
½ cup butter (¼ pound), softened
¼ cup hazelnuts, toasted and chopped fine
¼ pound dry macaroons, crumbled into small pieces
1 teaspoon vanilla
3 to 4 tablespoons additional chopped hazelnuts

Combine egg and sugar and beat until very thick and lemon colored, about 4 minutes with an electric beater. Add cocoa and beat until thoroughly blended. Beat in softened butter, then fold in the nuts and the macaroon crumbs. Add the vanilla and blend. Line a 7¾ x 3⅞ x 2¼-inch pan with lightly oiled wax paper; pour in the mixture, spread it evenly with a spatula, cover with foil and chill about 4 hours. Turn out on a cold serving dish, remove paper, sprinkle top with additional chopped nuts, return to the refrigerator and keep chilled until needed. Serves 6 to 8.

In many American households if a dessert isn't chocolate, it doesn't seem like a dessert at all. This delicious but very easy icebox cake was a Sunday dessert fixture during Sylvia Hirsch's childhood.

SUNDAY ICEBOX CAKE

1 cup butter (½ pound)
½ cup granulated sugar
1 cup confectioners' sugar
2 ounces bitter chocolate
¼ cup strong black coffee
4 eggs, separated
30 ladyfingers
1 cup heavy cream
1 tablespoon powdered sugar
1 teaspoon vanilla

Cream butter and sugar until light and fluffy. Combine confectioners' sugar, chocolate, and coffee in top of double boiler and cook, stirring frequently, until chocolate is melted. Beat egg yolks until light, then with chocolate away from heat, combine yolks and chocolate; return to heat and cook, stirring constantly, until thick and smooth. Add to butter mixture and blend thoroughly. Cool. Beat egg whites until stiff and fold into mixture gently. Split enough of the ladyfingers to line the bottom and sides of a lightly oiled loaf pan, arranging them flat-side out and touching one another. Pour on half of the chocolate mixture. Add a layer of whole lady-fingers laid crosswise. Pour in the remaining chocolate and add another layer of ladyfingers. Cover with wax paper and chill 4 hours. Unmold on a chilled serving plate. Whip cream until stiff and sweeten it with sugar. Add vanilla. Frost top and sides of cake. Sprinkle with shaved bitter chocolate if desired. Serves 6 to 8.

This Chocolate-Orange Icebox Cake calls for slices of plain sponge cake, but pound cake makes for an even richer dessert, and store-bought pound cake will be more than adequately disguised by the rich filling.

CHOCOLATE-ORANGE ICEBOX CAKE

Plain sponge cake or pound cake	1 teaspoon vanilla
	1 tablespoon orange liqueur
8 ounces German sweet chocolate	2 cups heavy cream
	1 tablespoon powdered sugar
3 tablespoons boiling water	1 tablespoon grated orange rind
3 tablespoons powdered sugar	1 tablespoon additional liqueur
4 eggs, separated	

Cut slices of cake ½ inch thick and of a size to line the bottom and sides of a lightly oiled loaf pan. Cut additional slices of the same thickness to make 2 or 3 additional layers of cake as desired. Cake should make the final layer when filling the pan for it gives a better base for the cake to stand on when it is eventually unmolded.

Melt chocolate with hot water in top of double boiler. Add sugar and stir until smooth. Remove from heat and cool 2 to 3 minutes. One by one, beat in the egg yolks, beating well after each addition. Add vanilla and orange liqueur. Beat the egg whites until stiff and fold gently into the mixture. Now, depending on whether you use 2 or 3 additional layers of cake, pour either half or one-third of the chocolate mixture into the cake-lined pan. Add a layer of cake, then more chocolate, and either the final layer of cake or repeat until the pan is filled. Cover with wax paper and chill 24 hours. Unmold on a cold serving plate. One hour before serving, whip cream and add the sugar, orange rind and additional liqueur bit by bit. Beat until stiff. Frost the top and sides of cake and return to the refrigerator to chill until needed. Serves at least 8.

The consistency that marshmallows give to a cream filling is particularly well-suited to icebox cakes. This cake has chopped pecans to contrast with the rich cream, and maraschino cherries for additional flavor.

CHOCOLATE MARSHMALLOW CAKE WITH PECANS

4 ounces German sweet chocolate	¾ cup halved maraschino cherries
6 tablespoons boiling water	1½ cups chopped pecans

6 eggs, separated
24 large marshmallows
30 ladyfingers

1½ cups heavy cream
2 tablespoons powdered sugar
¼ cup pecan halves

Melt chocolate with boiling water in the top of a double boiler. Beat the egg yolks until very thick and lemon colored. Gradually pour the hot chocolate over the egg yolks, beating as you do so. Return to double boiler with marshmallows. Cook over low heat, stirring constantly until the marshmallows are melted. Cool. Beat egg whites until stiff and fold into the chocolate mixture.

Line an 8 x 8-inch pan with wax paper. Split ladyfingers and line the bottom and sides of the pan with them, flat-side out and touching one another. Over the ladyfingers arrange the halved maraschino cherries in an even layer. Pour in half the chocolate mixture. Sprinkle with half the pecans. Add another layer of split ladyfingers. Add remaining chocolate, pecans and ladyfingers. Cover with wax paper and chill 24 hours. Unmold on a cold plate and remove paper. One hour before serving, whip cream with sugar. Spread over top and sides of cake. Garnish with pecan halves. Return to refrigerator until needed. Serves 10 to 12.

Packaged vanilla wafers are also excellent in combination with chocolate creams, as in this Chocolate Toffee Icebox Cake.

CHOCOLATE TOFFEE ICEBOX CAKE

8 ounces vanilla wafers,
  crumbled
2 ounces bitter chocolate
½ cup (¼ pound) butter
½ cup powdered sugar
3 eggs, separated

1 teaspoon vanilla
½ cup ground pecans
1 cup heavy cream
1 tablespoon additional
  powdered sugar

Coat the bottom and sides of an oiled 8 x 8-inch pan with crumbs. Shake out the excess and sprinkle half of the remaining crumbs evenly over the bottom. Melt chocolate in the top of a double boiler over hot (not boiling) water; cool. Cream butter with sugar until light and fluffy. Add chocolate to butter mixture and blend. Beat egg yolks until light and then beat them into the chocolate. Add vanilla and ground nuts. Mix thoroughly. Beat egg whites until stiff and fold into the mixture. Pour into pan. Sprinkle evenly with remaining crumbs. Spread with a spatula if necessary. Cover with wax paper and chill 3 to 4 hours. Before serving, whip cream and sweeten with additional sugar. Cut cake in squares in pan and top individual portions with cream. Makes 16 2-inch squares.

The trifle is an English dessert, popular in the early days of this country, made of cake and custard with or without whipped cream but always embellished with preserves or fruit of some sort and generally flavored with wine or brandy. This trifle is an icebox cake, however, made with graham cracker crumbs and a chocolate-cornstarch-pudding mixture. It is easy to make and relatively inexpensive but not a bit less good for being so.

CHOCOLATE GRAHAM CRACKER TRIFLE

2 ounces bitter chocolate
1 cup sugar
1 quart milk
6 tablespoons cornstarch
1 pinch salt

1½ teaspoons vanilla
16 to 20 graham crackers, crumbled fine
1 cup heavy cream
1 tablespoon powdered sugar

Melt chocolate in top of double boiler over hot water. Add sugar and blend. Gradually stir in 3 cups of the milk. Blend the remaining cup of milk with the cornstarch. Add this to the chocolate mixture with pinch of salt. Cook over hot water, stirring frequently, for 20 minutes. Cool and add vanilla. Sprinkle ⅓ of the crumbs in the bottom of an 8 x 8-inch pan. Pour on half the chocolate mixture. Add another ⅓ of the crumbs and the remaining chocolate. Top with remaining crumbs. Cover with wax paper and chill 24 hours. Cut in squares in the pan and serve each portion topped by some of the cream whipped stiff and sweetened with the powdered sugar. Serves 6 to 8.

Baked and Steamed Puddings

The popularity of pies and cakes and creams of all kinds in this country has pushed baked and steamed puddings into the background. There was a time—and not so very long ago—that these were highly esteemed, not only for family dinners but festive occasions as well. And in the latter half of the nineteenth century, some of those made with chocolate were thought of as *the* desserts for the most festive times. All chocolate puddings, however, have a marvelous richness, though many are simple and relatively easy to make. One of the best of the simple ones is this Baked Chocolate Custard.

BAKED CHOCOLATE CUSTARD

1⅛ cups light cream
1⅛ cups milk
6 ounces dark sweet chocolate
6 whole eggs

4 tablespoons sugar
1 pinch salt
1¼ teaspoons vanilla

Combine cream, milk and chocolate in the top of a double boiler and cook gently until the chocolate is melted; remove from heat. Beat the egg yolks until thick and lemon colored with sugar and salt. Slowly pour the chocolate mixture into them, stirring as you do so. Stir in vanilla. Pour through a sieve into a buttered 6-cup baking dish. Set in pan with 1 inch hot water and bake at 325° F. for 50 to 60 minutes or until done (a knife inserted at the center will come out clean). Remove from oven, cool and chill. If desired serve with lightly sweetened whipped cream. Serves 8 to 10.

MOCHA CUSTARD

Substitute ⅔ cup strong black coffee for part of the milk.

Similar, but with its special difference, is this Weimar Pudding with chocolate sauce.

WEIMAR PUDDING

¼ cup (½ stick) butter
¼ cup sugar
3 eggs, separated
1 teaspoon vanilla

3 tablespoons cocoa
1 pinch salt
¼ cup fine cake crumbs

Cream butter with sugar until light and fluffy. One by one beat in the egg yolks. Add vanilla. Combine cocoa, salt and crumbs. Fold into yolk mixture and blend thoroughly. Beat egg whites until stiff and fold in also. Divide equally among 6 buttered custard cups. Set in pan of hot water and bake at 400° F. for 30 minutes. To serve, turn out on dessert plates and pass chocolate sauce separately (page 24). Serves 6.

Chocolate puddings as such generally contain a noticeable portion of flour or cornstarch. Or, as in the foregoing, crumbs. Many are simple desserts, such as the following Plain Baked Chocolate Pudding. But simplicity does not imply a lack of goodness. On the contrary, where chocolate is concerned, quality and simplicity often go hand in hand.

PLAIN BAKED CHOCOLATE PUDDING

2 ounces bitter chocolate
2 eggs
1 cup sugar
2 tablespoons butter, melted
1 cup flour

2 teaspoons baking powder
1 pinch salt
1 cup milk
1 teaspoon vanilla

Melt chocolate in top of double boiler over hot (not boiling) water; cool. Beat eggs until thick and lemon colored, then beat again with sugar. Add melted butter and blend. Combine flour, baking powder and salt. Add milk to dry ingredients and mix thoroughly. Add the flour mixture to the eggs. Stir in chocolate and vanilla. Pour into a buttered 2-quart Pyrex baking dish, set in pan with 1 inch hot water and bake at 325° F. for 45 minutes. Serve warm with a chocolate sauce, preferably the Foamy Rum Sauce (page 26). Serves 8.

Bread pudding is one of the old-time favorites that should not be forgotten, particularly this mouth-watering version made with chocolate.

CHOCOLATE BREAD PUDDING

2 ounces bitter chocolate
3¼ cups milk
¼ teaspoon salt
3½ cups cubed, dry, crustless
   bread

3 eggs, separated
¾ cup sugar
1½ teaspoons vanilla
1 pinch mace or nutmeg
¼ teaspoon salt

Melt chocolate with milk in the top of a double boiler over hot water. Stir to blend thoroughly and add ¼ teaspoon salt. Place bread cubes in bowl and pour the chocolate milk over them. Beat the egg yolks with sugar until thick and lemon colored; add vanilla and spice. Combine with bread mixture and blend gently. Do not mash the bread cubes. Beat egg whites with pinch of salt until stiff. Fold into the bread mixture. Turn into a buttered 2-quart baking dish, set in pan with 1 inch of hot water and bake at 350° F. for 45 minutes. Serve warm with ice-cold very heavy cream or cold with whipped cream or any hot fudge sauce (see index).

Chocolate puddings take well to the added richness of fruits and nuts.

CHOCOLATE DATE-NUT PUDDING

2½ ounces bitter chocolate
½ cup white sugar
3 tablespoons butter
1½ cups sifted flour
1½ teaspoons baking powder
½ teaspoon cinnamon
1 pinch salt
¾ cup milk

1 cup pitted dates, cut in small
   pieces
½ cup chopped walnuts
½ teaspoon vanilla
½ teaspoon grated orange rind
2 cups boiling water
1 cup brown sugar, packed

Melt chocolate in the top of a double boiler over hot (not boiling) water; cool. Cream white sugar with 1 tablespoon of butter. Add chocolate and blend. Combine flour, baking powder, cinnamon, and salt. Sift together into bowl. Add dry ingredients and milk alternately to chocolate mixture, blending after each addition. Add dates (cut up, not chopped; chopping mashes them), nuts, vanilla and orange rind. Blend thoroughly. Spread in a buttered 9 x 9-inch pan. Combine boiling water with brown sugar and remaining 2 tablespoons butter in saucepan. Bring to a boil. Gently pour this hot syrup over the batter in the pan. Bake at 350° F. for 45 minutes. Serve warm with vanilla or lemon ice cream. Serves 6 to 8.

Steamed puddings are cooked in covered molds over or in boiling water. Their consistency as a rule is rich and moist. This is accented by the fact that they are usually served warm or even hot with a special sauce that has its own richness.

CHOCOLATE SPICE PUDDING

6 eggs, separated
1¼ cups sugar
1 cup grated bitter chocolate
2 tablespoons fine bread crumbs

1 teaspoon baking powder
1 pinch salt
1¼ teaspoons vanilla
½ teaspoon cinnamon
¼ teaspoon allspice

Combine egg yolks with sugar and beat until very thick and lemon colored. Add grated chocolate and all other ingredients *except* the egg whites. Blend thoroughly. Beat the egg whites until stiff and fold into the mixture. Butter the inside surface of the top of a double boiler, preferably of the sort that has a rounded bottom and sides with no indentation. Pour the pudding batter into this, cover tightly, place over (not in) boiling water and cook at the boil for 1 hour. Replenish the lower part of boiler with additional boiling water if necessary. Turn out on a hot serving dish when done and pass a Hard Sauce on the side . . . preferably flavored with brandy. Serves 6 to 8.

HARD SAUCE

¼ pound sweet butter
¼ pound fine sugar
Orange or lemon peel

Brandy or other flavoring as desired . . . vanilla, liqueur, etc.

Cream the butter until barely workable. Work the sugar with several strips of lemon or orange peel or both. Discard peel. (A bit of vanilla bean may be used instead if desired.) Slowly add the sugar to the butter. Cream until light and fluffy. Work in brandy a few drops at a time but never so much as to liquify the sugar. When thoroughly blended, chill.

Richer and of a decidedly different flavor is this Ambrosial Pudding which, with almonds and bittersweet chocolate, uses toasted crumbs of pumpernickel.

AMBROSIAL PUDDING

8 eggs, separated
¾ cup sugar
1 pinch salt
¾ cup ground blanched almonds
⅓ cup bittersweet chocolate,
   grated

1 cup coarse crumbs of day-old
   pumpernickel
¼ cup butter, melted
½ teaspoon almond extract

Beat egg yolks with the sugar and salt until very thick and lemon colored. Add ground almonds and grated chocolate; blend thoroughly. Toss crumbs with butter and toast in the oven at 225° F. until crisp and dry. Cool. Beat egg whites until stiff and fold into the yolk mixture. Fold in the toasted crumbs. Add almond extract. Pour into a buttered pudding mold, cover tightly, stand in a large pot with hot water to half the depth of the mold, cover pot and boil 45 minutes. Add more boiling water if necessary. Unmold pudding on a hot serving plate and serve hot or warm with cold whipped cream lightly sweetened and flavored with rum, curaçao or brandy to taste.

Richer still is this Steamed Almond-Chocolate Pudding.

STEAMED ALMOND-CHOCOLATE PUDDING

10 eggs, separated
1½ cups sugar
¾ cup bitter chocolate, grated
1 cup ground almonds

½ cup flour
2 teaspoons cinnamon
¼ teaspoon cloves
1 pinch salt

Beat egg yolks with sugar until thick and lemon colored. Add all the remaining ingredients (*except* the salt and egg whites) one by one, blending after each addition. Beat egg whites with salt until stiff and fold gently into the mixture. Pour into top of double boiler as directed in recipe for Chocolate Spice Pudding (page 66), cover and steam for 2 hours. Add more boiling water if necessary. Unmold on hot serving dish and serve with sweetened whipped cream flavored with vanilla, or with Sauce Sabayon (page 70).

Souffles

A soufflé is a baked dish of feather-light consistency, the texture of which is derived from the air entrapped in stiffly beaten egg whites which expands when exposed to heat. It may be a sweet dish, in which case it will be served as a dessert, or an unsweetened one, in which case it will be served with the main body of a meal; the egg whites, however, will always be present. Many dessert dishes that gain their lightness from whipped cream are called soufflés but they are really mousses. A confusion arises because of the fact that dessert soufflés may be either hot or cold. Whether cold or not, a soufflé is always baked (or cooked in some way) and always contains the egg whites. Mere lightness has nothing to do the name.

Whenever possible, soufflés should be baked and served in straight-sided soufflé dishes which are specially made for the purpose. Such dishes encourage the skyward climb. (Such a dish is perfect also for the mousses that pose as soufflés.) Hot soufflés, which we will deal with here, pose a problem of timing for the hostess for they must be served immediately when taken from the oven. They bake as a rule in from 35 to 40 minutes, and it is better to wait a few minutes for a perfect soufflé than to have an imperfect one served on the dot. With an eye to perfection, the wise hostess (if she be indeed the cook) will put a clock somewhere near her dining table so she can see it!

It seems somehow demeaning to refer to any good chocolate soufflé as a standard one; the following is precisely that nonetheless.

A FRENCH CHOCOLATE SOUFFLÉ

3 tablespoons butter
⅓ cup flour
½ cup sugar
1 cup cream

3 eggs, separated
2 ounces bitter chocolate,
  melted
1 teaspoon vanilla

Melt the butter in the top of a double boiler over hot water; add flour
and blend. Add sugar and blend. Slowly stir in the cream and cook,
stirring constantly, until smooth and thickened. Beat the egg yolks until
light. Add a few spoonfuls of the cream mixture to heat them, then
pour into the double boiler and cook 3 to 4 minutes longer, still stirring. Remove from heat and add the melted chocolate. Blend. Cool.
Beat the egg whites until stiff. Fold into the chocolate custard. Add
vanilla. Pour into a buttered 2-quart soufflé dish; set dish in pan with
1 inch warm water. Bake at 350° F. for about 35 minutes. Serve immediately with or without a sauce or with lightly sweetened whipped
cream or whipped cream flavored with any orange liqueur. Serves 4
to 6.

Many recipes for hot dessert soufflés call for a soufflé dish that has
been both buttered and sugared. In particular recipes we feel this is
essential; in others it is optional. Simply butter your soufflé dish, then
sprinkle bottom and sides with sugar. Invert the dish to shake out any
excess. A different and delicious effect may be had by sprinkling the
dish with cocoa instead of sugar.

Individual soufflés may be baked with any of the soufflé mixtures in
Pyrex or pottery custard cups instead of the larger soufflé dish. These
should be buttered, of course, and sugared if desired. They should be
filled about ⅔ full before baking and set in a pan of water as described
above. The baking time for individual soufflés is about the same as
that for a big one.

Special company deserves a special soufflé . . . although the family
should get one, too. This particular soufflé, somewhat on the order of
the famous one served at *La Tour D'Argent* in Paris, is part chooclate,
part vanilla and rum, with a layer of liqueur-flavored ladyfingers in
between; it is special indeed! Like the Paris creation, this is served as
a rule with a Sauce Sabayon.

COMPANY SOUFFLÉ

3 tablespoons butter
3 tablespoons flour
1 cup milk
½ cup sugar
1 pinch salt
6 egg yolks
2 ounces bitter chocolate, melted

¼ cup black coffee
1 teaspoon vanilla
1 tablespoon rum
8 to 10 ladyfingers
    Curaçao or Grand Marnier as needed
8 egg whites

Melt butter in the top of a double boiler over hot water. Add flour and blend. Gradually add the milk and cook, stirring constantly, until the mixture is smooth and thickened. Add sugar and salt. Stir until the sugar is dissolved. Beat the egg yolks until thick, add several spoonfuls of the hot mixture, then pour the yolks into the remaining mixture and cook 2 to 3 minutes, stirring gently. Remove from heat.

Melt chocolate with coffee over hot water. Divide egg yolk mixture in half. To one half add the chocolate and blend. To the other half add the vanilla and rum. Sprinkle the ladyfingers with just enough of the liqueur to moisten them. Beat the egg whites until just stiff. Divide the whites in half and gently fold half into each of the two yolk mixtures.

Butter a 2½-quart soufflé dish and sugar it. (See page 69). Pour in the chocolate batter. Cover this with a layer of ladyfingers. Cover the ladyfingers with the rum-vanilla batter. Bake at 375° F. for about 35 minutes. Serve immediately with the Sauce Sabayon or whipped cream flavored with the liqueur used in the recipe. Serves 8 to 12.

SAUCE SABAYON

5 egg yolks
1 pinch salt
¼ cup sugar, or to taste

2 cups rich milk or light cream
Liqueur to taste, about ¼ cup

Combine the egg yolks, salt and sugar in the top of a double boiler away from all heat. Beat with a rotary beater until very light. Add milk and blend thoroughly. Place over hot water and cook gently, still beating. When well thickened—and this means very well thickened—add the liqueur (Grand Marnier, curaçao or brandy). Cook a couple of minutes longer and serve hot—in a glass or china bowl (it will blacken a silver one).

Generally speaking, the Italians are not great dessert-eaters. When they do make a dessert, however, they make a good one—and as a rule a rich one. This Italian Nut Soufflé came from Florence.

ITALIAN NUT SOUFFLÉ

⅓ cup cocoa
¾ cup sugar
1¼ cups ground English walnuts
4 eggs, separated
1 pinch salt
1 teaspoon grated lemon rind

1 teaspoon vanilla
2 tablespoons very fine dry
    crumbs, preferably zwieback
    or such but plain bread will
    do ,

Combine cocoa, sugar and nuts. Blend. Beat the egg yolks until very thick and combine with the cocoa mixture. Add salt, lemon rind and vanilla. Blend. Beat the egg whites until just stiff and fold them gently into the batter. Pour into a buttered 9-inch soufflé dish sprinkled with dry crumbs. Bake at 350° F. for about 30 minutes. Serve with lightly sweetened whipped cream.

Pecans may be substituted for the walnuts if desired, but the dish will have a completely different flavor.

This soufflé with its lemon-flavored chocolate was served in Madrid. There, baked in individual dishes and served to twelve, it made a perfect ending for a perfect dinner.

SPANISH CHOCOLATE SOUFFLÉ

2 tablespoons butter
2 tablespoons flour
¼ cup light cream
½ cup sugar
¼ cup lemon juice
2 tablespoons cocoa

2 tablespoons grated lemon rind
4 egg yolks
5 egg whites
    Additional granulated sugar
    Powdered sugar

Melt butter in the top of a double boiler over hot water. Add flour and blend. Stir in cream and blend. Add sugar, lemon juice, cocoa and grated rind. Cook until thickened, stirring constantly. Remove from heat and cool. Beat the egg yolks until very thick and combine with the lemon mixture. Beat the egg whites until stiff and fold gently into the mixture. Fill 12 buttered individual soufflé dishes ⅔ full of batter. Sprinkle the top very lightly with a little additional granulated sugar. Bake at 350° F. about 15 minutes. Or, pour into a buttered 1½-quart soufflé dish, sprinkle with sugar and bake at 350° F. for about 40 minutes. Either way, sprinkle with powdered sugar just when taken from the oven. Serve with or without a sauce or whipped cream.

The macaroons used in the following recipe should be *dry* (as compared to fresh macaroons) but not dry to the point of hardness. The crumbs made from them should be rather coarse, and if such is possible, both dry and soft at once.

CHOCOLATE MACAROON SOUFFLÉ

3 tablespoons butter
3 tablespoons flour
1 cup rich milk
2 ounces bitter chocolate
¼ cup sugar
1 generous pinch salt

1 teaspoon vanilla
4 eggs, separated
¼ cup additional sugar
¼ pound macaroons, partially
   dried and crumbled

Melt butter in the top of a double boiler over hot water. Add flour and blend. Stir in the milk and cook until smooth and thickened, stirring constantly. Add chocolate and cook over very low heat until chocolate is melted, stirring from time to time. Add sugar, salt and vanilla. Stir until sugar is dissolved. Beat egg yolks until thick. Add several spoonfuls of the chocolate mixture and blend; then pour all into the double boiler. Cook gently 2 to 3 minutes, stirring. Remove from heat. Cool.

Beat the egg whites until just stiff and then beat in the additional sugar. When glossy and quite stiff, fold gently into the yolk mixture. Fold in the macaroon crumbs. Pour into a buttered and sugared 2-quart soufflé dish. Set in pan with 1 inch of warm water. Bake at 375° F. about 35 to 40 minutes. Serve immediately with vanilla-flavored whipped cream. Or the following:

COOKED CREAM

¾ cup sugar
1 cup heavy cream

3 heaping tablespoons cocoa

Combine all the ingredients in the top of a double boiler. Stir until sugar is completely dissolved. Then cook for 20 minutes, stirring occasionally. Remove from heat and cool. Chill for 2 hours. Then whip to whatever stiffness you desire. For a cake frosting, the cream should be very stiff, of course; if to be served by itself as dessert in parfait glasses, then it should be somewhat softer than the frosting. And if to be served as sauce, as with this delectable soufflé, then merely beat it to soft peaks.

Cakes

SOME THOUGHTS
ON CAKES AND BAKING

Before going into the vast and wonderful subject of chocolate cakes, there are certain matters concerning cakes in general that should be considered. Cake-making is not a difficult art but success with even the simplest cake depends on the attention and care that one gives to the details of procedure. These are worth mastering, because, while many commercial mixes give excellent results, and are easy to use and fool-proof in the bargain if you follow package directions, they cannot do more than give you a stereotyped cake with no special personality of its own. Homemade cakes, on the other hand, invite experimentation. Once the details of procedure have become a matter of rote, you may experiment at will with any cake, adding more or less of this or that for a different effect, changing flavors, accenting flavors, adding new ingredients for varied texture, changing frosting and fillings or adding to them to gain a change of flavor and appearance at the same time.

Here are the basic procedures that should be followed.

Assemble all needed utensils and ingredients before you begin to make your cake batter. Preheat the oven according to recipe directions.

Have all ingredients at room temperature before you begin your work (with the exception of heavy cream for whipping, which must be refrigerator-cold).

Be sure that you have at least one mixing bowl on hand large enough to hold all ingredients easily for the final step in mixing the batter. This bowl should have sides that round down into the bottom in an even sweep so that sides and bottom may be scraped easily with a rubber spatula or scraper to blend evenly.

Cake batters may be mixed either by hand or by electric beater. A portable electric beater is far better for average size cakes because it will work easily in any mixing bowl, and may be moved about to do its work in several. Bear in mind that whatever beating you do should conform to specific recipe directions. Over-beating is quite as injurious to a cake batter as under-beating. Cream and egg whites, however, are better whipped when whipped by hand.

TO STIR means to move spoon or other mixing utensil in a gentle circular motion. Stirring prevents scorching, lumping and other such disasters; it also mixes and blends.

TO BEAT (where some utensil other than an electric beater is meant) means to use a vigorous, somewhat circular motion, lifting and turning ingredients to blend them thoroughly and, at the same time, to add air to the mixture.

TO FOLD is to gently turn one ingredient over and around another so that the two will be mixed together while retaining their own identities.

TO CREAM is a softening process used for butter or other shortening. It gives the fat a smooth, workable consistency that permits its blending with other ingredients without melting it into an oil.

The procedures for creaming butter and sugar together, and for the proper beating of eggs or egg yolks are two of the most important in cake-making. A butter-sugar mixture when correctly creamed—the butter having been at room temperature to begin with—will be light and fluffy, but thick at the same time. This is also true of egg yolks that have been properly beaten. The yolks take on a light, lemon-yellow color as they thicken and increase in volume. And the more they thicken, the more their volume increases. This contributes much toward the ultimate lightess of any cake.

The greasing or not greasing of cake pans is determined by the kind of cake you are baking. Butter cake batters require greasing (and sometimes flouring as well) while sponge cake batters and angel food batters require ungreased pans. When greasing a cake pan, *always* use either unsalted butter or, better, a tasteless vegetable oil or fat.

To flour a cake pan, sprinkle the entire greased surface lightly and evenly with flour, then invert pan and shake out any excess.

If a long baking period is required, or if there is danger that the bottom of a cake may scorch in baking, first grease the pan, then line the bottom with a circle of wax paper and grease the paper as well.

Baking directions are given in all recipes for a degree of doneness that appeals to the average taste. As a general rule, the longer the baking, the drier and lighter the cake. So if you like a moist cake (as we do) pull your cakes from the oven five minutes before the end of the baking time. Then, although most books tell you to turn all but a few special cakes out on a rack immediately to cool, we suggest that you let them rest in the baking pans for at least five minutes. We also feel that many cakes are improved by being cooled completely in the pans before turning out, and we have specified this in certain recipes.

Always test cakes for doneness by using a cake tester or toothpick even though clock and thermometer say that they should be done. Stick it into the center of the cake and if it comes out clean the cake is done. Any sign of *moist* batter on the tester is a sure indication that some further baking is required.

Sometimes cakes are stubborn when it comes to turning them out of their pans. Our procedure in such cases is to make sure that the cake is free from the baking tin all around the edges, running a thin, sharp knife around the pan to loosen it if necessary. Then set the cake pan directly over a low flame for a very few seconds. The heat will loosen the cake almost immediately. Or, you may invert the cake pan so that the cake is over and resting lightly on the open palm of your hand. Then bang the pan a few sharp raps on your kitchen counter. Presto—the cake is in your hand. Let us say in passing that cakes when baked can take a surprising amount of punishment. While baking, they are delicate indeed. They need peace and calm and special conditions. Once baked, however, they take on amazing stamina. It is good to bear this strength of texture in mind when you are thinking of new ways to use your standard cake recipes. A world of desserts may be created with cakes cut this way or that to be used in combination with other ingredients, such as creams, preserves, fresh fruits, syrups, wines, spirits and liqueurs.

Bake all cakes as nearly in the center of your oven as possible. It is better to bake them in separate batches than to bake some on a rack at the top of the oven and others at the bottom.

PAN SIZES AND SHAPES

Many batters may be baked in different kinds of cake pans. The kind of a pan that you select will have much to do with the texture, consistency and even the quality of the finished cake. Batters suggested for layer cakes may be baked in loaf or ring pans, but in loaf pans they will require almost twice the baking time given for layer cake, and in ring pans they will require a length of time usually halfway between the two, the actual time depending on the depth of the batter in the ring and the diameter of the center opening, which is a heat conductor.

A round pan whose diameter equals the side of a square pan will hold approximately ¾ the amount of batter.

We might mention, also, that any cake batter may be used for cup-cakes as well. Fill muffin tins (greased or not as directed) or paper baking cups ⅔ full of the batter and bake about 20 minutes until done.

It is impossible to give an accurate number of servings for cakes because this depends on how the cakes are served, whether with dessert or as dessert, as a snack in the evening or, conceivably, as a meal in themselves with a tall glass of cold milk. Then, too, there are a good many people around (present company not excepted) who can bliss-fully eat their way through a large portion of a cake without any out-side help whatever. These servings, therefore, are merely approximate.

Pan sizes	Servings
13 × 9 × 2-inch rectangle	24 2-inch squares
	12 3-inch squares
8-inch square	6 to 8
8-inch layer cake (2 or 3 layers)	8
9-inch layer cake (2 or 3 layers)	10
10-inch springform	10 to 12
9 × 5 × 2¾-inch loaf	12 slices more or less
Tube pans	Minimum number the same as for layer cakes

FILLINGS AND FROSTINGS

With many of the cakes that follow we have given special frostings and fillings that seem to us to set the cakes off to their best advantage. In most cases, the frosting is used as the filling as well, but there is no reason why you should abide by our opinion on the matter. In fact, one of the pleasures to be derived from cake-making is in the success that you achieve using your own judgment and imagination. Another lies in the variety you can achieve by changing frostings and fillings or combining them in a different way, altering their flavors, their textures, setting new ones in juxtaposition. Before the cake recipes themselves, we have listed a selection of fillings and frostings that you may want to consider as you read the cake recipes. Visualize the look of the finished cake, its combination of colors. Mentally taste the flavors as the colors swim before you, and add, in your mind, by way of a finishing touch, the green of pistachios, the brown of walnuts or pecans or the waxy sheen of blanched almonds.

FILLINGS

Fillings, of course, are spread between layers of cake, layers which may be either baked as layers or cut from a single cake—from a loaf cake, for instance, or a flat sheet cake. It is difficult to give a precise rule for the amount of filling that you will need since this is largely a matter of personal choice. The amount used will obviously bear on the ultimate richness of the cake as well as its flavor and moisture. Anywhere from ½ cup to 1½ cups may be used to fill a 2-layer 9-inch cake. The lesser amount will suffice for jams and jellies which, as a rule, are spread rather thin. Often they are used as a glaze only, and often too they will be used in conjunction with a second filling. The larger amount would be required for some fluffy, creamy filling which in itself would become virtually a layer. It is well to bear in mind that for the average American taste, the filling and frosting of any cake are quite as important as the cake itself (perhaps even more so). Many American cakes are virtually confections because of the quantity and richness of their fillings and frosting.

Of the jams that are particularly good in combination with chocolate, apricot jam, strawberry jam and orange marmalade come immediately to mind. In addition to these, you might try cherry preserves or pineapple or plum preserves. Raspberry jam has special uses in connection with many European cakes and tortes (page 139).

It should be noted that a glaze of jam or other preserve has a two-fold purpose with cakes of any kind, whether layer or not. If cakes are to be held any length of time before filling and frosting, a thin layer of glaze spread over their surfaces will keep them moist and add to their flavor at the same time. To be most effective, such a glaze should be spread while a cake is still warm. Any jam or jelly will serve the purpose, but a true glaze is composed of jam or preserve heated with additional sugar, as in the following:

APRICOT GLAZE

A glaze of any jam can be made using this same method.

½ cup apricot jam   2 tablespoons sugar

Press jam through a fine mesh sieve and combine it in a small saucepan with the sugar. Cook over moderately high heat to 225° F. on the candy thermometer. Remove from heat immediately. Spread over warm cake while the glaze is itself still warm.

Red currant jelly (which is excellent for this purpose) and raspberry jelly need only to be heated. Added sugar (as above) will give extra richness, of course.

The use of cream or custard filling for cakes was widely popular in this country not so many years ago. It is unfortunate that it has passed out of favor. Custard—or *crème pâtisssière*—takes well to all kinds of flavorings. And it is excellent, too, when used in conjunction with some secondary filling such as the jams and preserves mentioned above. Both custard and jam in conjunction with chocolate open the door to a world of richness. So, as a point of departure, let's start with the Cream Filling.

CREAM FILLING—CRÈME PÂTISSIÈRE

6 tablespoons sugar
1 tablespoon cornstarch
⅛ teaspoon salt
2 egg yolks, slightly beaten

1 cup milk
1 rounded tablespoon butter
½ teaspoon vanilla

Combine the dry ingredients and mix with the slightly beaten egg yolks. Heat milk in a double boiler. Add enough of the hot milk to the egg yolk mixture to make a thick, smooth paste. Add the paste to the remaining hot milk. Cook 5 minutes over hot water stirring constantly; reduce heat and cook 10 minutes, stirring from time to time. Stir in the butter and blend. Remove from heat and add vanilla or other flavor as desired. Stir several times as the filling cools. Spread when cold. This thickens even more if refrigerated.

CHOCOLATE CREAM FILLING

Proceed as above but first melt 1½ ounces bitter chocolate in the milk.

MOCHA CREAM FILLING

Proceed as above but first melt 1 ounce bitter chocolate in the milk with 1 teaspoon instant coffee.

CREAMY CUSTARD FILLING—DOUBLE PASTRY CREAM

Proceed as in the Cream Filling and when this is cold, fold in ½ cup whipped cream, or as much as you desire.

This Orange Cream Filling, delicious with chocolate, is made somewhat differently.

ORANGE CREAM FILLING

½ cup sugar
2 tablespoons cornstarch
1 pinch salt
1 egg yolk

½ cup strained orange juice
1 tablespoon lemon juice
½ cup water
½ cup whipping cream

Combine sugar, cornstarch and salt. Blend with egg yolk in a small saucepan. Little by little stir in the orange juice. Add lemon juice and water. Blend. Place over low heat and cook, stirring constantly, until the sauce bubbles. Place pan over hot water and cook gently 10 minutes, stirring from time to time. Remove from heat. Stir several times as the sauce cools. Whip cream until stiff and fold into the cold orange sauce gently but thoroughly. Chill to thicken further before using if desired.

The following filling made with brown sugar is not only quick and easy but delicious as well, a rare combination.

BROWN SUGAR CHOCOLATE FILLING

1¼ cups dark brown sugar, packed
¼ cup grated dark sweet chocolate

¼ cup milk
1 pinch salt
1 rounded tablespoon butter
1 teaspoon vanilla

Combine the sugar, chocolate, milk and salt in the top of a double boiler and cook over hot water until smooth. Add butter and blend. Remove from heat and add vanilla. Beat as it cools until you reach the desired spreadable consistency, which is a matter of personal choice. Ground or finely chopped nuts, grated orange rind, or 3 to 4 tablespoons puréed prunes may be added if desired.

This is another of the richer fillings. In fact, it is just about as rich as a filling can be.

SWEET CHOCOLATE FILLING

4 ounces sweet chocolate
2 tablespoons heavy cream
  (or water)
2 small eggs

¾ cup powdered sugar
4 tablespoons butter
1 teaspoon vanilla

Melt chocolate with the cream in a double boiler. Beat the eggs and then gradually beat in the sugar. Add to the chocolate mixture and cook, stirring constantly, until smooth and very thick. Stir in the butter bit by bit. Remove from heat and cool. Add vanilla. Beat until creamy and of desired spreadable consistency.

This Cold Chocolate Rum Cream is delicious with any cake.

COLD CHOCOLATE RUM CREAM

1½ ounces bitter chocolate,
  cut up
4 tablespoons sugar
1 pinch salt

2 tablespoons light cream
1 cup whipping cream
1½ teaspoons rum (or vanilla or
  other flavor)

Combine chocolate, sugar, salt and light cream in top of double boiler and cook, stirring frequently, until the chocolate is melted. Remove from heat and cool, then chill. Beat the cream until stiff and then beat in the flavoring. Fold this into the cold chocolate mixture. Chill again. This filling must be used at the last minute, just before your cake is to be served. It is excellent for rolls of all kinds and makes a fine topping or frosting for special cakes and tortes. Double the recipe if you wish to use this to frost and fill an entire cake.

FROSTINGS

Aside from the flavors and richness that they add to cakes, frostings serve a practical purpose as well. They keep cakes moist. Used in conjunction with a glaze, they will keep a cake fresh in a cake box or, better, refrigerator for several days.

Frostings and icings in general usage are thought of as identical. If a distinction between them must be made (as it often is among professional chefs), then icings should be thought of as white and frostings as all other colors; icings as relatively simple, and frostings as relatively complex. Both are primarily of sugar, but butter, eggs, and cream are more prominent in frostings.

Most frostings should be used with a lavish hand, and when so used, applied with a modicum of easy artistry so they are themselves decorations. Well-frosted cakes have a look of richness that is as pleasing to the eye as any sugar rosebud or wreath.

It is difficult to state categorically the precise amount of frosting you will need for any cake, since, as with the fillings, the amount that is right to one cook, may be wrong to another. Always make more than enough frosting. What is left over will never go begging. Use it to frost slices of store-bought cake for children's snacks or lunches. Use it to fill ladyfingers.

As a guideline, though, use the following quantities:

For the top and sides of one 9-inch layer of cake use ¾ cup of frosting; to ascertain the amount needed for a multiple-layer cake, simply multiply ¾ by the number of layers in your cake. A 4-layer, 9-inch cake would take 3 cups.

For the top and sides of a 9½ x 5½ x 3-inch loaf use 1½ cups. If you split a loaf horizontally to make it into layers, add ½ cup for each needed layer of filling.

For a 16 x 5 x 4-inch loaf—top and sides—use 2½ cups.

For a 10 x 15-inch roll use 2 cups.

For 12 large cupcakes, allow 1½ cups frosting.

For an 8-inch square loaf use 1½ to 2 cups.

Other quantities may be computed roughly if you visualize the surface area of the cake in relation to that of the various cakes above. A rather flat, rectangular cake, for instance, would have approximately double the surface area of the loaf cake. But err always on the generous side. If your budget does not permit a free hand with the frosting, then make a cake that requires no other frosting than a dusting of powdered sugar. Do not compensate for a rich frosting by making an inexpensive and perhaps inferior cake. Popular opinion notwithstanding, the cake should be the main point of interest!

Most books state flatly that all cakes should be cold before they are filled and frosted. This is true of many, but it is *not* true of all. There is a wide range of cakes that are actually improved if filled and frosted while still warm, perhaps even hot from the oven. Follow specific recipe directions in this matter until you are experienced enough to make your own decisions.

Layer cakes will be sturdier if the flat undersides of two layers are placed facing each other. The bottom layer, in other words, would be filled bottom-up while the second layer would be put in place bottom-down. Third and fourth layers of a four-layer cake may repeat the pattern of the bottom two. In the case of a three-layer cake, after the filling has been spread over the second layer, let it stand for a few minutes at room temperature or, better, in the refrigerator, to give it a firmness before the third layer is put in place. If two top sides are used face to face, spread on a little extra filling to make up for their slightly curved surfaces.

To frost the outside surface of the cake, spread the whole cake with a thin coating of frosting, covering the sides first; then allow it to set a few minutes before applying the frosting in its full thickness, again spreading the sides first. Apply the final coat with a broad-bladed knife or narrow spatula. (An artist's palette knife will give excellent special effects.) Work with a wide, swirling motion. Come up on the sides in a curving stroke from the bottom, using generous globs of frosting. Whatever drops off your knife or spatula can be retrieved and reused without damage. Frost the top last. Pile the frosting high in the middle and work out from the center, or pile it in an even ring and work in from the edge. In either case use the wide curving stroke. If you have been generous with your frosting, your cake will be beautiful just as it is. If, however, you feel inclined to play with tubes and pastry bags, do so by all means, but remember that understatement can be more attractive than overstatement!

The addition of such things as chopped and slivered nuts or a final chocolate glaze should not be thought of as in the same category as sugary rosettes, however. Nuts of any kind add both texture and flavor as well as visual beauty; a glaze adds flavor and often texture as well, since on cooling or chilling the glaze may harden. Nuts may be applied in different ways. They may be spread over the surface of the cake or they may be pressed into a glaze or into the frosting on the sides. To accomplish the latter, chop or sliver more than the quantity you will need, sprinkle them around the base of the cake on paper or on the plate and then scoop them up against the sides of the cake with a spatula or similar implement. Some will adhere, some will fall back; but no matter. With little effort you can make enough of them stick to the cake so that it will have a professional appearance. Brush the remaining nuts gently away and use them for something else.

FLUFFY WHITE FROSTING

1½ cups sugar
½ teaspoon cream of tartar
⅛ teaspoon salt
½ cup hot water

½ cup egg whites (4 large ones)
½ teaspoon vanilla or other
flavoring, or to taste

Combine sugar, cream of tartar, salt and hot water in a saucepan. Bring to a boil and cook without stirring until it reaches the soft-ball stage (238° F. on your candy thermometer). Meanwhile beat the egg whites until stiff but not dry. Pour the hot syrup over the beaten whites in a thin stream, beating constantly as you do so. Continue beating until the frosting is light and creamy. Add vanilla or other flavoring; blend.

A WHITE FUDGE FROSTING

⅔ cup butter
1 cup granulated sugar
⅓ cup milk

3 cups confectioners' sugar
1 teaspoon vanilla or other flavoring, or quantity to taste

Melt the butter in a saucepan over low heat; add granulated sugar, blend and cook 2 minutes, stirring constantly. Add milk and stir until it comes just to a boil. Remove from heat and let cool 10 minutes. Gradually beat in the confectioners' sugar. When the frosting is creamy and of a good spreadable consistency, add the vanilla. Spread on cold layers of cake for filling and frosting.

As we mentioned a short while back, cake decoration should be practised in private until one has mastered at least the rudiments of the art, and an art it is, as you will learn once you try it. For those who want to practice, here is a simple Decorator's Frosting.

DECORATOR'S FROSTING

¼ cup sweet butter
2 cups confectioners' sugar
1½ tablespoons milk

1 teaspoon vanilla
1 pinch salt

Cream butter until soft. Work in half the sugar and continue to cream until light and fluffy. Now add the remaining sugar and milk alternately, blending and beating after each addition. When smooth and creamy, add vanilla and salt. Use with pastry bag or tube.

Orange frostings are delectable with chocolate cake. Here are two of them:

ORANGE BUTTER FROSTING

½ cup butter (¼ pound)
4 cups confectioners' sugar
1 teaspoon vanilla
1 pinch salt

2 egg yolks
3 to 4 tablespoons orange juice
2 teaspoons grated orange rind

Cream butter until soft; gradually work in half of the sugar, the vanilla and salt. Now beat the egg yolks with the orange juice and rind. Alternately add the remaining sugar and the egg mixture to the butter mixture, beating well after each addition. Continue beating until the frosting is light and creamy. Use for filling or frosting or both. Marvelous if finished with a chocolate glaze—or Allegretti Frosting (see page 87).

A BOILED YELLOW FROSTING

1⅔ cups sugar
3 tablespoons light corn syrup
½ cup water
3 egg yolks
¼ teaspoon salt

Grated rind of ½ orange
1 teaspoon grated lemon rind
1 teaspoon lemon juice, Cointreau or curaçao, or to taste

Combine sugar, syrup and water in a small saucepan, bring to a boil and cook without stirring until it reaches the hard-ball stage (250° F. on your candy thermometer). Meanwhile beat the egg yolks with the salt until light and lemon colored. Gradually pour the syrup into the yolks, beating as you do so. Add the grated rinds and continue to beat until the frosting is thick and creamy—and of a good spreadable consistency. Beat in the lemon juice or other flavoring. Fill and frost cake when cold.

For good measure, here is an orange frosting made with cream cheese:

A CREAM CHEESE-ORANGE FROSTING

2 3-ounce packages cream cheese
4½ cups sifted confectioners' sugar

1 scant tablespoon grated orange rind
2 tablespoons Grand Marnier or curaçao

Cream the cheese with half of the sugar and the orange rind. When light and fluffy, work in the remaining sugar and liqueur alternately until you get the desired consistency. Use all of the liqueur but only as much of the remaining sugar as you need. This will fill and frost a 2-layer, 9-inch cake.

To start the chocolate frosting, we have a simple one:

A BOILED ICING

¾ cup sugar
¼ cup water
1 ounce bitter chocolate, grated

2 egg yolks, beaten
1 pinch salt
¼ teaspoon vanilla

Combine sugar and water in a small saucepan and boil until a thick syrup. Add chocolate and cook over low heat until chocolate is melted. Pour hot chocolate slowly over beaten egg yolks, beating as you do so. Add salt and vanilla. Beat until thick and creamy. If too thick, thin with coffee, cream or water; or, for additional flavor, with sherry, rum or brandy.

This Brown Sugar Boiled Icing has a very different flavor.

BROWN SUGAR BOILED ICING

2 cups brown sugar, packed
⅔ cup water
1½ ounces bitter chocolate

¾ cup (⅜ pound) butter
¼ teaspoon vanilla
1 pinch salt

Combine sugar and water in small saucepan; bring to a boil and cook without stirring until it spins a thread (230° F. on your candy thermometer). Meanwhile melt chocolate with butter. Remove from heat and add vanilla and salt. Remove syrup from fire when proper temperature is reached and add the chocolate mixture. Beat constantly as it cools and continue beating until of a thick, spreadable consistency. If the frosting tends to separate at any point, add a teaspoon or two of cold water and continue beating. Fill and frost cake when cold.

The rich fluffy frostings that are the hallmarks of most American cakes were especially devised for the American taste. Many French frostings are rich, to be sure, but they have a different consistency. Many other French frostings are exceedingly plain, as is this one, for instance.

A FRENCH CHOCOLATE FROSTING

8 ounces semisweet chocolate
¼ cup whipping cream

2½ cups confectioners' sugar

Melt chocolate over hot water. Add cream and blend. Remove from heat. Gradually beat in the confectioners' sugar, and continue beating until smooth. Spread frosting while still warm.

This frosting has a marvelous sheen.

GLOSSY BLACK FROSTING

1 6-ounce package semisweet
  chocolate bits
2 tablespoons butter

3 tablespoons milk
1 cup sifted powdered sugar
1 pinch salt

Combine chocolate, butter and milk in double boiler and cook until chocolate is melted. Remove from heat and add sugar and salt. Beat vigorously as the frosting cools and continue to beat until of a spreadable consistency. Fill and frost cake when cold.

This frosting is as good as it is easy.

NEVER FAIL CHOCOLATE FROSTING

2 ounces bitter chocolate
1 14-ounce can sweetened
  condensed milk

1 pinch salt
1 teaspoon vanilla
1 tablespoon butter

Combine chocolate, condensed milk and salt in a double boiler and cook until chocolate is melted and the mixture is thick and smooth, about 10 minutes. Remove from heat. Add vanilla and butter. Place pan in bowl of cold water and beat until thick and creamy. If it gets too thick, thin with a little cream. Fill and frost 2-layer, 9-inch cake when cold.

Blender frostings take less than half a minute from start to finish.

BLENDER CHOCOLATE FROSTING

6 ounces semisweet chocolate
  bits
¼ cup strong, black, hot coffee
¼ cup confectioners' sugar
4 egg yolks

½ cup soft butter
1 tablespoon rum *or* 1 teaspoon
  vanilla or in combination to
  taste
1 pinch salt

Combine chocolate and hot coffee in blender. Blend 15 seconds. Add remaining ingredients and blend 15 seconds longer. Pour and scrape into bowl. Chill until of a spreadable consistency. Fill and frost a 2-layer, 8-inch cake.

This frosting is somewhat similar to the previous one though it is beaten by hand.

CHOCOLATE BUTTER WHIP

4 ounces bitter chocolate
5 tablespoons butter
½ cup milk
¼ teaspoon salt

2 eggs
2 cups powdered sugar
½ teaspoon vanilla

Melt chocolate with butter in a double boiler. Combine remaining ingredients in bowl and beat until blended. Place bowl in large bowl with ice-water or cracked ice. Add chocolate mixture and beat until stiff enough to spread. Fill and frost a 2-layer, 9-inch cake.

For a final touch of richness, cake frostings may be finished with an over-glaze of chocolate. Sometimes this is spread over the entire surface of the cake. Sometimes it is allowed to drip unevenly down the sides. An Allegretti Frosting is spread around the edge of the upper surface of the cake, over the basic frosting (which has been allowed to dry a bit), and is allowed to run down as it may. It is especially good over an orange frosting.

ALLEGRETTI FROSTING

2 ounces bitter chocolate   ½ teaspoon butter

Melt chocolate and butter together and when blended, spread around edge of cake and allow to drip down at will. Chill to harden.

For a glaze of a somewhat different consistency, try this Honey Glaze.

HONEY GLAZE

1 ounce bitter chocolate
1 ounce semisweet chocolate
1 teaspoon honey

2 tablespoons softened butter
1 pinch salt

Melt the chocolates together over hot water. Add the honey and blend. Add the butter and salt and stir until smooth. This recipe may be increased proportionately at will and the glaze, if desired, may be spread over the entire surface of another frosting (which has been allowed to dry) or it may be applied directly to the cake.

Or for still another consistency you can try Boiled Glaze.

BOILED GLAZE

⅓ cup granulated sugar
¼ cup water
2 ounces bitter chocolate

1 teaspoon butter
1 tablespoon milk or light cream

Combine sugar and water in small saucepan, bring to a boil and cook 30 seconds, stirring constantly. Melt chocolate over hot water and add the hot syrup slowly. Stir in the butter. Remove from heat and beat in cold milk. Continue to beat until of a spreadable consistency.

LOAF CAKES

American cakes fall chiefly into three major categories—butter cakes, sponge cakes and angel food cakes. They are also distinguished in many respects by their size and shape which they take, of course, from the pans they are baked in. Actually, people tend to think in terms of loaf cakes, layer cakes, cakes baked in tube pans, and flattish sheet cakes. The form of a cake does much to suggest the style and perhaps even the richness of its frosting. Sometimes the form of a cake will suggest that it have no frosting at all. Layers of cake, of course, suggest fillings as well as frostings. And loaf cakes and sheet cakes, perhaps because of the basic plainness of their forms, invite an added richness of ingredients. What's more, the very look of a sheet cake suggests that it be cut into square serving portions while still hot to be served hot with a sauce of some kind, for all the world like a pudding. (Plain chocolate sheet cake served hot with a curaçao-flavored Hard Sauce [page 66] makes a marvelous dessert.) So we have separated our cakes according to the pans they require. And we will start arbitrarily with loaf cakes.

In the old days, pound cake recipes meant what they said: a pound of each ingredient went into the mixing bowl, and the mixing went on and on for the better part of an hour, or even longer. Sometimes the eggs alone were beaten for an hour. Nowadays pound cake indicates a general type of cake, close-grained and of a marked richness despite the changed proportions.

CHOCOLATE POUND CAKE

5 ounces bitter chocolate
¼ cup strong black coffee
1½ cups butter
3 cups sugar
5 eggs
3 cups sifted cake flour

1 teaspoon baking powder
½ teaspoon salt
¼ teaspoon cinnamon
¾ cup rich milk
1 tablespoon brandy

Melt chocolate with the coffee over hot water; set aside and let cool. In a good-sized bowl, cream the butter until light and fluffy. Gradually work in the sugar. When thoroughly blended, beat in the eggs one at a time, beating 3 minutes after each addition. Combine the dry ingredients and sift them all together. Combine chocolate with milk and brandy. Add the dry ingredients and the chocolate mixture to the batter alternately, bit by bit, blending after each addition. Butter a 9 x 5 x 2¾-inch loaf pan and line it with wax paper. Butter the paper as well. Pour in the batter and bake at 325° F. until the cake tests done, about 1½ hours. If you prefer a moist cake, let it cool in the pan, then turn out on a rack and carefully peel off the paper. If you prefer a rather dry cake, turn it out on the rack immediately to cool. Serve unfrosted, but with a sprinkling of powdered sugar if you like. We prefer the cake well chilled.

Virtually all chocolate cakes, regardless of their butter content, or the number of eggs or quantity of sugar they contain, have a quality of richness about them. This one, though actually a simple cake, has the quality in extra measure.

RICH CHOCOLATE CAKE

3 ounces bitter chocolate
½ cup boiling water
2 eggs
1½ cups sugar
½ cup butter

1 pinch salt
1 teaspoon vanilla
¾ cup buttermilk
1 teaspoon baking soda
1½ cups sifted flour

Melt chocolate with boiling water; remove from heat and let cool. Beat eggs until thick and lemony; beat in sugar gradually, then butter and salt. When all are thoroughly blended, add chocolate and vanilla. Combine buttermilk and soda. Add buttermilk and flour alternately to the batter, beating after each addition. Pour into a greased, floured loaf pan—9 x 5 x 2¾-inches—and bake at 375° F. for 45 minutes or until the cake tests done. Let cake cool in pan, then turn out and frost as desired. Chill slightly before serving.

This delectable cake is reputedly of Roumanian origin, and its chief differences lies in the fact that it has a baked-in layer of nuts and chocolate.

ROUMANIAN SOUR CREAM CAKE

3 eggs
1¼ cups sugar
1 teaspoon vanilla
½ pint (1 cup) sour cream
1¾ cups sifted flour
1 teaspoon baking soda
1 teaspoon baking powder
4 tablespoons grated sweet chocolate
2 tablespoons finely chopped walnuts

Beat eggs until lemony, then beat with sugar. Add vanilla and sour cream and mix thoroughly. Sift flour with baking soda and baking powder. Add to the batter and blend. Pour half the batter into a buttered loaf pan—9 x 5 x 2¾ inches—sprinkle evenly with chocolate and walnuts, pour the remaining batter on gently. Bake at 350° F. for 1 hour. Let cake cool in pan, then turn out on a rack. Sprinkle with powdered sugar if desired.

Fruit cakes of any kind have a special richness all their own. With chocolate added they are virtually confections. This Black Coffee Fruit Cake is one of the best, and is especially good for the winter holiday season because it can be made well ahead of time.

BLACK COFFEE FRUIT CAKE

½ cup (¼ pound) butter
2 cups dark brown sugar
1½ ounces bitter chocolate
½ cup strong black coffee
2 tablespoons unsulphured molasses
2 eggs, beaten
3 cups sifted flour
3 teaspoons baking powder
½ teaspoon salt
¼ teaspoon baking soda
½ teaspoon cinnamon
¼ teaspoon cloves
¼ teaspoon mace
½ cup seedless raisins
½ cup currants
¼ cup candied orange peel, cut
¼ cup candied grapefruit peel, cut
¼ cup candied cherries, cut
¼ cup candied pineapple, cut

In a large mixing bowl, cream the butter and sugar. Melt chocolate with coffee over hot water; let cool. Add chocolate, molasses and beaten eggs to butter mixture and blend thoroughly. Set aside ½ cup of the flour. Combine the remaining flour with all the dry ingredients and then sift together. Dredge the cut-up fruits with the reserved ½ cup flour. Add dry ingredients to batter and blend. Fold in the fruits and any flour that has fallen from them. Blend. Butter a loaf pan, line the bottom with wax paper and butter the paper. Pour in batter and bake at 250° F. for 20 minutes. Now turn the heat up gradually every 10 minutes until it reaches 350° F. Bake at 350° F. until the cake tests done, about 1 hour and 20 minutes from start to finish. Let the cake cool in the pan. When cold, turn out and store as is in a tightly covered tin box, or—if to be served immediately or soon—ice with powdered sugar that has been brought to spreading consistency with a little cream and rum.

It is difficult to decide whether this creation should be listed as cake or pudding or soufflé. In its finished consistency it resembles all three. Perhaps because of that it is triply delectable with its quality reflected precisely in its name.

CROESUS CAKE

4 4-ounce bars German sweet chocolate	4 eggs, separated
½ cup sweet butter	4 teaspoons sugar
	4 teaspoons flour

Melt chocolate over hot water. Remove from heat and beat in the butter. Beat the egg whites until stiff and set aside. Beat the yolks until thick and lemon colored. Gradually beat in the sugar, then the flour, beating the latter until just blended. Combine yolk mixture with chocolate; blend. Gently fold in the beaten egg whites. Butter a 9 x 5 x 2¾-inch loaf pan and line it with wax paper; pour in batter and place in oven at 425° F. *Immediately* turn the heat down to 350° F. Bake 25 minutes. Let the cake cool completely in its pan on a rack. It will settle as it cools; it is supposed to. Remove from pan and chill 4 hours in the wax paper. Loosen paper before serving. Top with lightly sweetened whipped cream and curls of bitter chocolate. Serves 12 to 16.

LAYER CAKES
MADE FROM LOAF CAKES

In France, layer cakes are made from loaf cakes or flat cakes—oblong, square or round—cut horizontally to the desired thickness, then filled and frosted. In the early days in this country, before layer cakes had become standard, this was often our way with cakes as well. One of the finest of these was made in South Carolina just prior to the Civil War. Oddly enough, it was thought of not as a cake at all but rather as a pudding.

HAMPTON POLONAISE

1 loaf pound cake 9× 5 × 3 inches
1½ cups milk
1½ tablespoons cornstarch
4 egg yolks, beaten
¼ cup sugar
1 pound blanched almonds
¾ pound citron
1 tablespoon brandy
3 ounces bitter chocolate, grated fine
White Fudge Frosting (see page 83) using lemon juice to flavor instead of vanilla

Slice the pound cake in 8 layers of equal thickness. In a double boiler combine milk, cornstarch, egg yolks and sugar. Blend. Cook over moderate heat, stirring constantly, until very thick and smooth. Set aside. Halve 6 to 8 whole almonds and reserve. Cut 1 tablespoon of slivers from the citron; reserve. Grind the remaining almonds and citron together through the finest blade of your grinder. Add brandy and blend.

Divide the hot custard into two equal parts. To one add the grated chocolate; stir until the chocolate is dissolved. Return the custard to gentle heat for a few minutes if necessary. Add the almond mixture to the other half of the custard. Blend. Now fill the layers of pound cake with the two mixtures alternately, starting with the chocolate and ending with the chocolate. You will have three rather thicker layers of the almond filling. Put the cake together gently. Chill.

Prepare the icing as directed, but use strained lemon juice instead of vanilla and use enough of it so that the icing has a pronounced lemon flavor. Frost the entire cake thickly and smoothly with this icing. Decorate with the reserved almonds and citron. Chill again before serving. Serves 10 to 12.

Here is a chocolate loaf cake to be split and finished with its own special chocolate filling and frosting.

CHOCOLATE CAKE ISCHIA

For the cake:

4 ounces semisweet chocolate	2 teaspoons baking powder
⅔ cup butter	¾ cup sour cream
⅔ cup sugar	½ teaspoon soda
3 eggs	1 teaspoon vanilla
6 tablespoons light corn syrup	1 teaspoon almond extract
2 cups sifted flour	Fine dry bread crumbs

Melt chocolate over hot water; let it cool. Cream butter with sugar; when light and fluffy, beat in the eggs, one at a time. Beat several minutes after each addition. Beat in the corn syrup and the melted chocolate. Sift flour with baking powder. Blend sour cream with soda. Add dry ingredients and cream alternately to egg mixture, blending after each addition. Add vanilla and almond extract. Blend. Grease a 4½ x 11½ x 3-inch loaf pan. Sprinkle the inside with very fine dry bread crumbs. Shake out any excess. Pour in the batter and bake at 375° F. for 1 hour or a little longer. Cover cake with aluminum foil if the top seems to be browning too much during baking. Turn cake out on a rack to cool when done. Cut into 3 even layers when cold.

For the filling:

¾ cup milk	1 tablespoon gelatin
2 egg yolks, beaten	3 tablespoons cold water
3 tablespoons sugar	⅔ cup whipping cream,
2½ tablespoons cocoa	whipped stiff
2 teaspoons cornstarch	

Combine milk, egg yolks, sugar, cocoa and cornstarch in the top of a double boiler and blend. Cook over hot water, stirring constantly, until thick and smooth. Soften gelatin in cold water. When custard is nearly done, add gelatin and stir until dissolved. Remove pan from heat, set in bowl of ice water. Stir as it cools. When it is about to set, fold in whipped cream. Spread equally between layers of cake. Chill.

For the frosting—part 1:

1¼ cup confectioners' sugar,
sifted
  1 cup finely ground blanched
  almonds

1 egg white
½ teaspoon almond extract

In a mixing bowl combine the sugar and almonds; blend. Add unbeaten egg white and almond extract. Work the mixture quickly and
lightly with your fingertips until the consistency of pastry dough. Press
lightly together. Turn out on sheet of waxed paper. Press flat with
fingertips. Cover with another sheet of wax paper and gently roll paste
to size of top of cake. Remove top sheet of wax paper. Invert other
sheet so that almond paste goes into place on cake. Pat down gently.

For the frosting—part 2:

¾ cup sugar
3 ounces bitter chocolate

6 tablespoons milk
1½ tablespoons butter

Combine all the ingredients in the top of a double boiler. Cook, stirring
constantly, until the chocolate is dissolved. Continue to cook, stirring
frequently, until the mixture reaches the soft-ball stage (238° F. on
your candy thermometer) or forms a soft ball when a bit is dropped
in cold water. Remove pan from heat. Let cool to lukewarm. Spread
evenly over top and sides of cake. Sprinkle top of cake with the final
fillip,

⅓ cup finely shaved almonds

This cake will serve 16 to 20 and is well worth every second of the
effort involved!

RING AND
TUBE-PAN CAKES

Many batters besides those for angel food cakes are well suited to
baking in tube pans. These cakes are sometimes split horizontally and
filled like layer cakes, but most are frosted just as they are.

PLAIN CHOCOLATE RING CAKE

2½ ounces bitter chocolate
½ cup (¼ pound) butter
2 cups sugar
4 eggs, separated
2 cups sifted cake flour

2 teaspoons baking powder
¼ teaspoon baking soda
¼ teaspoon salt
1 cup buttermilk
1 additional pinch salt

Melt chocolate over hot water and cool. Cream butter and sugar until light. Add egg yolks and beat thoroughly. Add cooled chocolate and blend. Combine sifted flour with dry ingredients and then sift all together. Add dry ingredients and buttermilk to batter alternately, blending after each addition. Beat the egg whites with the pinch of salt until stiff. Fold gently into the batter. Pour into a greased 9-inch tube pan and bake at 375° F. 40 to 45 minutes. Cool in pan or turned out on rack as desired. Frost when cold with a chocolate frosting.

Springform pans are available with both flat bottoms and bottoms that have central tubes. This Chocolate Syrup Cake (one of the best cakes ever devised) calls for one of the latter, preferably 9 inches in diameter. It was developed by Sylvia Hirsch to get the most chocolaty chocolate cake possible.

CHOCOLATE SYRUP CAKE

¼ pound butter
1 cup sugar
4 whole eggs
1 cup sifted cake flour
½ teaspoon baking powder

1 generous pinch salt
1 1-pound can chocolate syrup
  (or equivalent homemade)
½ teaspoon vanilla

Cream butter and sugar until light and fluffy. One by one beat in the whole eggs, beating well after each addition. Combine sifted flour with baking powder and salt, then sift again. Add to egg mixture and blend. Add chocolate syrup and vanilla and beat until the batter is no longer streaky. Pour batter (which will be very thin) into a buttered and floured 9-inch springform pan as described above. Bake at 375° F. for 1 hour. Cool in pan right side up. When cold, remove ring and invert to free from tube and bottom. Set right-side-up on a serving dish and dust with powdered sugar.

Applesauce cakes are particularly American. This one combining applesauce and cocoa is especially good!

APPLESAUCE COCOA DELIGHT

½ cup (¼ pound) butter
1 cup dark brown sugar,
   packed
1 egg
1⅔ cups sifted cake flour
½ teaspoon salt
1 teaspoon baking soda

¾ teaspoon cinnamon
½ teaspoon cloves
3 tablespoons cocoa
¾ cup seedless white raisins
½ cup currants
½ cup finely chopped pecans
1 cup applesauce, heated

Cream butter and sugar until light. Add egg and beat thoroughly. Set ⅓ cup flour aside. Combine the remaining flour with dry ingredients and sift all together. Dredge the fruits and nuts with the ⅓ cup flour. Add dry ingredients to the butter-egg mixture and beat until just smooth. Add nuts and raisins and any extra flour. Blend. Fold in the warm applesauce. Mix thoroughly. Turn into a greased 9-inch tube pan and bake at 350° F. for 40 to 50 minutes or until the cake tests done. Cool in pan. When cold, frost if desired with 1 cup powdered sugar brought to spreadable consistency with a little cream and rum or all cream with a touch of vanilla. Or simply dust the cake with powdered sugar. This cake is also excellent if served hot, sliced fresh from the oven with ice-cold heavy cream or whipped cream lightly sweetened.

This cake, apparently, is a man's cake. Men think it wonderful, while women tolerate it at best. The authors are therefore divided on the matter, so you will have to decide for yourself.

SPICED CHOCOLATE FRUIT CAKE

½ cup (¼ pound) butter
1½ cups sugar
4 eggs
4½ ounces dark sweet chocolate,
   grated
½ cup finely chopped mixed
   citron, candied orange peel
   and candied lemon peel

2½ cups sifted cake flour
1½ teaspoons baking powder
1 pinch salt
½ teaspoon cloves
1¼ teaspoons cinnamon
¼ teaspoon nutmeg
1 scant cup milk (about ⅞ plus)

Cream butter and sugar until light. Add eggs and beat thoroughly. Add grated chocolate and finely chopped fruits. Combine sifted flour with dry ingredients and sift all together. Add dry ingredients and milk alternately to egg batter, blending after each addition. When all are combined, beat just until smooth. Pour into a buttered tube pan and bake at 350° F. 50 to 60 minutes or until the cake tests done. Cool in pan, then frost with a chocolate icing or simply dust with powdered sugar.

In the Hirsch household, this delectable Spiced Potato Cake (which, if you prefer, you may call a spiced chocolate cake) has been a standby for several generations. Old-fashioned though it is, it more than holds its own with any modern cake and in fact disappears faster than many of them.

GRANDMOTHER'S SPICED POTATO CAKE

1 cup butter (½ pound)
2 cups plus 2 tablespoons sugar
4 eggs, separated
1¼ cups grated bitter chocolate
1 cup ground English walnuts
1¼ cups finely grated cold boiled Irish (white) potatoes
1½ cups sifted cake flour

½ teaspoon cinnamon
2 teaspoons baking powder
¼ teaspoon salt
½ cup half-and-half (cream and milk)
1½ teaspoons vanilla
1 additional pinch salt

Cream butter and sugar until light and fluffy. Add egg yolks and beat thoroughly. Add chocolate, nuts and potatoes; beat again. Combine sifted flour with dry ingredients and then sift together. Add dry ingredients and half-and-half alternately to batter, blending after each addition. Add vanilla. Beat egg whites with pinch of salt until stiff. Pour into a greased and lightly floured tube pan. Bake at 350° F. for 50 to 60 minutes. Cool in pan or turned out on rack as desired. When cold, either frost or dust with powdered sugar.

In the old days, Marble cakes were made with a spice cake batter giving their dark striations, but since mid-nineteenth century, chocolate batters have been used as well. Many of these cakes are even more delicious than the old-timers.

SAMMY'S MARBLE CAKE

1 ounce bitter chocolate	2 teaspoons baking powder
⅓ cup plus 1 tablespoon butter	1 generous pinch salt
1 cup sugar	½ cup milk
2 eggs, beaten	1 teaspoon vanilla
1½ cups sifted flour	

Melt chocolate with 1 tablespoon butter over hot water and cool. Cream the remaining butter with the sugar until light and fluffy. Add the beaten eggs and beat together until thick. Combine flour with baking powder and salt and sift all together. Add flour mixture and milk alternately to the batter, blending after each addition. Pour ⅓ of the batter into a separate bowl and combine with the cooled chocolate. Add vanilla to the remaining batter. Drop the two batters by alternate spoonfuls into a well-greased and floured 9-inch tube pan. Bake at 350° F. for about 40 minutes or until the cake tests done. Cool in pan or turned out on rack as desired. Dust with plain powdered sugar or ice with your favorite frosting. If you are adept in applying frostings, swirl on two different kinds with a narrow spatula, one white and the other chocolate. If two frostings are used, swirl them up and down diagonally so that with each slice of cake the diner will have light and dark together.

Matzo flour gives cakes a special texture that many find delightful.

COCOA MATZO CAKE

7 eggs, separated	2 tablespoons cold water
1 cup plus 2 tablespoons sugar	Juice of 1 good-sized orange
¾ cup sifted matzo cake flour	Grated rind of orange
4½ tablespoons cocoa	⅓ cup finely chopped almonds,
¼ teaspoon salt	not blanched
	¼ teaspoon vanilla

Combine egg yolks with sugar and beat until very light. Combine sifted flour with cocoa and salt. Combine cold water and orange juice. Add dry ingredients and juice mixture alternately to the egg-yolk mixture, beating after each addition. Fold in grated rind, nuts and vanilla. Beat egg whites until stiff and fold in gently. Pour into ungreased tube pan or ring and bake at 325° F. for 45 minutes. Invert cake to cool in pan as directed on page 99. When cold, remove from pan and frost with any chocolate frosting, preferably one flavored with orange rind or orange liqueur or both.

Of delicious flavor and and interesting, crunchy texture is the Black Devil Cake, not to be confused in any way with devil's food.

BLACK DEVIL CAKE

4½ ounces bitter chocolate
½ cup butter (¼ pound)
3 eggs, separated
1¼ cups sugar
¾ cup sifted cake flour

1 teaspoon baking powder
1 generous pinch salt
¾ cup finely chopped pecans
1 teaspoon vanilla

Melt chocolate with butter in a double boiler; cool. Beat egg yolks with sugar until thick and lemon colored. Combine flour, baking powder and salt, then sift together. Beat chocolate into egg mixture, then slowly blend in the dry ingredients; then the nuts and vanilla. Beat the egg whites until stiff and fold into the batter gently but thoroughly. Grease and flour a 1½-quart ring mold. Pour in the batter and bake at 350° F. for 20 minutes. Cool in the pan or on a rack as desired. Frost when cold, perhaps with the Cream Cheese-Orange Icing (page 84) or any chocolate frosting or just sprinkle with powdered sugar.

The chiffon cake is a relatively new member of the American cake family. Its lightness is of the sponge cake order but its richness is much like that of pound cake. It calls for a liquid shortening, and thus the long process of creaming butter and sugar is eliminated. The ultimate texture of the cake is achieved by gently pouring the egg yolk batter over stiffly beaten egg whites, then folding it in, a simple operation for anyone.

Chiffon cakes, like angel food cakes, are invariably baked in ungreased pans, tube or ring, and they must be cooled in the pans in an inverted position. This hangs the cakes, as it were, stretching them to their fullest height and giving them maximum lightness. To do this, simply support the rim of an inverted cake pan on three cans or tumblers of equal height.

COCOA PUFF CAKE

¾ cup boiling water
½ cup cocoa
1½ cups sifted flour
1¾ cups sugar
1½ teaspoons baking soda
1 teaspoon salt

½ cup vegetable oil
7 unbeaten egg yolks
1 teaspoon vanilla
½ cup almond extract
1 cup egg whites (7 to 8)
½ teaspoon cream of tartar

Combine boiling water with cocoa; stir to blend thoroughly. Cool. Sift flour three times, then combine with sugar, soda and salt. Sift together into mixing bowl. Make a well in the center of the dry ingredients and add oil, egg yolks, vanilla, almond extract and cocoa. Beat until just smooth. Beat the egg whites with the cream of tartar until stiff. Slowly pour the cocoa batter over the beaten whites, folding it in gently as you do so. Pour batter into an ungreased 10-inch tube pan. Bake at 325° F. for 55 minutes. Invert tube pan for cake to cool, propping it on the end of the tube or supporting the edge of the rim as described above. Remove from pan when cold. Then frost with this special frosting:

SOUR CREAM FROSTING

1 6-ounce package semisweet
    chocolate bits
½ cup butter
½ cup sour cream
½ teaspoon vanilla

½ teaspoon almond extract
¼ teaspoon salt
2½ cups sifted powdered sugar
    (or more as needed)

Melt chocolate with butter in the top of a double boiler. Cool. Add remaining ingredients. Whip with wire whisk until of correct spreadable consistency (adding more sugar if needed), then frost the cooled cake. Chill before serving.

Angel food cakes need no introduction to most Americans. They are unusual in baking in two ways: first, they require no shortening at all and hence are diet cakes, if any cake can be called such, and second, an ungreased tube pan is always used for their baking. In fact, so essential to success is the absolutely fat-free pan that even a residue of grease left in a tube pan from a previous baking will keep the cake from rising properly.

Angel food cakes may be either iced or not, as desired, after they have been allowed to cool in the baking pan (with the pan inverted as for the chiffon cakes [page 99]). Many delightful desserts can be contrived with one of these feathery light cakes as a base. The soft center crumb of the cake may be removed, leaving a shell to act as container. The crumb may be combined with whipped cream and/or custard, preserved or candied fruits, and nuts to make the filling, and then chilled. Or the cake may be sliced into layers and filled if desired; but if you do slice it, use a pronged cake-cutter or a long-tined fork, piercing into the cake all around horizontally. The texture of an angel food cake is such that it tends to tear.

CHOCOLATE ANGEL FOOD CAKE

¾ cup sifted cake flour	¼ teaspoon salt
¼ cup cocoa	1 teaspoon cream of tartar
1¼ cups sugar	(be sure it is fresh)
10 egg whites (from large eggs)	1½ teaspoons vanilla

Combine flour and cocoa and sift together 4 or 5 times. Sift sugar. Beat the egg whites until they are beginning to hold a shape, then beat in salt and cream of tartar. Continue beating until stiff. Sift the sugar over the egg whites, folding in gently as you do so. Sprinkle on the vanilla and fold that in also. Sift the flour-cocoa mixture over the whites a little at a time, folding this in as well. Spoon the batter into an ungreased 10-inch tube pan. Run a knife blade gently through the batter to break up any large air holes. Bake 30 minutes at 275° F. Increase heat to 325° F. and bake 30 minutes longer. Invert to cool as directed on page 99. Turn out when cold and frost or dust with powdered sugar. Or, fill and top with chocolate-flavored whipped cream (see page 135). Chill before serving.

This batter may be used for angel food cupcakes if you happen to own a new muffin tin, or have cupcake papers on hand. Bake 25 to 30 minutes at 300° F. and invert the pan or the cups to let the cakes cool —an operation more easily performed with the pan, of course. These little cakes, if hollowed out, make excellent shells for individual desserts, using the center cake crumb, naturally, in combination with a rich custard or plain, sweetened or chocolate-flavored whipped cream.

A marble angel food cake may also be made by mixing half the amount of cocoa with half of the flour and leaving the other half of the flour plain. Then, following the procedure for Chocolate Angel Food Cake, divide the egg whites in half after the sugar and vanilla have been folded in. Sift the cocoa mixture over one half and the plain flour over the other. Spoon batters into the ungreased tube pan in alternate spoonfuls and bake as directed.

So-called Stuffed Angel Food Cakes are often put together and some-times even frosted with a gelatin mixture. The extent of additional flavorings and ingredients that can be combined with it, even when chocolate is the basic flavor, is endless. Here is a recipe that you can use either for its own sake or as a point of departure.

STUFFED ANGEL FOOD CAKE

1 10-inch angel food cake, 1 day old	1 cup milk
4 ounces bitter chocolate	2 tablespoons gelatin
1 cup powdered sugar	½ cup cold water
¼ teaspoon salt	2½ cups whipping cream
	Chopped pistachio nuts

Bake either a plain or a Chocolate Angel Food Cake as directed on page 101. Do this a day ahead of time so that the cake will dry a little. Cut it in 3 equal horizontal slices.

Melt chocolate in double boiler over hot water. Add sugar and salt. Blend. Slowly stir in the milk and cook over low heat until smooth. Soften gelatin in cold water. Combine with hot chocolate mixture and stir until dissolved. Remove pan from heat and stand in bowl of cold water. Stir as it thickens. Beat the cream until stiff but still with a soft smoothness to it. When the chocolate mixture is very thick and just on the verge of setting, fold in the cream. Blend gently. Spread between layers of cake and pile one on top of the other. Spread the remaining chocolate mixture over the entire surface of the cake. Sprinkle with chopped pistachio nuts and chill. Serves 12.

For a change, flavor the chocolate mixture with rum to taste or curaçao or brandy. Add extra chopped or slivered nuts between the layers. Arrange halved maraschino cherries between the layers and decorate the top of the cake with more cherries in a pretty pattern. Spread layers of plain angel food with raspberry jam or orange mar-malade before adding the chocolate filling.

FLAT, SQUARE, AND RECTANGULAR CAKES

Cakes baked in flat, rectangular or square pans are usually thought of as the plainest cakes. Many of them *are* plain, and many closely resemble such old-time puddings as cottage pudding, for instance. Many are actually served as puddings with a sauce or whipped cream. But they do not have to be plain, and an interesting variety is possible. Both layer cake and loaf cake batters may be baked in rectangular or square pans, of course; many of the batters usually baked in tube pans may also be baked in this way—those for angel food and chiffon cakes excepted. But certain batters seem to require these pans, which should always be buttered and are usually floured lightly. The cakes should be turned out to cool on racks if you like them dry, or cooled in the pans if you like them moist.

CHOCOLATE CHERRY CAKE

1 ounce bitter chocolate	⅔ cup buttermilk
2 tablespoons water	2 tablespoons juice from jar of
½ cup butter	maraschino cherries
1½ cups sifted flour	1 egg
1 cup sugar	⅓ cup halved, drained
1 teaspoon soda	maraschino cherries
½ teaspoon salt	

Melt chocolate with water in double boiler; cool. Put butter in mixing bowl. Combine flour with sugar, soda and salt. Sift three times. Add to shortening. Add buttermilk and cherry juice. Beat 2 minutes at low speed with electric beater. (See note below). Scrape down sides of bowl. Add egg and cooled chocolate. Beat 2 minutes longer. Scrape down bowl again. Butter an 8 x 8 x 2-inch pan and line it with wax paper. Butter the paper. Pour in the batter. Arrange halved cherries at intervals over top. Bake at 350° F. for 35 minutes. Cool cake in the pan with the pan set on a rack. When cool, turn out and strip off paper. Ice cake with a chocolate frosting. Decorate, if desired, with additional cherries.

Still using the same ingredients, this cake can be radically changed if you add the cherries directly to the batter. During baking they will sink to the bottom of the cake and this, when done, will have an almost candied consistency.

NOTE: In case you do not have an electric beater, 300 strokes by hand is the equivalent of 2 minutes electric beating at low speed.

FUDGE CAKE SQUARES

4½ ounces bitter chocolate
¾ cup (⅜ pound) butter
1 whole egg
3 yolks
2¼ cups sifted flour

1½ teaspoons baking powder
¼ teaspoon salt
1½ cups milk
1¾ teaspoons vanilla
Powdered sugar as needed

Melt chocolate in double boiler over hot water; cool. Cream butter and sugar until light and fluffy. Add the whole egg and yolks one at a time, beating well after each addition. Add chocolate and blend. Combine flour with baking powder and salt. Sift together. Add dry ingredients and milk alternately to the chocolate mixture, blending after each addition. Add vanilla. Pour into a greased and lightly floured 13 x 9 x 1½-inch pan. Bake at 350° F. for 35 minutes. Cool in pan. Turn out when cold and dust with powdered sugar or frost with a marshmallow icing. Or you might add richness to richness by topping the marshmallow icing with a chocolate drip glaze or Allegretti Frosting (page 87).

SOUR CREAM FUDGE CAKE

3 ounces bitter chocolate
¼ cup water
2 cups sifted cake flour
1½ cups sugar
1 teaspoon soda

1 teaspoon salt
⅓ cup butter
1 cup sour cream
2 eggs
1 teaspoon vanilla

Melt chocolate with water in a double boiler; let stand over the hot water while the batter is prepared. Combine flour, sugar, soda and salt. Sift together into a mixing bowl. Add butter and sour cream. Beat for 2 minutes with an electric beater at low speed. (This is equal to 300 strokes by hand.) Add chocolate, eggs and vanilla. Beat for 2 minutes longer. Scrape down sides of bowl.

Grease the bottom of a 13 x 9 x 1½-inch pan. Line pan with wax paper and grease the paper. Pour in batter. Shake pan to spread it evenly. Bake about 35 minutes at 350° F. or until the cake tests done— or until the cake shows a marked resilience when touched at the center with the fingertips. Cool cake 5 minutes in pan. Turn out on rack, peel off paper and let cool completely. Sprinkle with powdered sugar or frost as desired. Serves 12. The same batter may be baked in 2 9-inch layer cake pans.

This Fudge Cake is undoubtedly the easiest cake ever devised, but its quality is excellent. The entire cake is mixed in its 9-inch square baking pan. You have your cake, from start to finish, in about 35 minutes.

LAST MINUTE FUDGE CAKE

⅓ cup butter, melted and cooled

2 envelopes (2 ounces) no-melt bitter chocolate

1 egg

1 cup sugar

1¾ cup instant flour

½ teaspoon baking soda

½ teaspoon salt

½ teaspoon vanilla

¾ cup water

½ cup semisweet chocolate bits

¼ cup walnut or pecan halves (as desired)

Pour the cooled butter into the 9-inch square pan. Add no-melt chocolate, egg, sugar, flour, soda, salt, vanilla and water. Beat with a fork until smooth and creamy, about 2 minutes. Scrape bottom and sides of pan with a rubber spatula after 1 minute of beating to gather up any ingredients not incorporated in the batter. Spread batter smooth with spatula when done. Sprinkle with chocolate bits, then arrange the nuts in a pattern on top. Bake 30 minutes at 350° F. Cool in pan and cut in squares before serving.

Nut Candy Cake, as its name implies, is virtually a candy. But like so many other rich foods, it seems to benefit from still more richness. It is at its best with a marshmallow icing topped by a dripping of bitter chocolate.

NUT CANDY CAKE

3 ounces bitter chocolate
⅓ cup butter
1 cup sugar
2 eggs, separated
2 teaspoons grated orange rind
1½ cups sifted cake flour
½ teaspoon salt
1½ teaspoons baking powder
1 cup milk
1 teaspoon vanilla
¾ cup chopped pecans
½ cup additional sugar

Melt chocolate in double boiler over hot water. Cool. Cream butter with 1 cup sugar until light and fluffy. Add egg yolks and orange rind. Beat until thick. Add chocolate and blend. Combine flour with salt and baking powder and then sift all together. Add dry ingredients and milk alternately to chocolate mixture, blending after each addition. Add vanilla and nuts; blend thoroughly. Beat the egg whites until they hold soft peaks and then gradually beat in the extra ½ cup sugar. When they are stiff and satiny, fold them gently into the batter. Butter a 10 x 12-inch pan and line it with wax paper. Butter the paper. Pour in batter evenly and bake at 350° F. for 25 to 30 minutes. Let cool in pan. Turn out when cold and frost as desired. The marshmallow icing with chocolate drip glaze (page 87) is our preference.

Yeast-risen cakes were once extremely popular in this country, and they still are in Europe today. They have a special flavor and texture that sets them apart from other cakes. But they do take time, since the batter must be set to rise like bread dough, and this, in the popular mind, is equated with work. Most of them, however, are very simple.

A YEAST-RISEN CHOCOLATE CAKE

½ package active dry yeast
¼ cup lukewarm water
1 cup butter
2 cups sugar
3 eggs
4 ounces bitter chocolate
1 cup milk
½ teaspoon salt
2¾ cups sifted flour
1 teaspoon soda
3 tablespoons hot black coffee
1½ teaspoons vanilla

In a cup, combine the yeast and warm water (*not* hot water). In a bowl, cream the butter until light and fluffy. Gradually work in the sugar. When all is combined, add the eggs one at a time, beating after each addition. Melt chocolate in the milk over low heat, stirring frequently. Cool. Add salt to the sifted flour; add this mixture and the cooled chocolate milk alternately to the egg batter. Blend after each addition. Add the yeast and blend. Cover and let stand overnight at 75° to 80° F.

Next morning, dissolve soda in hot coffee. Add to risen batter with the vanilla. Stir quickly. Pour batter into a greased and floured 9 x 12 x 2-inch pan. Bake at 350° F. for 45 minutes or until the cake is done. Turn out on rack to cool. Dust with confectioners' sugar before serving.

There are unfortunate people around who are allergic to eggs and for them virtually all cakes are off limits. This is one they can enjoy, however, eggless and delicious.

EGGLESS COCOA CAKE

1¾ cups sifted cake flour	⅓ cup softened butter
1 cup sugar	1½ teaspoons vanilla
¼ cup cocoa	1 tablespoon vinegar
1 teaspoon soda	1 cup cold water
½ teaspoon salt	

Combine all the dry ingredients and sift them together into a mixing bowl. Add all the remaining ingredients and beat until the batter is *almost* smooth. Butter a 9-inch square pan, line it with wax paper and butter the paper. Pour in the batter and bake at 350° F. for 30 minutes. Serve either warm or cold with sweetened whipped cream, or if desired, with a sauce of some kind, a rum-flavored Hard Sauce, for instance, if the cake is served hot.

This Black Beauty Cake lives up to its name admirably.

BLACK BEAUTY CAKE

2 ounces bitter chocolate	½ teaspoon salt
½ cup boiling water	¼ cup butter (½ stick), softened
1 cup sifted cake flour	¼ cup buttermilk
1 cup sugar	¾ teaspoon vanilla
¼ teaspoon baking powder	1 egg
½ teaspoon baking soda	

Melt chocolate in boiling water; cool. Combine the dry ingredients and sift them together. Add dry ingredients and softened butter to chocolate and beat well. Add buttermilk, vanilla and egg and beat again, until just smooth. Grease and flour an 8 x 8 x 2-inch pan. Pour in batter and bake at 350° F. for 35 minutes. Cool in pan, then turn out and frost as desired.

SPECIAL CAKES

No matter how many cakes are created, there always seems to be room for more. Many are made possible by gimmicks, new ways of applying the traditional methods. Here are two of them; the first is a Chocolate Bar Cake that is baked in an iron skillet, the second, an upside-down cake.

CHOCOLATE BAR CAKE

½ cup cold water
½ cup cocoa
1½ cups sifted flour
1 teaspoon soda
½ teaspoon salt
1 cup dark brown sugar,
  packed

½ cup butter (¼ pound)
3 eggs
½ cup buttermilk
1 teaspoon vanilla
4 1-ounce milk chocolate bars

Add cold water to cocoa gradually; blend thoroughly. Combine flour, soda, salt and sugar; sift together into a large bowl. Add butter, eggs and ¼ cup of the buttermilk. Beat 3 minutes with electric beater, 6 to 7 minutes by hand. Add vanilla and the remaining buttermilk. Beat 2 minutes longer. Pour into greased 10-inch iron skillet. Place the chocolate bars at even intervals on top of the batter. Bake at 300° F. for about 30 minutes. Serve cake warm or cold, cut in pie-shape wedges. Top each portion with sweetened whipped cream or ice cream.

CHOCOLATE UPSIDE-DOWN CAKE

½ cup dark brown sugar, packed
½ cup white sugar
4 tablespoons cocoa
1 cup water
1 ounce bitter chocolate
1 cup sifted cake flour
¼ teaspoon salt

2 teaspoons baking powder
2 tablespoons butter
¾ cup additional sugar
½ cup milk
½ cup chopped pecans
1 teaspoon vanilla

Combine brown sugar, ½ cup white sugar, cocoa and water in a saucepan. Bring just to boil and stir until the sugar is completely dissolved, about 3 minutes. Set aside to cool. Melt chocolate over hot water and set aside. Combine flour, salt and baking powder. Sift together. Cream butter with additional sugar. Alternately add the sifted dry ingredients and milk to the butter-sugar mixture, blending after each addition.

Stir in melted chocolate, nuts and vanilla. Pour into a greased 1½-quart baking dish. Carefully spoon the cocoa syrup over the batter. Bake at 350° F. for 45 to 50 minutes. Cool in baking dish. When cold, turn upside down on serving plate. Serve with sweetened whipped cream.

ROLLS

Chocolate rolls are among the loveliest of all desserts. Although some people may think of them as more closely related to icebox cakes, and some as more closely related to puddings, we will put them here with cakes, for they are made of cake that is baked as a rule in a 10 x 15-inch jelly roll pan, buttered and lined with buttered wax paper. Despite their elegant appearance, chocolate rolls are very simple, but careful attention must be paid to a few basic details.

Cakes for chocolate rolls must be turned out of their pans while hot, either onto a clean towel (sometimes dampened, sometimes sugared) or a sheet of wax paper. Then, the wax paper on which they are baked is carefully peeled away; the edges of the cake are trimmed of all crust; and the cake is rolled (still hot or at least warm), using the edge of the towel or wax paper to gently nudge it up and over, curling the cake slowly in on itself like a wave.

The cake then cools completely in this position. Before serving, the cake is unrolled gently and spread with a filling (from 2 to 4 cups, depending on consistency, for a 10 x 15-inch sheet). The filling may be whipped cream, softened ice cream or something of a custard nature, such as the *Crème Pâtissière* (see page 87), or even a buttery frosting. Raspberry or apricot jam may be used in addition to whipped cream; orange marmalade makes for a delectable variation, or you might use fresh raspberries or strawberries (lightly sweetened) as they do in Denmark. Once the cake is spread, it is quickly and gently rolled up once more, loosely so that the filling is not squeezed out. And the whole roll is usually chilled for an hour or longer, or even slipped into the freezer. Then, too, you may frost the whole roll if you like, or top it with whipped cream, or simply dust it with powdered sugar. Whipped cream, lightly sweetened and perhaps flavored, is our choice. This may be topped in turn with curls of bitter chocolate, a dusting of cocoa or a sprinkling of either chopped or slivered nuts. Green pistachios make a lovely topping.

A "PLAIN" CHOCOLATE ROLL

The cake:

5 eggs, separated	3 tablespoons cocoa
1 cup powdered sugar	1 pinch salt
1 tablespoon flour	

Beat egg yolks until light; add sugar and beat until very thick. Beat the egg whites until stiff and fold gently into the yolk mixture. Combine flour, cocoa and salt and bit by bit sift it over the batter, folding it in after each addition. Grease a 10 x 15-inch jelly roll pan and line it with wax paper. Grease the paper. Pour on the batter evenly. Bake at 350° F. for 20 minutes. Turn out on a clean dish towel lightly dampened. Trim edges of cake with very sharp knife. Roll while warm and let cool. When cold, unroll gently, fill, reroll, then ice.

The filling:

1 cup whipping cream	2 tablespoons cocoa
½ cup powdered sugar	1¼ teaspoons vanilla

Whip the cream until just stiff, then whip in sugar and cocoa. Add vanilla and whip again. Spread over cake evenly, reroll cake and spread on frosting.

The frosting:

½ cup powdered sugar	1 teaspoon vanilla
1 tablespoon cocoa	2 tablespoons cream

Blend the dry ingredients and add vanilla. Bit by bit work in as much of the cream as you need to make a smooth paste. Spread this evenly over the roll and chill 2 hours before serving.

Note:

Ice cream makes a fine filling for chocolate rolls, and for a cake baked in a 10 x 15-inch pan, you will need 1 quart of it. Soften just to spreadable consistency. Spread evenly over cake, roll and place in the freezer compartment of your refrigerator (or deep freeze) long enough for the ice cream to set. Such rolls may be frosted either just before serving with whipped cream or a "made" frosting; or the latter may be spread on the cake when filled and frozen with it. For this, place the frosted roll in the freezer uncovered and leave until the frosting has set, then wrap as desired. Such a cake may be frozen for several days or longer. Thaw in the refrigerator an hour or so before serving.

This chocolate roll is the favorite of the Hirsch household, so it comes by its name logically enough.

THE FAVORITE CHOCOLATE ROLL

5 eggs, separated
¾ cup sugar
6 ounces sweet chocolate
3 tablespoons cold water
1 pinch salt

1 teaspoon vanilla
¼ cup grated bitter chocolate
1 cup heavy cream
¼ cup additional sugar
½ teaspoon vanilla

Combine egg yolks and sugar and beat until very light. Melt sweet chocolate with cold water in double boiler; cool. Add sweet chocolate to yolk mixture and beat again. Add salt and vanilla. Beat egg whites until stiff and fold gently into the batter. Butter a 10 x 15-inch jelly roll pan and line it with wax paper; butter the paper. Pour in batter evenly and bake at 350° F. for 10 minutes. Reduce heat to 300° F. and bake 5 minutes longer. Remove cake from oven. Cover cake in pan with a cold dampened towel. Chill 1 hour in refrigerator. Remove cloth. Sprinkle top of cake evenly with grated chocolate. Lay a sheet of wax paper over the cake and invert. Remove pan. Remove buttered paper carefully. Trim edges with a sharp knife. Whip cream and sweeten and flavor it with the additional sugar and ½ teaspoon vanilla. Spread over cake and roll gently. Dust with powdered sugar and chill until needed. If desired, the powdered sugar may be mixed with a little cocoa.

Even richer is this roll which uses both sweet and bitter chocolate and is flavored with rum.

DOUBLE CHOCOLATE RUM ROLL

For the cake:

5 eggs, separated
¾ cup sugar

3 tablespoons sifted flour
1 pinch salt

Combine egg yolks and 5 tablespoons of the sugar; beat until light. Add flour and salt and beat until just blended. Beat the egg whites until stiff and fold them gently into the batter. Butter a jelly roll pan and line it with wax paper; butter the paper. Pour the batter into the pan evenly and bake at 350° F. for about 10 minutes or until lightly browned. Turn cake out onto wax paper; peel paper from bottom, trim sides with a very sharp knife and then sprinkle the surface with the remaining sugar. Roll and let cool completely. Chill.

For the filling:

6 ounces sweet chocolate
1 ounce bitter chocolate
3 tablespoons cold water

3 tablespoons butter
3 tablespoons rum

Melt chocolates with the cold water and butter in a double boiler. When smooth, stir in the rum. Cool. When the sauce is cold, unroll the cake and spread it evenly with the chocolate mixture. Reroll gently and spread the remaining chocolate mixture over the top. Chill again. Before serving sprinkle with

½ cup grated sweet chocolate
Powdered sugar as desired

2 to 3 tablespoons chopped
  pistachios or almonds

The candy filling of this chocolate roll offers a complete change.

CHOCOLATE CANDY ROLL

2 eggs, separated
6 tablespoons sugar
½ teaspoon vanilla
6 tablespoons sifted flour

1 teaspoon baking powder
1 pinch salt
4 ounces dark sweet chocolate
¼ cup strong black coffee or rum

Combine egg yolks and sugar and beat until very thick. Add vanilla and beat again. Combine flour with baking powder and salt and sift together into the batter. Beat until smooth with a wide, scooping motion to get air into the mixture. Beat the egg whites until stiff and fold into the batter gently. Butter a 12 x 10-inch pan and flour it lightly. Shake out any excess. Pour the batter in evenly and bake at 425° F. 7 minutes. While cake is baking dampen a clean towel and sprinkle it with sugar. When the cake is done, turn it out onto the sugared towel and trim the edges. Melt chocolate with coffee or rum over hot water. While still hot, spread it evenly over the cake. Roll the cake up in the cloth gently and chill. When the candy filling has hardened, it is ready to serve. Sprinkle with powdered sugar if desired.

VENETIAN SPONGE ROLL

2 ounces bitter chocolate
2 tablespoons butter
2 eggs
1 cup sugar
¼ cup hot water

¾ teaspoon vanilla
1¼ cups sifted cake flour
2 teaspoons baking powder
1 generous pinch salt

Melt chocolate with butter in top of double boiler; cool. Beat eggs until light and lemon colored; add sugar and continue to beat until thick. Add hot water and blend. Add chocolate and vanilla; blend. Combine flour, baking powder and salt. Sift all together twice. Fold into the chocolate batter. Butter a 10 x 15-inch pan and line it with wax paper; butter the paper. Pour in the batter evenly and bake at 350° F. for 20 minutes. Turn out on a dampened towel. Carefully remove buttered paper. Trim edges of cake with a sharp knife. While cake is still warm, spread with a Cold Chocolate Rum Cream (page 80), roll gently and chill. Dust with powdered sugar befor serving.

ONE-LAYER CAKES
BAKED IN SPRINGFORM PANS

Springform pans are especially useful for large cakes or cakes which require special handling when being taken from the pan after baking. These pans consist of flat metal bottoms and removable sides which are simply unclamped, leaving the cake to cool on a baked-in dish, as it were. The most useful size for general household purposes is 9 inches in diameter and 3 inches deep. They come larger, however; in fact, much larger, and they are good to remember for impressive dessert cakes for large parties. For small parties you might try this French chocolate cake, *Gâteau au Chocolat,* for which we give two versions, neither of which is for calorie counters.

GÂTEAU AU CHOCOLAT #1

1 pound sweet chocolate	⅔ cup soft sweet butter
1 teaspoon water	¼ teaspoon salt
1 tablespoon flour	4 eggs, separated
1 tablespoon sugar	

Melt the chocolate with 1 teaspoon water over hot, not boiling, water. Remove from heat and stir in flour, sugar and softened butter. Stir until completely smooth. Add salt. Beat egg yolks until thick, then stir them slowly into the chocolate mixture, blending them completely. Beat the egg whites until they hold soft peaks (they must not be dry) and fold them gently into the batter. Line an 8-inch springform pan with wax paper. Butter the paper very lightly. Pour in the batter. Bake at 425° F. 15 minutes—no longer! Though your cake will not look done, it will come to the proper consistency as it cools in the pan. When cold, remove from springform and carefully take off paper. Decorate with lightly sweetened whipped cream if you desire, but any kind of frosting is superfluous. Serves 6.

GÂTEAU AU CHOCOLAT #2

5 ounces sweet chocolate	½ cup sugar
4 tablespoons water	5 tablespoons sifted flour
5 eggs, separated	Grated rind of 1 orange

Melt chocolate with water in double boiler; cool. Beat egg yolks with sugar until thick and lemon colored. Add chocolate and flour. Blend thoroughly. Beat egg whites until they hold soft peaks and fold gently into the batter. Fold in the grated orange rind. Line an 8-inch spring-form pan with wax paper and butter the paper lightly. Pour in the batter and bake at 350° F. 45 minutes. Remove rim of springform when cake is done. Let cool on rack. And prepare this frosting:

The frosting:

4 egg yolks	4 tablespoons orange juice
¾ cup light corn syrup	1¼ cups butter
6 ounces sweet chocolate	2 tablespoons rum

Beat egg yolks until light. Boil corn syrup until it spins a thread. Pour the hot syrup into the egg yolks, beating constantly as you do so. Continue beating until quite stiff. Melt chocolate with orange juice. Add butter and blend thoroughly. Cool. Combine cool chocolate mixture with egg yolk mixture. Blend. Beat until smooth and of spreadable consistency. Add rum. Spread over cooled cake. Top frosting with

½ cup chopped almonds
Powdered sugar

This chocolate nut cake has all sorts of surprises in it, not the least of which is the presence of left-over mashed potatoes:

LEPRECHAUN CAKE

3 ounces bitter chocolate	1 pinch salt
1 cup butter	¼ teaspoon nutmeg
2 cups sugar	1 cup buttermilk
4 eggs	1 teaspoon cinnamon
1 cup leftover mashed potatoes	1 cup chopped pecans or
2 cups sifted flour	walnuts or almonds
1 teaspoon baking soda	

Melt chocolate in double boiler over hot water; cool. Cream butter until light, then work in sugar. When all is thoroughly blended, add eggs and beat until thick. Add potatoes and chocolate; blend. Combine dry ingredients and sift together. Add to batter alternately with butter-milk, blending after each addition. Fold in chopped nuts. Butter and flour a 9-inch springform pan. Pour in batter and bake at 350° F. for 45 minutes. Cool in pan, then remove rim and turn cake onto rack. Frost with the Sour Cream Chocolate Frosting (page 120), or simply serve with sweetened whipped cream.

LAYER CAKES

The layer cake as such is an American invention and its possibilities are endless. One can make a layer cake taller or shorter at will; using the same kind of cake and the same number of layers, one can make a new and different cake by changing the frosting and the filling; one can combine two or even more fillings in one cake. After filling and frosting, one can add a drip glaze, or bury the cake under a beautiful white snow of grated coconut. Fresh fruits, candied fruits, and pre-serves can be used not only to decorate a layer cake but to add flavor, and, of course, variety, to fillings.

French layer cakes, seldom if ever known as such, are made as a rule from a basic butter cake, the *Genoise*, split horizontally into layers. Our layer cakes are *baked* in layers . . . as every American knows. Most are baked in round pans, 8, 9 or 10 inches in diameter and 1 inch deep. Some are baked in rectangular pans or square pans. But the object of all is identical, a series of layers put together with rich fill-ing between to achieve height, and in many cases the greater the height the better.

AN 8-LAYER CHOCOLATE CAKE

For the cake:

4 ounces bitter chocolate
1 cup black coffee
½ cup (¼ pound) butter
1 pound dark brown sugar
2 eggs
½ cup buttermilk

1 teaspoon vanilla
2½ cups sifted cake flour
½ teaspoon salt
2 teaspoons baking soda
¼ teaspoon allspice

Melt chocolate with coffee in a double boiler; remove from burner but leave chocolate mixture over the hot water. Cream butter until soft; gradually work in the sugar and beat until light and fluffy. Add eggs, one at a time, beating after each addition. Add buttermilk and vanilla; blend. Combine flour with other dry ingredients and sift together. Add flour mixture and chocolate alternately to egg batter, blending after each addition. Grease and flour 4 9-inch layer cake pans. Divide batter evenly among them. Shake pans lightly to settle batter. Bake at 375° F. for 12 minutes or until done. Turn layers out on a rack to cool. When cold split each in half horizontally with a serrated knife. Place layers cut-side up and spread *seven* of them as follows:

The filling:

1½ cups sour cream
1 cup finely shredded almonds
or pecans

¾ cup orange marmalade
½ cup strawberry preserves

Spread seven layers with equal amounts of sour cream. Sprinkle these with equal amounts of the nuts. Cut the pieces of rind in the marmalade if necessary and then beat it (if necessary) with a fork to get a spreadable consistency. Spread this on 4 layers over the nuts. Mash the strawberries in the preserves to get an even consistency and then spread this on 3 layers. Put the layers alternately on top of one another. Frost the cake with a double recipe of the Chocolate Butter Whip (page 87).

This is a 4-layer cake of marvelous richness, excellent for a party of 12 or so. With 4 cake pans required, you will undoubtedly have to bake the cake in shifts, but since the layers must be cooled on a rack, the pans used for the first 2 layers may be used over again for the next lot.

CHOCOLATE BLOSSOM CAKE

For the cake:

10 ounces semisweet chocolate	3 cups powdered sugar
1¼ cups butter	¼ teaspoon salt
12 eggs	1½ cups sifted cake flour

Melt chocolate and butter together in the top of a double boiler; blend thoroughly and let cool. Do not let it get cold, however. Beat the eggs until thick and lemon colored. Add the powdered sugar and salt and beat until the sugar is completely dissolved, about 5 minutes. Divide this mixture in half. Now sift the flour twice again. Fold half of the flour into half of the egg batter. Fold in half of the chocolate-butter mixture bit by bit. Blend thoroughly. Butter 2 9-inch cake pans and line them with wax paper. Butter the paper. Pour in the mixed batter. Bake at 350° F. for 25 minutes or until the cake tests done. Let the layers cool 3 to 4 minutes in the pans, then turn out on a rack and carefully remove buttered paper. Wash pans and dry them thoroughly. Butter them again. Add remaining sifted flour and chocolate to the other half of the egg batter and proceed as above. While the layers are baking prepare this frosting:

CHOCOLATE CREAM FROSTING

6 ounces bitter chocolate	1 cup heavy cream
½ cup butter	2 teaspoons vanilla
6 cups powdered sugar	

(For the final topping you will need ¼ cup—or more as desired—semisweet chocolate curls; see page 10.)

Melt bitter chocolate in top of double boiler; cool. Cream butter until light. Add the powdered sugar to the butter gradually, alternating it with the cooled chocolate and the heavy cream. Beat vigorously after each addition so that the mixture becomes increasingly smooth and rich. Add vanilla a few drops at a time as you go along. Spread cold layers of cake with frosting, then put together gently. Frost sides of cake, then top. Sprinkle with chocolate curls and chill several hours before serving.

This is a 3-layer cake baked in 9-inch pans. It has a slightly different flavor because of the special chocolate used.

GERMAN CHOCOLATE CAKE

1 package Baker's German
    sweet chocolate
½ cup hot water
1 cup plus 2 tablespoons butter
2 cups sugar
4 eggs, separated

1½ teaspoons vanilla
2½ cups sifted cake flour
½ teaspoon salt
1 teaspoon baking soda
1 cup buttermilk

Melt chocolate with hot water in double boiler; cool. Cream butter and sugar until light. Add eggs yolks and beat until thick. Add chocolate and vanilla. Blend thoroughly. Combine flour with salt and baking soda. Sift together. Add the dry ingredients and the buttermilk alternately bit by bit to the egg batter, blending after each addition. Beat the egg whites until stiff but not dry and fold gently into the batter. Butter and flour 3 9-inch cake pans. Pour in the batter and shake the pans to set it evenly. Bake at 350° F. for 35 minutes. Cool in pans. When cold, turn out and frost with the following:

COCONUT FROSTING

1 cup commercial half-and-half
1 cup sugar
3 egg yolks
½ cup (¼ pound) butter

1 teaspoon vanilla
1 can coconut, grated
1½ cups slivered, toasted
    almonds

Combine half-and-half, sugar, egg yolks and butter in a saucepan. Blend. Cook over low to medium heat 12 minutes, stirring constantly, or until well thickened. Add vanilla, coconut and slivered almonds. Remove from heat and beat until cool and of a spreadable consistency. Spread layers and put them together gently. Put remaining frosting just on the top of the cake. Let it drip unevenly down over the sides. Chill and serve.

Or, if desired, use this delectable Spiced Chocolate Icing for filling and frosting the *entire* cake.

SPICED CHOCOLATE ICING

½ cup butter
2 ounces bitter chocolate
1 tablespoon honey
½ teaspoon vanilla
¾ teaspoon allspice

¼ teaspoon instant coffee
3½ cups sifted confectioners'
    sugar
6 to 7 tablespoons cream

Place butter in a saucepan over low heat and let it brown slightly. Add chocolate and let it melt, stirring frequently. Add honey, vanilla, allspice and instant coffee. Blend. Remove from heat. Alternately beat in sugar and cream. Continue beating as the frosting cools. Spread on cold cake. Refrigerate the cake for at least 1 hour after frosting.

Sponge cakes have no shortening, of course, and so would be excellent cakes for dieters, were it not for the fact that they are usually iced, as is this one of 3 8-inch layers with its special Creamy Frosting.

3-LAYER SPONGE CAKE

4 ounces bitter chocolate
1 cup milk
2 cups sugar
4 eggs, separated
1¼ cups sifted cake flour

2½ teaspoons baking powder
¼ teaspoon salt
¾ teaspoon vanilla
1 cup raspberry jam

Melt chocolate in double boiler; add milk and 1 cup of the sugar. Blend. Stir until smooth. Remove from heat. Beat egg yolks until thick and lemon colored. Beat in the remaining cup of sugar. Add the chocolate mixture and blend. Combine flour with baking powder and salt. Sift together and fold into the batter. Add the vanilla and blend. Beat the egg whites until stiff and fold them into the batter gently. Bake in 3 UNgreased 8-inch pans at 325° F. for 20 minutes. Cool cakes in pans. Then turn out. Spread two of the layers with ½ cup of the raspberry jam each. Put cake together gently and frost with the following:

CREAMY FROSTING

½ pound bitter chocolate
1 cup milk
4 egg yolks

3 cups sugar
2 tablespoons butter
2 teaspoons vanilla

Melt chocolate with milk in a double boiler. Beat the egg yolks with 6 tablespoons of sugar until thick. Add the remaining sugar to the chocolate and cook until sugar is completely dissolved. Add egg-sugar mixture and butter. Blend and cook 1 minute longer, stirring constantly. Cool and then stir in the vanilla. Beat frosting as it cools until it has a thick, creamy consistency. This may be spread just on the surface of the jam-filled cake or part of it may be used as additional filling over the layers of jam, the remainder on the surface as always.

From New Orleans we have a 2-layer sponge 8-inch cake with a very special point of difference . . . rum.

CREOLE SPONGE CAKE

4 ounces bitter chocolate	2 cups sugar
¾ cup milk	1 cup sifted cake flour
¼ cup light rum	1 teaspoon baking powder
4 eggs, separated	1 pinch salt

Melt chocolate with milk in a double boiler; when thoroughly blended, add rum and cook about ½ minute. Remove from heat. Beat egg yolks until thick and lemon colored. Gradually beat in the sugar. Continue to beat until smooth and very thick. Combine flour with baking powder and salt. Sift together. Add dry ingredients and the cooled chocolate mixture alternately to the egg batter, blending after each addition. Beat the egg whites until they are just stiff. Fold them into the batter. Pour batter into 2 ungreased 8-inch pans and bake at 350° F. for 30 to 35 minutes. Let layers cool in pans 10 minutes, then turn out to cool completely on a cake rack. Frost with the following, which was created about twenty years ago by the late Helen Evans Brown of Pasadena. It is, of course, a standard frosting today.

SOUR CREAM CHOCOLATE FROSTING

1 cup semisweet chocolate bits	1 pinch salt
½ cup sour cream	

Melt chocolate bits over hot water. Remove from heat and cool slightly. Stir in sour cream and salt. Beat until creamy. Fill and frost cake when cold.

This luscious cake gains both richness and flavor from sour cream.

SOUR CREAM CHOCOLATE CAKE

½ cup cocoa	½ teaspoon baking soda
¾ cup boiling water	½ cup sour cream
½ cup (¼ pound) butter	2 cups sifted cake flour
2 cups sugar	1 pinch salt
1 teaspoon vanilla	3 egg whites

Dissolve the cocoa in boiling water. Cool. Cream butter and sugar until light and fluffy. Add cocoa and vanilla. Blend. Dissolve soda in the sour cream. Stir into the cocoa mixture. Sift flour and salt four times. Beat the egg whites until stiff. Fold flour and egg whites alternately into the cocoa batter. Blend gently. Grease and flour 2 8-inch layer cake pans. Pour in the batter evenly and bake at 350° F. for 20 minutes. Let layers cool in pans. When cold, turn out and frost with a rich, dark, extra-chocolaty frosting such as the following:

BITTERSWEET CHOCOLATE FROSTING

3 ounces bitter chocolate
1 ounce German sweet chocolate
1 cup evaporated milk

1 cup sugar
1 teaspoon vanilla

Combine the first 4 ingredients in the top of a double boiler and cook, stirring frequently, until the consistency of a thick custard. Add vanilla and blend. Remove from heat and cool. Whip to desired consistency. Fill and frost the layers when cold, using an extra generous amount for filling.

Brown sugar adds a special flavor to this cake which, rightly, is called a *marvel.*

BROWN SUGAR MARVEL

½ cup (¼ pound) butter
1 pound brown sugar
2 eggs
2½ cups sifted cake flour
1 teaspoon baking soda

½ teaspoon salt
1 cup buttermilk
¼ cup plus 1 tablespoon cocoa
½ cup hot water
1¼ teaspoons vanilla

Cream butter and brown sugar until light and fluffy. Add eggs and beat until thick and smooth. Combine flour with soda and salt. Sift together. Add dry ingredients and buttermilk alternately to batter, blending after each addition. Dissolve cocoa in hot water. Stir this into batter and blend. Add vanilla. Grease and flour 2 9-inch cake pans. Pour batter into pans evenly and bake at 300° F. 25 minutes; increase heat to 375° F. and bake 10 minutes longer. Let layers cool in pans or turn out to cool as desired. When cold, fill and frost, preferably with this:

CHOCOLATE WALNUT FROSTING

6 tablespoons milk
2 ounces bitter chocolate
½ cup butter
4 cups powdered sugar

1 generous pinch salt
1½ teaspoons vanilla
½ cup chopped walnuts

Combine milk and chocolate in double boiler and cook until chocolate is melted. Cool. Cream butter. Sift sugar. Gradually work sugar into butter. Beat until light and fluffy. Add chocolate mixture bit by bit, beating to get the right consistency. Add salt, vanilla and chopped walnuts. Frost cake layers when cold and chill cake at least 1 hour before serving. This amount of frosting will do for 24 cupcakes as well.

This brown sugar cake with a special character all its own is delectable with either the Milk Chocolate or White Marshmallow Frosting given below.

BROWN SUGAR FUDGE CAKE

4 ounces bitter chocolate
¾ cup butter
1¾ cups dark brown sugar
1 whole egg
3 egg yolks

2¼ cups sifted flour
1½ teaspoons baking soda
¼ teaspoon salt
1½ cups milk
1½ teaspoons vanilla

Melt chocolate over hot water; cool. Cream butter and sugar together until light and fluffy; add whole egg and beat well. Add the yolks, one at a time, beating after each addition. Add the chocolate and beat again. Combine flour, soda and salt. Sift together. Add dry ingredients and milk alternately to the egg batter, blending after each addition. Add vanilla. Grease and flour 2 9-inch pans. Pour in batter evenly and bake at 350° F. for 40 minutes. Let layers cool 5 minutes in pans, then turn out on rack to cool completely. Fill and frost when cold.

MILK CHOCOLATE FROSTING

¼ pound sweet milk chocolate
  (candy bars)
1 egg

1 cup whipping cream
½ teaspoon vanilla, or to taste

Melt chocolate over hot water; remove from heat and beat in egg. Return to heat for a minute, stirring constantly. Remove entirely and let cool, stirring frequently. Whip cream and fold it into the chocolate mixture. Add vanilla and fold in also. This is also delectable flavored with rum, sherry or curaçao.

WHITE MARSHMALLOW FROSTING

Follow directions for the Chocolate Marshmallow Froth (see page 125) but omit the chocolate.

Still another brown sugar cake with still another texture, this has been a favorite in Dallas for many years, as has its special icing.

LINDA'S FAVORITE CAKE

2 ounces bitter chocolate	2 eggs
1 teaspoon baking soda	½ cup sour cream
½ cup boiling water	1½ cups sifted cake flour
½ cup (¼ pound) butter	1 teaspoon vanilla
2 cups (packed) brown sugar	

Melt chocolate in double boiler. Remove from heat. Dissolve soda in boiling water and stir into chocolate. Set aside. Cream butter and sugar until light and fluffy. Add eggs and beat until thick. Add sour cream and beat again. Bit by bit, add the sifted flour and blend. Add chocolate and vanilla and blend again. Fold repeatedly; do not beat. Grease and flour 2 9-inch pans. Pour in the batter evenly and bake at 350° F. for 20 to 22 minutes or until the cake tests done. Let layers cool in pans. Frost with the following:

LINDA'S SPECIAL ICING

2 ounces bitter chocolate	1 scant cup sugar
1 bar Bakers' German sweet chocolate (4 ounces)	1 tablespoon butter
	1 pinch salt
1 cup coffee cream	1 teaspoon vanilla

Melt the two chocolates together in the top of a double boiler over hot, not boiling water. Add all the other ingredients except the vanilla and cook, stirring frequently, until the mixture clings to the spoon. Remove from heat and let cool. Add vanilla. Beat to a spreadable consistency.

This Black Velvet Cake is made with coffee and brandy.

BLACK VELVET CAKE

⅔ cup butter
1⅔ cups sugar
3 eggs
⅔ cup cocoa
2¼ cups sifted cake flour
¼ teaspoon baking soda

1¼ teaspoons baking powder
¼ teaspoon salt
1 cup black coffee
⅓ cup brandy
1¼ teaspoons vanilla

Cream butter and sugar together, add eggs and beat until very light and fluffy. Combine cocoa, flour, soda, baking powder and salt. Sift together. Combine coffee, brandy and vanilla. Add dry ingredients and coffee mixture alternately to egg mixture, blending after each addition. Beat until just smooth. Grease and flour 2 9-inch cake pans. Pour in batter evenly and bake at 350° F. for 35 minutes. Cool in pans or turned out on rack as desired. When cold, fill and frost with the following:

BOILED BUTTER FUDGE ICING WITH PECANS

2 cups sugar
2 ounces bitter chocolate
2 tablespoons light corn syrup
¾ cup milk

2 tablespoons butter
1 pinch salt
1 teaspoon vanilla
½ cup finely chopped pecans

Combine sugar, chocolate, syrup and milk in saucepan and cook over moderate heat, stirring constantly, until sugar is dissolved. Cook without stirring until it reaches the soft-ball stage—238° F. on your candy thermometer. Remove from heat. Add butter and salt and blend. Place pan in bowl of ice water and beat to spreadable consistency as it cools. Add vanilla and chopped pecans. Beat again and set aside until needed. If it should be *too* thick, add a little cream to thin.

This easy cake is a good one for beginners. Simple as it is to make, its quality and taste are wholly professional.

THE COCOA WONDER

7 tablespoons cocoa
2 cups sifted cake flour
1½ cups sugar
1 teaspoon baking powder
¼ teaspoon salt

2 eggs
¾ cup (1½ sticks) butter
1 cup cold water
½ teaspoon vanilla

Combine all the dry ingredients and sift them together into a mixing bowl. Add the remaining ingredients and beat until smooth. Grease and flour 2 8-inch cake pans. Pour in batter evenly and bake at 350° F. for 40 minutes. Cool in pans or turned out on rack as desired. Fill and frost when cold with the following:

CHOCOLATE MARSHMALLOW FROTH

1½ cups sugar
1½ cups water
2½ ounces bitter chocolate
14 large marshmallows, cut up

2 egg whites
1 pinch salt
⅛ teaspoon cream of tartar
¼ teaspoon vanilla

Combine sugar and water in a saucepan and boil until the soft-ball stage is reached, 238° F. on your candy thermometer. Remove from heat. Add chocolate and marshmallows and let stand until they are melted, stirring from time to time. Beat egg whites until they hold soft peaks, then beat in salt and cream of tartar. Pour the hot chocolate mixture in a thin stream over the beaten whites, beating constantly as you do so. Beat until of a spreadable consistency. Add vanilla and blend. Fill and frost cake when cold, then chill.

Vinegar cakes (as well as vinegar pies) were popular in the old days. They deserve to be brought back into fashion.

VINEGAR CHOCOLATE CAKE

2 ounces bitter chocolate
½ cup (¼ pound) butter
1½ cups sugar
2 eggs
¾ teaspoon vanilla

2 cups sifted cake flour
½ teaspoon salt
1 cup buttermilk
1 teaspoon baking soda
1 tablespoon cider vinegar

Melt chocolate in double boiler; cool. Cream butter and sugar until light and fluffy. Add eggs and beat until thick. Add vanilla, then the melted chocolate. Blend. Combine flour and salt and sift together. Add dry ingredients and buttermilk alternately to the egg batter, blending after each addition. Dissolve soda in vinegar and add to batter. Blend. Grease and flour 2 9-inch cake pans. Pour in batter evenly. Bake at 375° F. for 20 to 25 minutes. Cool in pans or turned out on rack as desired. When cold frost with the following:

SWEET BUTTER ICING

1½ ounces bitter chocolate
1 cup (½ pound) sweet butter
1 egg yolk
¾ teaspoon vanilla

2½ cups powdered sugar
1 teaspoon instant coffee
1 pinch salt

Melt chocolate in a double boiler. Cool. Cream butter and then beat with the egg yolk until thick. Gradually beat in the chocolate and all the remaining ingredients. Continue beating until of a spreadable consistency. Fill and frost cake.

You must follow this recipe with special care for a part of its ingredients will be used as frosting for the finished cake.

THE BIRTHDAY SPECIAL

4 ounces bitter chocolate
2 3-ounce packages cream
    cheese
½ cup (¼ pound) butter
½ teaspoon vanilla
1½ pounds confectioners' sugar
¼ cup hot water

2¼ cups sifted cake flour
1½ teaspoons soda
1 teaspoon salt
¼ cup additional butter
    (⅛ pound)
3 eggs
¾ cup milk

Melt chocolate in double boiler; cool. Cream the cheese with ½ cup butter and vanilla. When smooth, add *half* of the sugar; blend. Alternately work in the hot water and the remaining sugar. Add half of the melted chocolate; blend. Measure 2 cups of this mixture and set aside for the frosting.

Now combine flour, soda and salt; sift together. Add the additional ¼ cup butter to the remaining chocolate mixture and blend thoroughly. Add the eggs one at a time to the chocolate mixture, beating after each addition. When all are in beat 1 minute with electric beater at low speed (150 strokes by hand). Add sifted dry ingredients and milk alternately to the chocolate batter, blending after each addition. Grease and flour 2 9-inch cake pans. Pour in batter evenly and bake at 350° F. for 30 to 35 minutes, or until the cake tests done. Cool in pans or turn out on rack as desired. (We prefer to cool this in the pans.)

While cake is cooling, beat the reserved chocolate-cheese mixture to spreadable consistency. When cake is cold, fill and frost.

VIENNESE CHOCOLATE CAKE

4 ounces bitter chocolate	1 teaspoon soda
1 cup sugar	¼ teaspoon cinnamon
1 cup water	⅛ teaspoon cloves
2⅓ cups sifted flour	¼ teaspoon allspice
½ teaspoon salt	½ teaspoon instant coffee
1 teaspoon baking powder	3 eggs
1 cup (½ pound) butter	½ cup buttermilk
1 additional cup sugar	

Combine chocolate, sugar and water in a double boiler and cook until the chocolate is melted, stirring frequently. Let cool to lukewarm. Combine flour, salt and baking powder. Sift together. Cream butter until light, then add the extra cup of sugar, the soda, spices and coffee. Beat until light and fluffy. Beat the eggs in one by one. Add ½ cup of the sifted flour mixture and blend. Add the chocolate mixture and blend. Add the remaining flour mixture and buttermilk alternately, blending after each addition. Beat 30 seconds.

Grease and flour 2 9-inch cake pans. Pour in the batter evenly and bake at 375° F. for 30 minutes. Cool for 10 minutes in the pans, then turn out on cake rack. When cold, fill and frost with the following:

ORANGE-CHOCOLATE FROSTING

3 cups powdered sugar	½ cup grated dark sweet chocolate
2 tablespoons cream, or more if needed	2 tablespoons strong black coffee
5 tablespoons butter	3 tablespoons orange juice
	1 tablespoon brandy

Sift the sugar, then combine it with all ingredients—except the brandy —in the top of a double boiler. Cook until chocolate is melted, stirring constantly. When smooth and thick, add brandy. Remove from heat and beat as it cools. If it gets too thick, add a little more cream to thin. Fill and frost cold cake.

The secret of the next cake lies in the fact that it contains stewed fruit. The fruit itself cannot be detected as such but it gives a magic touch.

CHOCOLATE SECRET CAKE

1½ ounces bitter chocolate
1¼ cups stewed, drained, pitted
   prunes or apricots, chopped
 6 tablespoons butter (¾ stick)
 ¾ cup sugar
 2 eggs

1⅓ cups sifted cake flour
1⅓ teaspoons baking powder
 ¼ teaspoon baking soda
 ¼ teaspoon salt
 ½ cup milk
 ½ teaspoon vanilla

Melt chocolate in double boiler; cool. Chop the pitted, stewed fruit. Cream butter and sugar together until light and fluffy. Add eggs and beat until thick. Add chocolate and blend. Combine flour, baking powder, soda and salt; sift together. Add dry ingredients and milk alternately to egg batter, blending after each addition. Add vanilla. Add the chopped fruit and beat until smooth. Grease and flour 2 8-inch cake pans. Pour in the batter evenly and bake at 375° F. for 25 minutes. Cool in pans or turned out on rack as desired. (We prefer this cake cooled in the pans.) When cold, fill and frost with the following:

DIVINE CHOCOLATE ICING

2 cups dark brown sugar,
   packed
8 ounces bitter chocolate
2 tablespoons light corn syrup

¼ cup cream
2 tablespoons butter
2 teaspoons vanilla
1 pinch salt

Combine sugar, chocolate, syrup and cream in saucepan and cook over low heat, stirring constantly, until both sugar and chocolate are melted. Now, increase heat slightly and boil without stirring until the syrup reaches the soft-ball stage, 238° F. on your candy thermometer. Remove pan from fire. Add butter. Immerse pan in bowl of ice water and beat as it cools. Add vanilla and pinch of salt and continue beating until of the right consistency. Fill and frost cake. Chill before serving.

The majority of our cakes have been frosted with chocolate frostings not only because we are chocolate addicts, but also because in this way we can give you more chocolate recipes in a limited space. They are all double chocolate cakes in a sense, but this next one just happens to be called a Double Dutch Chocolate Cake.

DOUBLE DUTCH CHOCOLATE CAKE

For the cake:

3 ounces bitter chocolate	2½ cups sifted flour
2 tablespoons butter	2½ teaspoons baking powder
4 eggs	1 pinch salt
2 cups sugar	1 cup milk

Melt chocolate with butter in a double boiler; cool. Beat eggs until very light, then beat with sugar until smooth and thick. Add chocolate mixture and blend. Combine flour, baking powder and salt, then sift together. Add dry ingredients and milk alternately to the chocolate mixture, blending after each addition. Grease and flour 2 9-inch cake pans. Pour in batter evenly and bake at 350° F. for 30 minutes. Cool cake in pans. Turn out when cold to fill and frost with the following:

For the frosting:

3 tablespoons Droste's Dutch cocoa	1 cup milk
¼ cup sugar	1½ teaspoons vanilla
1 tablespoon cornstarch	2 cups whipping cream
	¼ cup shaved bitter chocolate

Blend cocoa, sugar and cornstarch with cold milk in the top of a double boiler away from heat; place over hot water and cook, stirring constantly, until smooth and thick. Add vanilla and cool. Whip cream until stiff. Add 1 cup whipped cream to the cocoa mixture and blend gently. Fill and frost the cake with this mixture. Pile the remaining whipped cream on top of the cake or swirl it around the edge in an elaborate crown. Sprinkle the cream with the shaved bitter chocolate. Candied cherries or drained maraschino cherries may be added for color. For additional flavor a bit of maraschino cherry juice may be whipped into the cream.

It is said that a new hat is good for female spirits; this is a cake that should also lift the spirits, and for the male as well as the female. For the frosting and filling Maillard's semisweet chocolate is essential.

CHOCOLATE DREAM CAKE

For the cake:

4 ounces bitter chocolate	1 cup sifted flour
1 cup milk	1 teaspoon baking powder
5 eggs, separated	1 pinch salt
2 cups sugar	

Melt chocolate with milk in a double boiler; cool. Beat egg yolks with sugar until very thick and light. Combine flour with baking powder and salt and sift together. Add dry ingredients and cooled chocolate mixture alternately to egg yolks. Beat egg whites until stiff and fold into batter. Butter and flour 2 9-inch cake pans. Divide batter evenly between them and bake at 325° F. for 25 minutes. Cool in pans. Turn out when cold and fill and frost with the following:

For the filling and frosting:

5 ounces Maillard's semisweet chocolate	3 tablespoons water
	3 egg yolks, beaten
3 tablespoons sugar	1½ cups whipping cream
1 pinch salt	

Combine chocolate, sugar, salt and water in the top of a double boiler. Cook over hot water, stirring frequently, until smooth and thick. Remove from heat. Cool slightly, then beat in the beaten egg yolks bit by bit. Stir from time to time as the mixture cools. When cold, whip cream until stiff and fold into the chocolate. Fill and frost cake, then chill well before serving.

Housewives used to keep a variety of wines, spirits and liqueurs in the kitchen and doused their cakes generously with whatever struck their fancy as they came hot from the oven. This seemingly hit-or-miss method achieved not only a marvelous variety of flavors, but also gave the cakes a seeming richness because of the moisture. This cake uses somewhat this same approach.

FLORENCE'S CHOCOLATE CAKE

For the cake:

4 ounces bitter chocolate	1 pinch salt
½ cup (¼ pound) butter	1⅓ cups milk
2 cups sugar	1 teaspoon vanilla
4 eggs, separated	4 to 6 tablespoons Tia Maria
2 cups sifted cake flour	(or Kahlua or curaçao)
2 teaspoons baking powder	

Melt chocolate in a double boiler, then cool. Cream butter until light and fluffy, then work in 1½ cups of the sugar. When thoroughly blended, beat in the egg yolks one at a time. When very thick, add the chocolate and blend. Combine flour with baking powder and salt, then sift together. Add flour and milk alternately to the chocolate mixture, blending after each addition. Add the vanilla. Beat the egg whites until they hold soft peaks, then beat in the remaining ½ cup sugar. When glossy, fold them into the batter gently but thoroughly. Grease and flour 2 9-inch cake pans. Pour in batter evenly. Bake at 350° F. for 35 minutes. When cake comes from oven, dribble 2 to 3 tablespoons of liqueur over each layer. Let cool in pans. Turn out when cold and frost with the following:

For the frosting:

2 ounces bitter chocolate
½ cup Tia Maria (or whatever liqueur was used for cake)
4 tablespoons butter

2 cups sugar
½ cup milk
½ cup finely chopped almonds

Melt chocolate in double boiler; cool. Add liqueur and blend. In a saucepan melt the butter; add sugar and milk. Bring to a boil, then reduce heat and cook over low heat 10 minutes. Remove from heat and let cool slightly. Combine syrup with chocolate mixture. Beat until thick enough to spread. If the icing should harden before the cake is frosted, add a very little hot water and beat again. When cake is filled and frosted, sprinkle the top of the cake evenly with the chopped almonds.

DEVIL'S FOOD CAKE WITH BUTTERMILK

2 cups sugar
½ cup plus 1 tablespoon cocoa
1 cup buttermilk
½ cup (¼ pound) butter
2 eggs

2 cups sifted cake flour
1 teaspoon baking soda
½ teaspoon salt
1½ teaspoons vanilla

Combine 1 cup of the sugar with the cocoa and ½ cup of the buttermilk; beat well and set aside. Cream the butter with the remaining 1 cup sugar until light and fluffy. Beat in the eggs one at a time. Combine flour with soda and salt. Sift together. Add dry ingredients and remaining ½ cup buttermilk to the egg mixture alternately, blending after each addition. Add vanilla. Beat the cocoa mixture briefly once more and add that also. Blend. Grease and flour 2 9-inch cake pans. Pour in batter evenly and bake at 350° F. for 30 to 35 minutes. Cool layers in pans. Turn out when cold. Fill and frost with Never-Fail Chocolate Frosting (page 86).

One of the many remarkable things about layer cakes is that a very small difference in the way the cakes are put together can make a big difference in the cakes themselves. The difference in this cake comes from the finely chopped pecans which are evenly sprinkled over the bottom of each cake pan before the batter is added . . . and the special use of the grated chocolate.

CHOCOLATE PECAN SURPRISE

1 cup finely chopped pecans
2½ cups sifted flour
4½ teaspoons baking powder
1 teaspoon salt
1½ cups sugar
⅔ cup softened butter

1¼ cups milk
1 teaspoon vanilla
⅔ cup egg whites, 4 large or 5 medium
2 ounces semisweet chocolate, grated

Grease and flour 2 9-inch cake pans. Sprinkle the bottom of each evenly with finely chopped nuts. Combine flour, baking powder, salt and sugar. Sift together into a mixing bowl. Add butter, milk and vanilla. Beat with an electric beater at medium speed for 1½ minutes (225 strokes by hand). Add the *unbeaten* egg whites. Beat 1½ minutes longer. Now ladle ¼ of the batter carefully into each prepared cake pan. Do not disturb the nuts. Sprinkle half of the grated chocolate over each pan evenly. Cover the chocolate gently with the remaining batter. Bake at 350° F. for 35 to 40 minutes. Cool cake in pans 15 minutes before turning out. Then cool completely on racks. Frost with the layers nut-side up. And use the following:

For the frosting:

2 ounces bitter chocolate
¼ cup granulated sugar
¼ cup water
4 egg yolks, beaten

½ cup butter
1 teaspoon vanilla
2 cups sifted confectioners' sugar

Combine chocolate, granulated sugar and water in a saucepan. Cook over low heat, stirring constantly, until chocolate is melted and the mixture is smooth. Remove from heat. Let cool a minute and then slowly beat in the beaten egg yolks, a little at a time. Continue beating until light and creamy. Cool.

Now cream the butter and work in the vanilla and confectioners' sugar. Set aside ⅓ of this butter mixture to decorate cake. Add the remaining ⅔ to the chocolate mixture and beat until smooth. Fill and frost the cake with the chocolate icing. Then decorate the top with rosettes of the white icing. If you have any candied violets, use those as well. This is a special cake and it should be treated accordingly.

For many years Beatrice was cook in the Hirsch household in Dallas and at times she doubled as nurse for the children as well. For the youngest Hirsch daughter she devised this Banana Cake.

BEA'S BANANA CAKE

½ cup (¼ pound) butter
1½ cups sugar
1 cup mashed bananas
3 eggs
¾ teaspoon vanilla
2½ cups sifted cake flour
½ teaspoon salt

2 teaspoons baking powder
4 tablespoons cocoa
1 cup half-and-half (cream and milk)
1 to 2 bananas sliced as desired and depending on size

Cream butter and sugar together until light and fluffy. Add mashed bananas and eggs and beat until thick and light. Add vanilla. Combine flour with other dry ingredients and sift together. Add dry ingredients and half-and-half alternately to banana mixture, blending after each addition. Grease and flour 2 9-inch cake pans. Pour in batter evenly and bake at 375° F. for 20 to 25 minutes. Cool in pans. When cold, cover one layer with sliced bananas, then fill and frost the cake with the following:

UNCOOKED MOCHA FROSTING

½ cup (¼ pound) butter
1¾ cups sifted powdered sugar
1 tablespoon cocoa
1 pinch salt

3 to 4 tablespoons strong black coffee
1 teaspoon rum

Cream butter until soft, then work in sugar and cocoa. Beat until creamy. Add salt. Bit by bit add the coffee, beating after each addition. Add the rum. Continue beating until the frosting is creamy and of a spreadable consistency. Fill and frost the cake and chill before serving. For other cakes, vanilla may be used instead of the rum or both may be used together.

Most recipes for chocolate spice cakes omit ginger for some reason. This one uses ginger in quantity. Its flavor suggests that a bit of chocolate in many gingerbreads would be to their advantage.

GINGER CHOCOLATE CAKE

1 ounce bitter chocolate	¾ teaspoon salt
1¼ cups milk	4½ teaspoons baking powder
¾ cups butter	1½ teaspoons ginger
1½ cups sugar	½ teaspoon *each* cinnamon and
3 eggs	nutmeg
3 cups sifted cake flour	1½ teaspoons vanilla

Melt chocolate with ¼ cup of the milk in a double boiler; cool. Cream butter and sugar together until light and fluffy. Add eggs, one at a time, beating well after each addition. Add chocolate and blend. Combine flour with all dry ingredients and sift together. Add dry ingredients and remaining milk to egg mixture alternately, blending after each addition. Add vanilla and blend. Grease and butter 2 9-inch cake pans. Pour in batter carefully and bake at 375° F. for 25 minutes. Cool layers in pans for 5 minutes, then turn out on racks and cool completely. Fill and frost with a white icing (see index). Chill before serving.

Although many chiffon cakes are baked in tube pans, as we have seen, some are baked as layer cakes, too.

A BITTER CHOCOLATE CHIFFON CAKE

2½ ounces bitter chocolate	1 teaspoon salt
1¾ cups sifted cake flour	⅓ cup vegetable oil
1½ cups sugar	1 cup buttermilk
¾ teaspoon baking soda	2 eggs, separated

Melt chocolate in a double boiler; cool. Combine flour, 1 cup of the sugar, soda and salt. Sift together into a mixing bowl. Make a well in center of dry ingredients and pour in the vegetable oil and the buttermilk. Beat 2 minutes with a rotary beater. Add egg yolks and chocolate and beat until thoroughly blended. Beat egg whites until they form soft peaks, then beat in the remaining ½ cup sugar. When stiff, fold into the batter. Grease and flour 2 9-inch cake pans. Pour in batter evenly and bake at 350° F. for 25 minutes. Cool cakes in pans. Turn out on rack and split layers horizontally with a serrated knife. When completely cold, fill and frost with Whipped Cream Brown Fluff Icing. Chill cake before serving.

WHIPPED CREAM BROWN FLUFF ICING

2 cups whipping cream	1 pinch salt
1 cup sifted powdered sugar	¼ teaspoon vanilla
½ cup cocoa	

Whip the cream until just barely stiff, then whip in gradually the sifted sugar, cocoa and salt. When all is incorporated and smooth, add vanilla. Fill and frost cake when cold. Chill cake before serving.

Cakes with other than chocolate batters but with chocolate fillings or frostings or both are often called chocolate cakes, too. An elegant example is this French orange cake with orange filling and chocolate frosting which we, for the ease of it, will call an Orange Chocolate Cake.

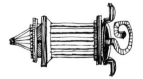

ORANGE CHOCOLATE CAKE

For the cake:

⅔ cup sugar	1 generous pinch salt
4 eggs, separated	1¼ cups sifted cake flour
Grated rind of 1 orange	Extra pinch of salt
⅓ cup strained orange juice	1 tablespoon additional sugar

Beat sugar and egg yolks together until of a thick custard consistency. Add orange rind, juice and pinch of salt. Beat lightly again. Then, bit by bit, beat in the flour. Beat the egg whites with an extra pinch of salt until they form soft peaks. Sprinkle them with the tablespoon sugar and beat again until stiff. Blend ¼ of the whites through the batter, then very gently fold in the remainder. Turn into 9-inch buttered and floured layer cake pan 1½ inches deep. Fill evenly to the rim all around. Bake at 350° F. for 30 to 35 minutes or until the cake is puffed and brown and starting to pull from the sides of the pan. Cool 6 to 7 minutes in the pan. Loosen around edges with a sharp knife if necessary and turn out on a rack to cool completely. When cold, split horizontally in two with a sharp knife.

For the orange filling:

6 tablespoons sweet butter	2 egg yolks
1⅔ cups sugar	Grated rind of 1 orange
2 eggs	¼ cup strained orange juice
	1 tablespoon curaçao

Combine all the ingredients in a double boiler and cook over hot water, stirring constantly, until the mixture has the consistency of honey. Do not stop stirring for a second. When done, remove from heat, set in bowl of cold water and beat to desired thickness. Spread between layers when cold.

For the frosting:

CSOKOLÁDÉ TÖLTELÉK

4 ounces bitter chocolate	2 eggs, beaten
2 tablespoons hot water	½ cup (¼ pound) sweet butter
1 cup confectioners' sugar	

Melt the chocolate in a double boiler; add the hot water and blend. Add sugar and the beaten eggs; stir 1 minute. Remove from heat but leave the chocolate mixture over the hot water. Stir for 3 minutes as it gradually cools and thickens. Cool to lukewarm as quickly as possible, preferably by immersing the top of the double boiler in a bowl of cold water. When lukewarm, add the butter—2 tablespoons at a time—and beat vigorously after each addition. When all the butter has been beaten in, and the frosting is of a spreadable consistency, store in refrigerator until needed (it will never harden).

CUPCAKES

Small cakes may be made from flat sheet cakes cut into desired shapes —diamonds, squares, fingers—or from any cake batter baked in cup-cake pans or special paper cupcake cups. For those baked individually in pans or paper cups the oven as a rule should be set at 375° F. for a baking time of approximately 20 minutes. Cups or pans should be filled in most cases about ⅔ full of batter. When done and thoroughly cooled, the cupcakes may be frosted with any desired icing or frosting.

Cupcakes may also be hollowed out and used as shells for creams or custards or sweetened whipped cream. Preserves and some cake filling may be used in combination if desired. Or the little cakes may be filled with chopped candied fruit and topped with Cold Chocolate Rum Cream (page 80) or the Cooked Cream (page 78).

For small cakes cut out from sheet cakes, try any of the fudge cakes in this book. All of these, when cut, should be frosted on the sides as well as on top, and they should stand a while before serving so that the frosting will have a chance to set. Bear in mind that most of these will be eaten with the fingers, so choose a frosting with some firmness.

LITTLE BROWN CUPCAKES

½ cup (¼ pound) butter	1 teaspoon baking soda
1 cup sugar	½ teaspoon salt
¼ cup cocoa	½ cup milk
1 egg	1½ teaspoons vanilla
1½ cups sifted flour	½ cup boiling water

Cream butter with sugar until light and fluffy. Add cocoa and egg. Beat until thick. Combine flour, baking soda and salt, then sift together. Alternately add dry ingredients and milk to egg mixture, blending after each addition. Add vanilla and lastly the hot water. Beat 5 minutes with electric beater. Fill greased muffin tins ⅔ full of batter. Bake at 350° F. for 25 to 30 minutes. Cool cakes on rack, then frost as desired. Yield, 24.

CHOCOLATE CHIP CUPCAKES

2½ cups sifted cake flour
2¼ teaspoons baking powder
½ teaspoon salt
½ cup (¼ pound) butter
1 cup strained honey

½ cup sugar
3 eggs, separated
1 teaspoon vanilla
½ cup milk
1 cup semisweet chocolate bits

NOTE: Handle this batter as little as possible after the chocolate bits have been added to prevent their sinking to the bottom.

Combine flour, baking powder and salt; sift together three times. Cream butter and then cream with honey; add half of the sugar and blend. Add the egg yolks, one at a time, beating well after each addition. Add vanilla. Add dry ingredients and milk alternately to the batter bit by bit, blending until just smooth. Beat egg whites until they form soft peaks, then beat in the remaining sugar. When they are stiff, fold them gently into the batter. Fold in the chocolate bits. Spoon the batter into greased muffin tins, filling each cup ⅔ full. Bake at 375° F. for 20 minutes. Let cool in pans set *on* rack for 5 minutes. Remove cakes to rack and cool completely. Frost when cold. Or, if you like, serve the cakes warm without any frosting. Yield, 24.

BROWN SUGAR CUPCAKES

½ cup (¼ pound) butter
1 cup brown sugar, packed
1 egg
1½ cups sifted cake flour
½ cup cocoa

½ teaspoon baking soda
¼ teaspoon salt
½ cup buttermilk
1 teaspoon vanilla

Cream butter and sugar together until light and fluffy. Add egg and beat until thick. Combine the dry ingredients and sift together. Add dry ingredients and buttermilk alternately to the egg mixture, blending after each addition. Add vanilla and blend. Fill greased muffin tins ⅔ full of batter. Bake at 375° F. for about 20 minutes. Cool in pans or turned out on rack as desired. When cold, spread with any desired frosting. Yield, about 18 cupcakes.

These cupcakes have the lightness of their name.

FEATHER CUPCAKES

1 ounce bitter chocolate
½ cup (¼ pound) butter

1½ cups sifted cake flour
1½ teaspoons baking powder

1 cup sugar

1 egg

1 tablespoon grated orange rind

¼ teaspoon salt

½ cup milk

¾ teaspoon vanilla

Melt chocolate over hot water; cool. Cream butter and sugar together until light and fluffy. Beat in egg until mixture is thick; add orange peel and blend. Combine dry ingredients and sift together. Add dry ingredients and milk alternately to the egg mixture, blending after each addition. Add vanilla. Beat until just smooth. Fill greased muffin tins ⅔ full of batter and bake at 375° F. for 20 minutes. Cool cakes in pan or turned out on rack as desired. Spread with a frosting when cold, perhaps one of the orange frostings (see index). Yield, 18.

Children love these little cakes!

CHOCOLATE SWIRLS

½ cup (¼ pound) butter

1½ cups sugar

3 eggs, beaten

2 cups sifted flour

4 teaspoons baking powder

¼ teaspoon salt

½ cup milk

1 teaspoon vanilla

2 rounded tablespoons cocoa

Cream butter and sugar together until light and fluffy. Add beaten eggs and beat until very thick. Combine flour, baking powder and salt, then sift together. Add dry ingredients and milk alternately to egg mixture, blending after each addition. Add vanilla and blend. Divide batter in two equal parts. Add the cocoa to one and blend thoroughly. Drop a spoonful of each batter into greased muffin tins, repeating with some of each until the cups are ⅔ full. Bake at 375° F. for about 20 minutes. Cool in pan or turned out on rack as desired. When cold, spread with chocolate frosting. Yield, about 24 cupcakes.

TORTES

Tortes, or *torten,* are cakes of European origin in which the batter, while much like that of sponge cakes, uses crumbs, finely chopped or ground nuts, or coarse meal in place of all or a major portion of its flour. They are on the whole not difficult to make, and when filled and frosted they have great elegance. Inasmuch as they contain no butter or other shortening, they are less rich than, say, a pound cake, but most of them more than make up for the omission of butter by calling for quantities of cream or butter-cream (and chocolate at that) for the finishing touches. They may also take jam or preserves or a fruit glaze in addition to frosting, and sometimes an extra chocolate glaze to give the *coup de grâce*. They are marvelous cakes, wonderfully flavorful and delightful for their characteristic consistency.

Most tortes are baked in ungreased pans—spring-form or tube—from which the bottoms may be removed for convenience when the cakes are done. Some are baked in greased layer cake pans, however, while others are baked as sheet cakes, then split horizontally to make many thin layers with filling in between. Some of these, exceptions to the general rule, call for a considerable quantity of flour and are for all the world like layer cakes though not baked as such. American layer cakes may well have come from these special tortes, such as the following Dobos Torte. Many European versions of this famous cake have it made from a *Génoise* batter which is baked in 9 thin 8-inch layers. Our version, with its own delectable batter, is made with a modest six layers.

HUNGARIAN DOBOS TORTE

With this cake, you start with the frosting!

For the frosting:

4 ounces bitter chocolate	¼ cup water
1 cup (½ pound) sweet butter	6 egg yolks
1 teaspoon vanilla	10 hazelnuts, toasted and
1 cup sugar	chopped

Melt chocolate in double boiler; let cool. Cream butter with vanilla until light and fluffy. Combine sugar and water in a small saucepan and cook over low heat, stirring constantly, until sugar is dissolved. Cover saucepan and boil 5 minutes. Uncover and cook to thread stage, 234° F. on your candy thermometer. Remove from heat. Beat egg yolks until very thick with a rotary beater. Gradually pour in the sugar syrup in a thin stream, beating as you do so. Continue beating until the mixture is the consistency of softened butter. Cool; then beat this into the butter-vanilla mixture. Gradually beat in the chocolate. When thick and smooth, add the hazelnuts. Refrigerate until needed.

For the torte:

1 cup sifted flour	6 eggs, separated
2 tablespoons cocoa	½ cup sugar

Sift flour and cocoa together; set aside. Beat egg yolks with half of the sugar until thick and lemon colored. Beat egg whites until they form soft peaks, then beat in the remaining sugar. Beat until stiff. Now gently spread the beaten yolks over the whites. Sift the flour-cocoa mixture over the yolks. Fold whites, yolks and flour very gently together, lifting and turning bit by bit. Grease bottoms only of 6 8-inch cake pans with removable bottoms. Divide batter evenly among them and bake at 350° F. for 15 minutes. (It will probably be necessary to bake 3 pans at a time.) When cakes are done, remove them to cooling racks and cool right side up.

When cakes are cold, remove frosting from refrigerator and beat until creamy. Spread frosting ⅛-inch thick on four of the layers. Set them gently in place on top of one another. Set the unfrosted fifth layer over the fourth and place the torte in the refrigerator. Return the unused frosting to the refrigerator also. Place the *sixth* layer on a buttered cookie sheet. Lightly brush an area 3 inches wider than the cake with butter all around it. (This layer is to be glazed with caramel and the buttered surface prevents its sticking.) With the back of a knife mark 16 even-sized wedges on the top of the cake running out from the center like the spokes of a wheel. Press them down gently so they are visible, but do not cut the cake.

For the Caramel Glaze (which gives this torte its name, "Dobos," a *drum*):

Melt ¾ cup sugar in a heavy iron skillet over moderate heat. Cook until smooth and a golden brown, stirring constantly. Do not scorch. Remove from heat. Quickly pour this over the sixth layer and spread evenly with a knife. You will have to work fast for the caramel hardens quickly. Remove cake and remaining frosting from refrigerator. Beat frosting again until creamy. Spread it ⅛-inch thick over the unfrosted fifth layer. Set the caramel-coated layer on top. Now with a hot buttered knife cut down through the caramel glaze directly over the marks made in the top of the cake. If you do not at least partially separate the caramel thus you will be unable to cut the cake for the glaze hardens in a glossy sheen. With the remaining frosting, spread the sides of the torte. This coating of chocolate should be as smooth as the caramel. Return torte to refrigerator to chill before serving. Then cut with a knife dipped in hot water or, better, heated and rubbed with sweet butter. It should be noted that purists in Hungary do *not* frost the sides of this torte at all but use the chocolate only as a filling. In our estimation, the additional chocolate makes it better.

In a Mexican variation of the Dobos Torte, the chocolate filling is made with semisweet chocolate and only ¼ cup additional sugar. For additional flavor, 1 rounded teaspoon of instant coffee is added to the mixture (or ¼ cup strong black coffee may be used instead of water). And the hazelnuts are omitted. They *are* used (and in quantity), however, to coat the sides of the torte after frosting.

Different versions of the Dobos Torte have been made in all parts of the world for many years. Most, like the original, have had many layers; and most have had chocolate only in their frosting and filling. This version, from Dallas, was created with a chocolate batter. And a good version it is, authentic or not!

CHOCOLATE DOBOS TORTE

For the torte:

3 ounces bitter chocolate
½ cup sifted cake flour
½ teaspoon baking powder
¼ teaspoon salt
4 eggs

¾ cup sugar
¼ teaspoon soda
3 tablespoons cold water
2 tablespoons additional sugar

Melt chocolate in a double boiler, then cool. Combine flour, baking powder, salt and eggs in a mixing bowl. Beat with a rotary beater, adding the ¾ cup sugar gradually. Continue beating until the batter is thick and light. Add the soda, cold water and 2 tablespoons sugar to the cooled chocolate; blend. Quickly fold this into the batter. Blend quickly. Grease a 15 x 10 x 1 inch jelly roll pan and line it with wax paper. Pour in the batter. Bake at 375° F. for 18 to 20 minutes. Turn cake out on a clean dish towel. Remove paper from cake and trim edges with a sharp knife. Cool on rack.

When cake is cold, cut into even quarters, 7½ x 5 inches. With a sharp knife cut each quarter in half horizontally, which will give you eight thin layers of cake. Fill and frost with Bitter Chocolate Frosting. Chill before serving.

This luscious dessert can be varied, of course, by using different frostings and fillings, or by alternating different fillings between the eight layers. Or you might use the Bitter Chocolate Frosting just as filling and then frost the torte with the Orange Cream Cheese Frosting (page 84).

BITTER CHOCOLATE FROSTING

4½ ounces bitter chocolate
½ cup butter
3 cups sifted confectioners' sugar

⅓ cup milk
2 egg whites, unbeaten
1 teaspoon vanilla

Melt chocolate with butter in a double boiler. Combine sugar, milk, egg whites and vanilla, blend thoroughly and add to chocolate. Blend quickly. Remove from heat and place in deep bowl of ice water or cracked ice. Beat constantly as the frosting cools to bring it to a proper spreadable consistency. Let stand at room temperature until needed.

The *Sachertorte* is probably the most famous chocolate cake of all time, not only because it has been made continuously and to great acclaim for 133 years, but also because a lawsuit as to what was and what was not a proper *Sachertorte* lasted for seven years in Vienna. And although the verdict was handed down in favor of Eduard Sacher, son of the renowned Frau Sacher who though not the creator of the torte perhaps added most to its fame, there are still those in Austria who insist that the torte at Demel's is the real one. Needless to say, if the Austrians themselves argue the pros and cons of this matter, people elsewhere have become even more confused. All kinds of recipes have purported to be the one and only *Sachertorte* and they have varied from straight-forward cakes to straight-forward tortes (with odd mixtures of both methods in between) but almost all abide by the use of jam and chocolate frosting in combination. The *real Sachertorte* is indeed a torte and calls for crumbs amongst its ingredients. It calls also for apricot jam and chocolate frosting. Tortes using strawberry or raspberry jam instead of the apricot jam are delicious, to be sure, but they are variations on the theme. And cakes utilizing apricot jam and chocolate together are equally delicious but they are cakes, not tortes. So it is for you to decide what cake or torte you prefer; what it is called will not in any way affect its quality. The fact remains, however, that there is only one real *Sachertorte* . . . but which?

SACHERTORTE #1 (from Vienna)

4 ounces sweet chocolate
½ cup (¼ pound) butter
¾ cup (scant) confectioners'
    sugar
5 eggs, separated
1 tablespoon grated lemon rind
1 teaspoon cinnamon
½ teaspoon allspice

1⅛ cups dry, fine, even-sized,
    toasted white bread crumbs
1 generous pinch salt
Apricot jam
Bitter Chocolate Frosting
    (see page 143)
Whipped cream

Be sure that all the ingredients are at warm room temperature before you begin. Melt chocolate in double boiler; set aside to cool. Cream butter with sugar. When well blended, add the chocolate. Beat the egg yolks into the mixture one at a time. Stir in lemon rind and spices, then the dry crumbs a few at a time. Beat the egg whites with a pinch of salt until stiff but not dry. Fold them gently into the batter. Pour into 2 *greased* 8-inch layer cake pans (preferably with removable bottoms) and bake at 325° F. for about 25 minutes. Cool, with sides of pans removed. When cold, spread one layer generously with apricot jam and top with second layer. Spread the second layer thinly with jam and let stand about 10 minutes. Frost top and sides with the Bitter Chocolate Frosting (page 143). Just before serving, top as desired with very lightly sweetened, chilled whipped cream. Serves 8 to 10.

SACHERTORTE #2 (from Hungary)

1 cup plus 2 tablespoons sifted
    flour
4 ounces finely grated semisweet
    chocolate
½ cup (¼ pound) sweet butter

⅔ cup sugar
6 egg yolks
7 egg whites
⅓ cup strawberry preserves
⅓ cup strawberry jelly

Divide the sifted flour into 4 equal portions. Grate the chocolate. Cream butter until light and fluffy with half of the sugar. Beat the egg yolks into the butter one at a time, beating well after each addition. Beat the egg whites until they form soft peaks, then beat in the remaining sugar. Beat until stiff but not dry. Gently spread the egg whites *over* the yolk mixture. Sprinkle the whites evenly with grated chocolate. One at a time, sift the portions of flour over the batter mixture, folding gently after each addition. Do *not* stir nor beat. The batter when done should be just blended. Butter an 8 x 10-inch pan and line it with wax paper. Butter the paper. Pour in batter and bake at 350° F. for 25 minutes. Cool in pan. Remove from pan and gently peel off the wax paper, starting from the center. When torte is cold, split in half to make 2 layers. Spread strawberry preserves over the bottom layer; top with second layer and then spread this with the jelly.

For the frosting:

3 ounces semisweet chocolate   ½ cup (¼ pound) sweet butter

Melt chocolate in top of double boiler. Remove from heat and stir in the butter. Continue to stir until thoroughly blended. Cool slightly, then spread evenly over cake. Chill torte until frosting is firm. Top with chilled, very lightly sweetened whipped cream just before serving. Serves 12.

And lastly we have this delectable creation which by rights should be called an Easy *Sachertorte*.

SACHERTORTE #3 (from Sylvia Hirsch)

5 ounces sweet chocolate   1 cup powdered sugar
1 tablespoon water   1¼ cups sifted cake flour
¾ cup (1½ sticks) butter   ⅓ to ½ cup apricot jam
6 eggs, separated

Combine chocolate and water in the top of a double boiler and heat until chocolate is melted. Add butter and stir until smooth. Remove from heat. Pour into mixing bowl. Beat egg yolks well and pour slowly into chocolate mixture, beating constantly. Add sugar and beat until smooth. Let mixture cool for 10 minutes. Beat the egg whites until stiff but not dry. Fold flour and egg whites alternately into the chocolate mixture. Blend gently but do not stir or beat. Butter and flour a 9-inch springform pan about 2 inches deep. Pour in the batter, running it evenly to the sides, and bake at 325° F. for 30 minutes. Remove side of pan and let cool. Warm apricot jam over hot water and spread over torte; let stand for 20 minutes. Frost with the following:

For the frosting:

3 ounces bitter chocolate   1 egg
¾ cup powdered sugar   1 egg yolk
2 tablespoons hot water   5 tablespoons butter

Melt chocolate over hot water. Remove from heat and stir in sugar and 2 tablespoons hot water. Blend. Beat whole egg and yolk together slightly and then beat into chocolate mixture. Add butter, 1 tablespoon at a time. Beat until desired consistency. Spread over cake while still warm, then cool. Serves 10 to 12.

Another Viennese favorite is this torte which has a marbled effect:

THE POLKA DOT TORTE

5 eggs, separated
¾ cup sugar
1 teaspoon grated lemon rind
¾ cup ground almonds
¼ teaspoon salt

1½ tablespoons cornstarch
2½ ounces dark sweet chocolate, grated
3½ tablespoons very fine, dry bread crumbs

Combine egg yolks, sugar and lemon rind; beat until very thick and light in color. Add nuts and blend. Beat the egg whites with the salt until stiff. Fold them gently into the yolk mixture. Divide this batter in half. Over half of it sift the cornstarch and blend gently. Over the other sprinkle the chocolate and bread crumbs bit by bit, folding in gently as you go. Drop the batters by alternate spoonfuls into an ungreased 9-inch springform pan. Bake at 350° F. for 50 to 60 minutes. Cool in the pan, then release sides. To serve, top with sweetened whipped cream or simply dust with powdered sugar. Serves 10 to 12.

This Hungarian torte gains its distinctive, subtle flavor from poppy seeds and brandy.

HUNGARIAN POPPY SEED TORTE

9 eggs, separated
½ cup plus 2 tablespoons sugar
2 tablespoons brandy
1 tablespoon lemon juice
  Grated rind of ½ lemon
½ cup ground poppy seeds
  (or bruised)

½ cup ground almonds
¾ teaspoon cinnamon
¾ cup grated dark sweet chocolate
¾ teaspoon baking powder
1 pinch salt

Beat egg yolks with sugar until light and lemon colored. Add brandy, lemon juice and rind, poppy seeds, almonds, cinnamon, chocolate and baking powder. Beat to blend thoroughly. Beat the egg whites with salt until stiff but not dry. Fold them gently into the yolk mixture. Turn into a *greased* 10-inch springform pan and bake at 350° F. for 45 minutes or until done. Cool in pan, then release sides. Dust with powdered sugar before serving. Serves 10 to 12.

One of the best tortes ever made is this Date Sponge Torte which seems to be the better for standing twenty-four hours before serving.

It is delectable served simply with a dusting of powdered sugar, but if topped with whipped cream flavored with Grand Marnier or curaçao it is superb. Tortes and superlatives seem to go together!

DATE SPONGE TORTE

4 ounces bitter chocolate
1 cup milk
2 cups sugar
4 eggs, separated
1¼ cups sifted cake flour
2½ teaspoons baking powder

¼ teaspoon salt
¾ teaspoon vanilla
1 cup pitted chopped dates
2 tablespoons grated orange rind
½ cup ground pecans

Melt chocolate in the top of a double boiler. Add milk and 1 cup of the sugar. Cook until smooth, stirring constantly. Cool. Beat the egg yolks with the remaining sugar until light and lemon colored. Add the chocolate mixture and beat again. Combine flour with baking powder and salt and sift together. Add to batter with vanilla and blend. Add dates, orange rind and ground nuts. Stir until just smooth. Beat the egg whites until stiff but not dry. Fold gently into the batter. Pour into an ungreased tube pan and bake at 325° F. for 50 to 60 minutes. Cool in pan. Remove when cold and dust with powdered sugar or (and better) top with the whipped cream described above. Serves 10 to 12.

This Texas torte is every bit as elegant as any devised in Vienna.

TEXAS PECAN TORTE

3 cups pecan halves
6 eggs, separated
1½ cups sugar
3 tablespoons flour

1 teaspoon salt
3 tablespoons Jamaica rum
½ cup whipping cream
2 tablespoons powdered sugar

One cup at a time, whirl pecans in a blender until very fine. Set aside. Beat the egg yolks until very light, then beat in sugar, flour, salt, 2 tablespoons of the rum and the ground nuts, adding the ingredients one at a time. Beat the egg whites until stiff but not dry. Fold them gently into the batter. Grease 3 8-inch layer cake pans or 2 10-inch pans and line them with wax paper. Grease the paper. Pour the batter into the pans evenly. Bake at 350° F. for about 25 minutes. Cool in the pans, then remove carefully. About two hours before serving, whip the cream with the powdered sugar until stiff and then flavor it with the remaining tablespoon of rum. Spread this as filling between the layers. Then frost with the following:

For the frosting:

1 cup semisweet chocolate bits   ½ cup sour cream

Melt chocolate bits in double boiler and cool. Fold in sour cream. Blend and spread over top of torte. Chill torte before serving. Serves 8 to 10.

At least once a year, when raspberries are in season, treat yourself to this Whipped Cream Torte with Raspberries.

WHIPPED CREAM TORTE WITH RASPBERRIES

1⅓ cups sifted flour   6 eggs
2 tablespoons cocoa   4 egg yolks
3 tablespoons sweet butter   1¾ cups sifted powdered sugar

Sift flour with cocoa. Divide into four equal parts and set aside. Melt butter and set aside. Combine whole eggs, egg yolks and powdered sugar in the top of a double boiler. Place over (not touching) simmering water. Beat with a rotary beater for 5 minutes or until the mixture is light and just heated through. Remove top of double boiler from lower section. Continue to beat egg mixture until very thick and cooled. One by one, sift the portions of flour and cocoa over the yolks, gently folding the flour in after each addition. Do not stir or beat. Fold in the melted butter. Continue to fold until just blended. Pour into 2 greased 9-inch layer cake pans. Bake at 350° F. for 25 minutes. Cool in pans 15 to 20 minutes, then remove gently to racks. And for the filling and frosting prepare the following:

For the filling and frosting:

2 cups ripe red raspberries   ½ cup sifted powdered sugar
2 cups whipping cream   1 teaspoon rum

Set aside a few whole raspberries to use on top of the torte when frosted. Slightly crush the remainder. Whip cream with sugar until stiff. Divide it in half. Add the crushed berries and rum to one half. Spread this over one layer of the torte, piling it evenly. Put the second layer in place and top this with the plain, sweetened whipped cream. Decorate with whole berries. Chill at least 1 hour before serving. Serves 10 to 12.

The flavor and consistency of the ground nuts used in any torte do much to affect its finished quality (pecans are relatively soft, for instance, while almonds are relatively hard). In the same way, the crumbs used give their own special flavor and consistency. In the following Chocolate Walnut Torte, for example, you may use either graham cracker crumbs or the crumbs of vanilla wafers; each gives equally fine—but very different—results, the graham cracker crumbs tending to be somewhat heavier.

CHOCOLATE WALNUT TORTE

9 eggs, separated
1¼ cups sugar
1 cup ground walnuts
½ cup crumbs, graham cracker
  or vanilla wafer

⅓ cup grated dark sweet
  chocolate
¼ teaspoon vanilla
1 generous pinch salt

Beat the egg yolks until thick and lemon colored; add sugar and beat until smooth. One by one, blend in nuts, crumbs and chocolate. Add vanilla. Beat egg whites with salt until stiff but not dry. Fold gently into batter. Pour batter into a *greased* 9-inch springform pan and bake at 350° F. for 45 minutes. Cool in pan, then remove rim. Frost when cold with a chocolate frosting, or one of the orange frostings or one of the cream cheese or sour cream frostings. Serves 8 to 10.

This torte uses soda cracker crumbs to give an unusual quality.

CHOCOLATE CRACKER TORTE

9 eggs, separated
1 cup sugar
2 cups ground almonds
1 cup seedless raisins
1 teaspoon baking powder
8 ounces dark sweet chocolate,
  grated

7 soda crackers rolled to fine
  crumbs
  Strained juice of 3 lemons
¼ cup rum
1 pinch salt

Beat egg yolks with sugar until thick and lemon colored. One by one add almonds, raisins, baking powder, chocolate, crumbs, lemon juice and rum, blending after each addition. Beat the egg whites with a pinch of salt until stiff but not dry. Fold gently into the batter. Pour into an ungreased 9-inch springform pan and bake at 350° F. for 50 to 60 minutes. Cool in pan before removing rim. Dust with powdered sugar before serving or frost with a chocolate frosting when cold. Serves 8 to 10.

This torte has not only a spice flavor but almonds and brandy as well.

CHOCOLATE BRANDY TORTE

For the torte:

10 eggs, separated	Grated rind of 1 lemon
2 cups sugar	Strained juice of 1 lemon
4 ounces bitter chocolate, grated	2 cups ground almonds
	2 ounces best brandy
1 tablespoon cinnamon	1 pinch salt
1 teaspoon cloves	1 cup sifted fine cracker meal

Beat egg yolks until lemon colored, then add sugar and beat until thick and smooth. One by one blend in chocolate, spices, lemon rind and juice, almonds and brandy. Beat the egg whites with pinch of salt until stiff but not dry. Fold egg whites and cracker meal alternately and gently into the batter. Pour batter into a *greased* 10-inch springform pan and bake at 350° F. for 50 to 60 minutes. Cool in pan before removing rim. When cold frost with the following:

For the frosting:

1 tablespoon butter	1 tablespoon rum
1 cup powdered sugar	Cream as needed

Cream butter and sugar until light and fluffy, then add rum and beat until smooth. Thin to desired spreadable consistency with cream. Frost top of torte only. Sprinkle center with shaved sweet chocolate if desired or decorate around edge of torte with chocolate curls (see page 10). Serves 10 to 12.

The combination of ground nuts and whole eggs or egg whites has been used in many countries (including our own) for cakes which while not truly tortes are much like them. They are thought of, however, simply as desserts more often than not, or at times as cakes, and again, more correctly, as confections. Such is the almond garland devised in Copenhagen of ground almonds and sugar and egg whites, with melted chocolate for frosting and a garnish of whole almonds and spun sugar. Such also is the following Almond Cake, created in the nineteenth century in Alabama.

ALMOND CAKE

1 pound unskinned almonds
12 eggs, separated
2 cups sugar

3 ounces semisweet chocolate,
  finely grated

Grind almonds with skins. Beat egg yolks until very thick, then beat with sugar until smooth. Add almonds and blend. Add chocolate. Beat egg whites until stiff but not dry. Fold gently into the batter. Bake in an ungreased tube pan at 350° F. for 1 hour and 10 minutes. Cool like an angel cake (page 99). Dust with powdered sugar before serving. Serves 8 to 10.

The *Dacquoise* is one of the richer glories of the French cuisine.

DACQUOISE

5 egg whites
⅛ teaspoon cream of tartar
¾ cup sugar
1 cup ground blanched almonds
½ cup additional sugar

½ cup zwieback crumbs
2 tablespoons each flour and
  cornstarch
½ teaspoon vanilla

In a large bowl beat the egg whites with the cream of tartar until they are frothy. Gradually beat in the ¾ cup sugar and continue beating until the whites will stand in peaks. In a bowl blend the ground almonds, additional sugar, crumbs, flour, cornstarch and vanilla. Fold this mixture evenly and gently into the meringue.

Now grease a baking sheet and dust it lightly with flour. Shake off any excess. With an 8-inch pie plate as guide, mark 2 circles in the flour. Spoon the meringue into a pastry bag with ½-inch tube and pipe the mixture onto the pan starting with a circle around the circumference drawn in the flour, then continuously spiralling it inward to the center until the whole circle is filled. Repeat to fill the second circle. Bake at 250° F. for 45 minutes or until the meringues are firm to the touch. Remove from oven and let cool completely. Then put them together with the following filling and frosting:

For the frosting (a Mocha Butter Cream):

2 ounces bitter chocolate
1 cup sugar
⅓ cup water
5 egg yolks

1¼ cups sweet butter, softened
3 tablespoons each powdered
coffee and curaçao or other
orange-flavored liqueur

Melt chocolate in double boiler and set aside. In a saucepan combine sugar and water. Bring to a boil and cook, stirring occasionally, until the syrup spins a thread, 236° F. on your candy thermometer. Beat egg yolks until thick and lemon colored. Gradually beat in the hot syrup. Cool. Then beat in the butter and chocolate. Beat until smooth. Beat in the coffee and liqueur and continue to beat until thick enough to spread.

Spread half of this mixture over one layer of the *Dacquoise*. Put the other layer in place and spread with the remaining filling. Sprinkle with sifted powdered sugar before serving and top the sugar with some shavings of bitter chocolate. Serves 8.

Cookies

In countries where they are made at all, cookies and similar small cakes frequently have a way of reflecting national tastes very directly. In many instances, they are linked with special feast days that have a cultural as well as religious significance. But in the United States where cookies are consumed by the millions, they have never had a national quality at all, nor have special ones been associated with special days or times of year. In the United States, cookies for the most part are simply cookies, whether of the highly spiced German varieties, the anise-flavored Italian, the large, rather stodgy, only faintly sweet English type, or the rich, buttery, rather sophisticated cookies of France. In the old days most of them were homemade, to be kept always on hand in generous cookie jars; today (more's the pity), most come from the supermarkets. Cookies once had the individual character of every household. Now, like so much else, they have been standardized, good maybe, but endlessly the same—vanilla, lemon, almond, ginger, mixed spice and, of course, chocolate.

If it seems that chocolate cookies, on the whole, have had less popularity than other kinds (and it does seem so if one judges by the number of chocolate cookie recipes as compared to those for, say, vanilla or pecan or almond cookies or plain sugar wafers) then this is probably because of the fact that chocolate cookies have a tendency to burn more easily than others. All cookies require watching, of course; they are cooked at high heat as a rule . . . some of them at a very high heat. But chocolate cookies (to be at their best) require double watching, as it were. The presence of chocolate (which itself burns easily) makes them doubly vulnerable. But even so they are really very easy!

There are several basic types of cookies, and chocolate in one form or another may be used in all of them to marvelous effect. There are drop, meringue, rolled, molded and refrigerator cookies. Most, unless otherwise specifically stated, are baked on greased cookie sheets at

325° F. for from 8 to 15 minutes. Some are soft (or should be), while others are crisp. *Soft cookies* should be stored in airtight metal containers to keep their proper consistency. A slice or two of apple stored with them will be an added safeguard. *Crisp cookies* should be stored so that they have a free circulation of air. All should be cooled *in a single layer on racks;* do not pile them on top of one another. Many can be converted into rich little cakes by the addition of frosting; some may take a frosting and then a glaze; some may be put together in pairs with a filling between. With a bit of imagination, one can devise all kinds of taste treats and surprises by combining different fillings and frosting or frostings and glazes. Lemon cookies, for instance, are delicious with chocolate frosting, or chocolate cookies with orange frostings. Chocolate cookies may be spread with a thin layer of marshmallow frosting, then glazed with bitter chocolate, or given added richness by means of a simple Confectioners' Icing . . . confectioners' sugar brought to paste consistency with a little water. Their possibilities are endless.

Drop cookies, all things considered, are' the easiest to make. It must be borne in mind, however, that they spread on the cookie sheet when they go into the oven, so drop them far enough apart to allow for an increase in their circumference. What looks like a little batter dropped from a spoon may make a rather big cookie. Try one to test for size before baking the first sheet. This way you will know for certain what any particular batter is going to do.

SOUR CREAM DROPS

2 ounces bitter chocolate	1⅓ cups sugar
1¾ cups sifted flour	1 teaspoon vanilla
1 teaspoon baking powder	1 egg
½ teaspoon soda	½ cup sour cream
½ teaspoon salt	½ cup chopped walnuts
⅔ cup butter	

Melt chocolate over hot water, then cool. Combine flour with baking powder, soda and salt, then sift together 4 times. Cream butter until smooth, then add sugar, vanilla and egg and beat until light and fluffy. Add cooled chocolate and blend. Add sour cream and blend. Add flour mixture and mix thoroughly. Add chopped nuts. Drop by teaspoonfuls 2 inches apart on a lightly greased cookie sheet. Bake at 425° F. for 9 to 10 minutes. Cool on sheet, then remove. Store in covered tin. Makes 4 dozen.

SOFT CHOCOLATE DROPS

Make like the Sour Cream Drops of preceding recipe but substitute 1⅓ cups moist brown sugar (packed) for the white sugar, and reduce the chocolate to 1½ ounces.

Either of these cookies may be frosted, of course; and for a quick and easy frosting you might try the following:

EASY COOKIE FROSTING

1½ cups sifted powdered sugar   2 tablespoons cream
 2 tablespoons cocoa   2 tablespoons softened butter

Combine all ingredients in a mixing bowl and beat until smooth and of a spreadable consistency.

Years ago, one of the best cooks in Dallas used to make these Chocolate Orange Turtles as gifts for her friends on special occasions.

CHOCOLATE ORANGE TURTLES

3 to 4 ounces dark sweet   1 cup finely chopped preserved
   chocolate   orange rind
½ cup cream   ½ cup chopped almonds
3½ tablespoons sugar   ¼ cup flour
1 pinch salt

Melt chocolate over hot water and set aside. Combine cream with all the other ingredients and drop batter from a teaspoon onto a greased and floured cookie sheet. Bake at 350° F. for 8 to 10 minutes. The cookies will be very thin. Cool on the pan. Lift carefully and turn over. Coat the bottom of each with melted chocolate. Let dry thoroughly before serving. Makes 3½ to 4 dozen.

These Brown Sugar Chip Cookies seem to be favorites with everybody.

BROWN SUGAR CHIP COOKIES

½ cup (¼ pound) butter
¼ cup brown sugar
½ cup white sugar
1 egg
1 cup plus 2 tablespoons sifted
flour
½ teaspoon salt

½ teaspoon baking soda
1 tablespoon cold water
1 teaspoon hot water
½ teaspoon vanilla
6 ounces chocolate bits
½ cup chopped pecans

Cream butter with brown sugar and white sugar until light and fluffy. Add egg and beat until smooth and thick. Combine flour and salt, then sift together. Work flour gradually into the egg batter. Dissolve soda in 1 tablespoon water. Add to batter and blend. Add hot water, vanilla, chocolate bits and chopped nuts. Blend thoroughly. Drop from a teaspoon onto a greased cookie sheet and bake at 375° F. for 10 minutes, or until brown. Cool on rack. Makes about 40.

Years ago, Sylvia Hirsch's grandmother made these Oriental Poppies —one of her specialties—on Friday afternoons in preparation for the Sabbath. She was a cook who measured by eye rather than by cup or spoon, so her recipe is necessarily an approximation.

ORIENTAL POPPIES

¾ cup poppy seeds
½ cup hot milk
½ cup (¼ pound) butter
½ cup sugar
1¼ cups sifted flour
1 teaspoon baking powder

1 pinch salt
½ teaspoon cinnamon
3 ounces dark sweet chocolate,
grated
¾ cup currants or white raisins
¼ teaspoon vanilla

Soak poppy seeds in hot milk for a few minutes. Cream butter and sugar until light and fluffy. Combine flour with baking powder, salt and cinnamon, then sift together. Add dry ingredients and the poppy seed-milk mixture alternately to the butter mixture, blending after each addition. One by one add the chocolate, raisins (or currants) and vanilla. Blend. Drop from a teaspoon onto a greased cookie sheet and bake at 350° F. for 15 to 20 minutes. Let cool on a rack. Dust with sifted powdered sugar before serving.

These Chocolate Fruit Drops are wonderful to have on hand in the winter holiday season.

CHOCOLATE FRUIT DROPS

½ cup milk
1¼ cups sugar
3 ounces bitter chocolate
½ cup (¼ pound) butter
2 eggs
1½ cups sifted cake flour
1 pinch salt

1½ teaspoons baking powder
1¼ teaspoons vanilla
1¼ cups mixed chopped fruits
(dried apricots, figs, dates, raisins, etc.)
1 cup chopped pecans

Combine milk, ¼ cup of the sugar and chocolate in top of double boiler and cook, stirring frequently, until chocolate is melted. Cool. Cream butter with remaining sugar until light and fluffy. Add eggs and beat until smooth. Add chocolate mixture and beat again. Combine flour with salt and baking powder, then sift together. Add gradually to the chocolate mixture. Blend. Add vanilla and blend. Fold in chopped fruits and nuts. Drop by teaspoonfuls onto a greased cookie sheet and bake at 375° F. for 6 to 8 minutes. Cool on baking sheet several minutes, then transfer to rack. Sprinkle with sifted powdered sugar before serving. Makes 4 dozen.

Chocolate Mincemeat Drops are also wonderful for the holidays. They're particularly good with an ice-cold, velvet-smooth, orange-flavored custard or floating island.

CHOCOLATE MINCEMEAT DROPS

1 ounce bitter chocolate
¼ cup (½ stick) butter
½ cup plus 2 tablespoons dark brown sugar, packed
1 egg

1¼ cups sifted flour
1¾ teaspoons baking powder
1 pinch salt
¼ teaspoon vanilla
1 cup mincemeat

Melt chocolate over hot water, then cool. Cream butter and sugar together until light and fluffy. Add egg and beat until thick and lemon colored. Add cooled chocolate and blend. Combine flour with baking powder and salt, then sift together. Add to batter and blend thoroughly. Add vanilla and mincemeat and blend. Drop from a teaspoon onto a greased cookie sheet and bake at 400° F. for 8 to 10 minutes. Cool on baking sheet. Dust with powdered sugar before serving. Makes 2½ dozen.

Chocolate Flutes are not only pretty to serve at a buffet supper but delectable as well. Inasmuch as the Flutes themselves may be made ahead of time, they present little problem to the hostess.

CHOCOLATE FLUTES

½ cup (¼ pound) butter
⅔ cup granulated sugar
2 egg whites
1¾ cups sifted flour
2 tablespoons cocoa
¼ cup water
½ teaspoon vanilla
⅔ cup semisweet chocolate
  pieces

2 tablespoons butter
1 cup chopped blanched
  almonds
1 quart heavy cream
4 to 5 tablespoons powdered
  sugar
1 tablespoon Grand Marnier, or
  more to taste

Cream ½ cup butter with sugar until light and fluffy. (If you use an electric beater, have it at medium speed.) Now beat in the unbeaten egg whites, then the flour, cocoa, water and vanilla. (With an electric beater this latter operation should be done at low speed.) Now on a greased cookie sheet spread one heaping teaspoonful of batter into a 3½ inch square, using the back of the spoon to spread it out evenly. Make 3 to 5 more similar squares on the same cookie sheet spacing them about 3 inches apart. Bake at 375° F. 5 to 6 minutes. Remove from oven. With a spatula invert the squares one by one and quickly roll them into a tube or flute shape. Let cool on a rack with each "tube" resting on its overlapping flap. Do not roll them too tightly. Proceed to make additional batches until you have made 42 to 44 all told. When all are completely cold, store tightly covered until needed.

Before supper or at a convenient hour ahead of time, melt chocolate in a double boiler over hot water. Add 2 tablespoons butter and stir until blended. Spread both ends of the tubes all the way round and 1 inch in depth with the melted chocolate. While this is still soft, sprinkle it with the chopped almonds. Let cool and set.

One hour before serving whip the cream and sweeten with the powdered sugar. Add Grand Marnier to taste and whip again. Using a cake decorator or pastry bag with tube No. 3, fill the tube from both ends with the cream. Refrigerate as soon as filled. Keep chilled until needed. If possible in this last part of the operation have a bit of the cream protrude from each tube.

ORANGE NUT MACAROONS

2 egg whites
½ cup sugar
1 pinch salt
2 tablespoons grated orange rind

2 ounces grated dark sweet
  chocolate
⅓ cup ground blanched almonds

Beat egg whites until they hold soft peaks, then beat in sugar and salt. When just stiff enough to hold soft, rounded peaks, fold in orange rind, chocolate and nuts. Grease a cookie sheet and line it with wax paper; grease the paper as well. Drop the batter by teaspoonfuls onto the paper and bake at 325° F. for 25 to 30 minutes. Lift off paper with a spatula and cool on a rack. Makes about 2½ dozen.

Kisses are meringues, and thus chiefly a matter of beaten egg whites and sugar. Chocolate kisses are delectable.

BITTERSWEET KISSES

6 egg whites
1 cup sugar
1 pinch salt

4½ ounces dark, sweet chocolate,
  grated
1 teaspoon vanilla

Beat the egg whites until they hold soft peaks; then beat in gradually the sugar and salt. When the meringue is stiff and satiny, fold in the grated chocolate and vanilla. Grease and flour a cookie sheet. Drop the meringue by teaspoonfuls on the sheet and bake at 250° F. for 50 to 60 minutes. Cool on a rack before storing. Makes 3½ dozen.

These Spiced Nut Kisses get their special flavor from cinnamon and almonds.

SPICED NUT KISSES

1¼ cups sugar
2½ tablespoons cocoa
½ teaspoon cinnamon

1 pinch salt
2 egg whites
½ cup ground almonds

Combine sugar, cocoa, cinnamon and salt; then sift together. Beat the egg whites until they hold soft peaks; gradually beat in the sugar mixture. When the meringue is stiff and glossy, fold in the ground almonds. Drop by teaspoonfuls onto a greased cookie sheet and bake at 250° F. for 50 to 60 minutes. Makes 2 to 2½ dozen.

Rolled cookies require a batter similar to that for pastries. If it is too soft to roll properly on a very lightly floured board with a very lightly floured roller, chill it a few minutes. Any excess flour tends to toughen cookies, even the small amount that they gather from the pastry board.

CHOCOLATE CRISPS

3 ounces bitter chocolate	1 teaspoon vanilla
½ cup (¼ pound) butter	2¼ cups flour
1 cup sugar	½ teaspoon salt
2 eggs, beaten	¾ teaspoon baking powder

Melt chocolate over hot (not boiling) water; then cool. Cream butter and sugar together until light and fluffy. Add beaten eggs and beat until thick and smooth. Add chocolate and blend. Add vanilla. Combine flour, salt and baking powder, then sift together. Add dry ingredients to egg batter and blend. Turn out on a very lightly floured board and roll out into a rectangle of ⅛-inch thickness. Cut in strips 1 x 3 inches. Arrange on a greased cookie sheet and bake at 375° F. for 10 minutes. Let cool on a rack. Makes about 6 dozen. The dough, of course, may be cut into other shapes with a cookie cutter if desired.

These Chocolate-coated Hazelnut Cookies are great favorites in Austria. In the Hirsch household, they are often served with cream desserts.

CHOCOLATE-COATED HAZELNUT COOKIES

1½ cups flour	¾ cup powdered sugar
¼ teaspoon cinnamon	½ cup ground hazelnuts
3 tablespoons cocoa	¾ pound semisweet chocolate
¾ cup sweet butter (1½ sticks)	¼ cup apricot jam
1 teaspoon grated lemon rind	¼ cup whole blanched almonds
½ teaspoon lemon juice	

Combine flour, cinnamon and cocoa and sift together twice. Cream butter with lemon rind, juice and sugar until light and fluffy. Add hazelnuts and blend. Gradually work in the flour mixture. Cover bowl and let dough stand 15 minutes. Melt chocolate over hot water and set aside. Turn cookie dough out on a lightly floured board and roll to ¼-inch thickness. Cut out with round cookie cutter not larger than 2 inches diameter, arrange on a greased cookie sheet and bake at 350° F.

for 15 minutes. Cool on rack. When cold, invert half of the cookies and spread each with a thin layer of apricot jam. Press the jam-covered cookies and the plain ones together bottom to bottom. Coat one side of each "sandwich" with cooled melted chocolate, let this harden and then coat the other side so that the entire "sandwich" is evenly covered. Press 1 whole blanched almond on each while the chocolate is still soft. Then let cool completely. Makes 2 dozen.

Ground almonds give additional richness to these Chocolate Spritz Cookies.

CHOCOLATE SPRITZ COOKIES

8 ounces dark sweet chocolate
½ cup (¼ pound) butter
2 cups sugar
2 eggs
1 cup flour
1 teaspoon baking powder

1 pinch salt
¼ teaspoon cinnamon
¼ teaspoon cloves
1¼ teaspoons vanilla
⅓ cup ground almonds
(not blanched)

Melt chocolate over hot (not boiling) water; cool. Cream butter with sugar until light and fluffy. Add eggs and beat until thick and lemon colored. Combine flour with baking powder, salt and spices; then sift together. Add these dry ingredients gradually to the egg batter and blend. Add vanilla. Add ground almonds and stir in thoroughly. Turn the dough out on a lightly floured board and roll to ¼-inch thickness. Cut out with a cookie cutter. Arrange cookies on a greased and floured cookie sheet and bake at 350° F. for 10 minutes. Cool in the pan 2 to 3 minutes, then remove to a platter. Do not pile on top of one another. Makes about 4½ dozen.

Refrigerator cookies are thin and crisp, made from a dough that has chilled for several hours. The dough, as a rule, is made into a roll whose diameter is the same size as the eventual cookies. This is then wrapped in waxed paper and it may be stored for several days or a week before using—or it may be frozen. Before baking, the roll (or as much as is needed of it) is cut with a sharp, thin-bladed knife into slices of equal thickness. These are then baked on a greased cookie sheet at 350° or 375° F. Leftover dough may be rewrapped and stored until needed. Chocolate Snaps are among the best of the refrigerator cookies.

CHOCOLATE SNAPS

2 ounces bitter chocolate
⅓ cup butter
1 cup sugar
2 eggs, beaten
½ teaspoon vanilla

1½ cups flour
¼ teaspoon baking soda
½ teaspoon salt
½ cup finely chopped pecans

Melt chocolate over hot (not boiling) water and then cool. Cream butter and sugar together until light and fluffy. Add beaten eggs and beat until thick and smooth. Add chocolate and vanilla. Blend. Combine flour, soda and salt, then sift together. Add dry ingredients to batter and blend. Add nuts and mix thoroughly. Form into 2 2-inch rolls, wrap in wax paper and chill until firm. Slice ⅛-inch thick, arrange on a greased cookie sheet and bake at 375° F. for 8 minutes. When done, cool on a rack before storing. Makes 4 dozen.

These Chocolate Jam Tarts are really crisp lemon-flavored chocolate cookies sandwiched together with raspberry jam. A soft chocolate frosting may be spread on one side only, or they may be coated all over with a chocolate glaze.

CHOCOLATE JAM TARTS

1 cup (¼ pound) butter
½ cup sugar
2 cups sifted flour

¼ teaspoon salt
Grated rind of ½ lemon
Strained juice of ½ lemon
½ cup chopped walnuts

Cream the butter and sugar together until light and fluffy. One by one work in the flour, salt, lemon rind and juice and the chopped nuts. Blend until smooth. Form into a roll 2 inches in diameter and wrap in wax paper. Chill until firm enough to slice. Slice very thin and bake on a greased cookie sheet at 375° F. until lightly browned, about 10 minutes. Cool on rack. When all are done and cooled, spread the bottom of half of them with raspberry jam. Cover the jam-spread cookies with the unspread ones, fitting them bottom to bottom. Frost one side only with your favorite chocolate frosting or, as with the Chocolate-coated Hazelnut Cookies (see page 160), spread both sides with a chocolate glaze. Let the glaze set, of course, before serving. Makes about 4 dozen.

No matter how many of these Rich Nut Cookies you make, you will find that you never have enough of them.

RICH NUT COOKIES

1 cup (½ pound) butter
1 cup sugar
2 eggs
½ cup ground almonds
½ pound (8 ounces) dark sweet
    chocolate, grated
4 cups sifted flour

1 teaspoon baking powder
1 pinch salt
¾ teaspoon cinnamon
⅛ teaspoon cloves
¼ teaspoon vanilla
3 tablespoons milk
    Additional granulated sugar

Cream butter and sugar until light and fluffy. Add eggs and beat until smooth and thick. Combine nuts and grated chocolate. Add to butter mixture and blend. Combine flour, baking powder, salt and spices, then sift together. Add dry ingredients and vanilla and milk alternately to batter, blending after each addition. Mix well. Shape into roll 2 inches in diameter, wrap in wax paper and chill. Slice in thin rounds about ⅛-inch thick. Arrange on a greased baking sheet and sprinkle each cookie lightly with granulated sugar. Bake at 350° F. for about 10 minutes. Cool on rack when done. Makes about 3½ dozen.

Molded cookies are made from a dough similar to that used for rolled cookies. Bits of it are taken from the main mass of dough and rolled or molded by hand into some desired shape—ball or cylinder. These are then placed on a greased cookie sheet at specified intervals and they may or may not be then flattened by hand or spatula. They are baked as a rule like most other cookies at 350° to 375° F. The following molded cookies have black pepper added to them for a delightful bite.

BLACK PEPPER CHOCOLATE COOKIES

1½ teaspoons baking powder
¼ teaspoon salt
1½ cups sifted flour
¾ cup cocoa
¾ cup butter (1½ sticks)
½ teaspoon freshly ground
  black pepper

¾ teaspoon cinnamon
¼ teaspoon allspice
1½ teaspoons vanilla
1 cup sugar
1 egg

Combine baking powder, salt, flour and cocoa, then sift together. Cream butter with spices and vanilla until light. Add sugar to the butter mixture and blend until smooth. Add egg and beat until thick. Gradually work in the flour mixture. Roll the dough into small balls about 1 inch in diameter. Place them on a greased cookie sheet 1½ inches apart. Flatten each with a spatula to about ¼-inch thickness. Bake at 375° F. for 12 minutes. Remove from cookie sheet when done and cool on a rack. Serve plain or coat with a chocolate glaze (see index) when cold. If glazed, let the glaze set before serving the cookies. Makes 3 to 4 dozen.

Chocolate Sticks are delectable served with ice cream or a similar dessert. They may be frozen if desired.

CHOCOLATE STICKS

3 egg whites
1 pinch salt
1¾ cups powdered sugar
½ pound almonds, ground

4 ounces sweet chocolate,
  grated
1 tablespoon sifted cornstarch
Granulated sugar

Beat the egg whites with salt until stiff but not dry. Gradually beat in the powdered sugar until the meringue is smooth and glossy. Fold in almonds, grated chocolate and sifted cornstarch. Blend gently. Shape by tablespoonful into 48 "sticks" (cylinders). Roll these lightly in granulated sugar. Place on a greased baking sheet and bake at 250° F. for 25 to 30 minutes. Makes 4 dozen.

Cookies baked in sheets and cut when done may be served plain, but more often they are made rich with butter and sugar, nuts and fruits, multiple flavorings. Some of these have gained baking fame under their distinctive names: Bishop's Cake, Fudge Squares, *Lebkuchen* and, of course, Brownies.

CHOCOLATE BUTTER COOKIES

1 ounce bitter chocolate
1 cup (½ pound) butter
1 cup sugar
1 egg, separated
  Strained juice of 1 lemon
  Grated rind of lemon

2 cups sifted flour
½ cup chopped pecans
1 pinch salt
¼ teaspoon vanilla

Melt chocolate over hot water; cool. Cream butter with sugar until light and fluffy. Add the egg yolk and beat until thick and smooth. Add chocolate, lemon juice and rind and blend. Sift the flour and add to the batter gradually. Add nuts, salt and vanilla. Mix thoroughly. Pat dough to ¼-inch thickness on an ungreased cookie sheet. Brush top with egg white beaten to a froth. Bake at 300° F. for 20 minutes. Cut into squares while hot. Cool in pan or on rack as desired.

Bishop's Cake, if baked in a loaf pan, becomes a cake, a chocolate fruit cake. But when baked in a flat, rectangular pan (11 x 7 inches or thereabouts) it has a different texture and qualifies as cookie.

BISHOP'S CAKE

3 eggs, well beaten
1 cup sugar
1½ cups sifted flour
1½ teaspoons baking soda
¼ teaspoon salt
8 ounces semisweet chocolate

2 cups chopped walnuts, not too fine
1 cup cut-up pitted dates
1 cup mixed chopped candied fruits

Combine beaten eggs with sugar and beat until very thick and lemon colored. Combine flour, soda and salt, then sift together. Chop or cut the chocolate into pea-size pieces (it must not be too fine). Add chocolate, nuts, dates and mixed fruits to flour mixture and toss together. Fold in the egg mixture gradually. Grease an 11 x 7-inch pan and line it with wax paper. Grease the paper as well. Pour in the batter and bake at 325° F. until done, about 30 to 35 minutes. Cool in the pan and cut into squares as desired.

These Iced Fudge Squares are just about as rich as cakes of this kind can be, which makes them just that much more delectable as accompaniments to a velvety rich cream.

ICED FUDGE SQUARES

½ cup plus 2 tablespoons butter
  (1¼ sticks)
4 ounces bitter chocolate
2 cups sugar
1½ cups sifted flour
1 generous pinch soda

¼ teaspoon baking powder
¼ teaspoon salt
6 eggs, beaten
1 teaspoon vanilla
Marshmallows

Melt butter and chocolate together over hot (not boiling) water. Remove from heat and stir in sugar. Combine flour, soda, baking powder and salt, then sift together. Add beaten eggs to chocolate mixture and blend. Add vanilla. Gradually stir in the dry ingredients. Mix thoroughly but do not beat. Spread batter in 2 greased 9-inch square baking pans. Bake at 350° F. for about 18 minutes. At the end of 15 minutes, place whole marshmallows at even and rather close intervals over surface of cake. Return to oven and let them rise. When cake is done, spread the marshmallows with a buttered knife or spatula. Let cake cool in pan. Frost with Bitter Chocolate Frosting (page 143), cut into small squares and chill before serving.

Among the old-time favorites that still enjoy great popularity, *Lebkuchens* stand near the top of the list. Like fruit cakes, they may have a variety of ingredients—orange peel, citron, candied fruits—or they may be merely spiced.

OLD-FASHIONED LEBKUCHEN

3 cups flour sifted twice before
  measuring
1 cup finely cut citron
1½ cups pecans
2 whole eggs
6 egg yolks
1½ cups sugar
½ cup (¼ pound) butter,
  softened

2 cups dark corn syrup
1 cup grated German sweet
  chocolate
1 teaspoon baking powder
1 teaspoon cinnamon
½ teaspoon allspice
½ teaspoon cloves
½ teaspoon ginger
1 pinch salt

Take ½ cup of the flour and sprinkle it over the citron and nuts, coating them evenly. Set aside. Beat whole eggs and egg yolks until thick and lemon colored. Add sugar and beat until smooth. Add butter and beat again. Add syrup and chocolate; blend. Add floured citron and nuts; mix thoroughly. Sift remaining flour with all the dry ingredients. Gradually work this into the batter. Grease a cookie sheet and line it with wax paper. Grease and flour the paper and shake off any excess of flour. Spread batter in pan (or pans) and place in oven preheated to 450° F.

Turn heat completely off immediately. Let pan stand in hot oven 10 minutes. Now light oven at 350° F. and bake 25 minutes. Cool in pan, then frost with the following:

For the frosting:

1 cup powdered sugar   1 teaspoon vanilla
                                        Cream or whiskey as desired

Add vanilla to sugar and blend. Add cream or whiskey or both drop by drop, working the paste to a smooth, spreadable consistency as you do so. Spread over *lebkuchen* when cold and cut into squares as desired. Let age 1 week before serving.

For very unusual *Lebkuchen*, try these:

LEBKUCHEN SQUARES

2½ cups sifted flour   1 cup unsulphured molasses
1½ teaspoons baking powder   1 tablespoon lemon juice
1 teaspoon cinnamon   Grated rind of 1 lemon
¾ teaspoon salt   8 ounces candied orange peel
½ teaspoon allspice   chopped fine
¼ teaspoon nutmeg   8 ounces ground almonds
7 eggs, separated   8 ounces dark sweet chocolate,
2 cups powdered sugar   grated
1 cup dark brown sugar,
  packed

Combine flour, baking powder, cinnamon, salt, allspice, and nutmeg, then sift together. Combine 7 egg yolks with 4 whites and beat until very light. Add both the sugars and beat until smooth. Add molasses, lemon juice and lemon rind; blend. Gradually work in the dry ingredients. Add orange peel, nuts and chocolate, bit by bit, blending after each addition. Spread dough about 1½ inches thick in a greased 10 x 15-inch pan. Bake at 350° F. for 20 minutes. While still warm, ice with the following:

For the icing:

3 egg whites   1 tablespoon hot water
3 cups sifted powdered sugar   2 tablespoons rum

Beat the egg whites until stiff but not dry, then beat in sugar and hot water. Continue beating until smooth and glossy. Beat in rum. Spread over warm *lebkuchen* and cut in squares as desired. Makes about 3 dozen 2-inch squares.

It should be obvious by now that we are fond of the chocolate-orange combination. Here it is again in Orange Molasses Squares.

ORANGE MOLASSES SQUARES

3 eggs
1½ cups dark brown sugar,
   packed
1½ cups flour
1½ teaspoons cinnamon
½ teaspoon cloves
¼ teaspoon allspice
½ teaspoon baking soda

1 pinch salt
¼ cup unsulphured molasses
2½ ounces bitter chocolate,
   grated
½ cup chopped candied orange
   rind
1¼ cups finely chopped almonds

Beat eggs until light and lemon colored; add sugar and beat until smooth and thick. Combine flour with spices, baking soda, and salt, then sift together. Add dry ingredients and molasses alternately to the egg batter. Mix thoroughly. Add grated chocolate, orange rind and chopped nuts. Blend. Grease a 10 x 12-inch pan and line it with wax paper; grease the paper as well. Pour in the batter and bake at 350° F. until the cake leaves the sides of the pan, about 18 minutes. Cool in pan and ice with the following:

For the icing:

1½ cups powdered sugar

1 to 2 tablespoons cream
   Bourbon whiskey

Combine sugar and cream in bowl and mix thoroughly. Add whiskey drop by drop, beating as you do so, until icing is of a spreadable consistency. Spread over cake when cold and cut into squares as desired. Makes about 30 2-inch squares.

These are the best brownies we have ever tasted, and all who have had them seem to agree.

DEBBIE'S BROWNIES

4 ounces bitter chocolate
½ cup (¼ pound) butter
1 cup sugar
2 eggs
½ cup sifted flour

1 teaspoon vanilla
1½ cups chopped pecans or
   walnuts (they give very
   different results)

Melt chocolate over hot (not boiling) water; cool. Cream butter and sugar until light and fluffy; add eggs and beat until smooth. Add flour and blend. Stir in vanilla, nuts and chocolate. Spread batter in a greased jelly roll pan and bake at 350° F. for 20 to 25 minutes. Frost while still hot with the following:

For the frosting:

¾ cup powdered sugar   Cream as needed

Add just enough cream to the sugar to bring it to smooth, spreadable consistency. Spread over cake while hot, then let cool in the pan. Makes 36.

The honey and orange peel give these Brownies a distinctive flavor.

HONEY BROWNIES

2 ounces bitter chocolate
½ cup (¼ pound) butter
½ cup dark corn syrup
½ cup honey
2 eggs, well beaten

½ cup sifted flour
¼ teaspoon baking powder
1 pinch salt
½ cup chopped candied orange
    peel, very fine

Melt chocolate over hot (not boiling) water; cool. Cream butter and cream again with syrup and honey. Add well-beaten eggs and beat until smooth. Combine flour, baking powder and salt and then sift together. Add to batter and blend. Add chocolate, orange peel and vanilla. Mix well. Pour into a greased and floured 8 x 8 pan and bake at 300° F. for 45 minutes. Cool in pan and cut into squares as desired. Dust with powdered sugar before serving. Makes 18 to 24.

These little bourbon balls are sometimes called Kentucky Colonels.

KENTUCKY COLONELS

8 ounces vanilla wafers, crushed
2 heaping tablespoons cocoa
1 cup chopped pecans

½ cup light corn syrup
¼ cup bourbon whiskey
Powdered sugar

In a mixing bowl combine all the ingredients except the sugar. Mix thoroughly. Form into small balls about ¾ to 1 inch in diameter. Roll in powdered sugar and store in a tightly covered container with wax paper between layers. This is one recipe you can double or triple without fear of failure. The confections are delicious and keep very well indeed. Makes 3 dozen.

These Bavarian Chocolate Balls are made with walnuts, and rose water gives them its fragrance. Or you may use orange-flower water instead. Lacking both, use brandy.

BAVARIAN CHOCOLATE BALLS

½ pound shelled walnuts
½ pound sweet chocolate
9 slices commercial zwieback

½ teaspoon cinnamon
1½ tablespoons powdered sugar
2 tablespoons rose water

Put the nuts, chocolate and zwieback together through the fine blade of a food chopper. Add cinnamon and sugar. Bit by bit add the rose water and blend. Add more than the 2 tablespoons if needed. The crumbs should be just moist enough to stick together. Roll into 36 small balls. Roll in additional powdered sugar and store in an airtight container with wax paper between layers. These may be frozen if desired.

Pies, Tarts
and Pastries

Chocolate pies and similar pastries may sometimes seem to be more puddings and creams than pies; often they are much like icebox cakes, or they may be called *cake* as with the Chocolate Cheesecake (page 184). But they are pies.

Chocolate pies, speaking generally, are of two kinds: with either baked or unbaked filling. The fillings of unbaked pies are often precooked, and require no further cooking once placed in the shell. Crusts may be baked or unbaked or partially baked. Sometimes the entire pie will be made with chilling instead of cooking; or crust and filling may be baked together. But what seems to make a pie a pie is the containment of filling in shell and the way in which filling and shell are served together. In the days when, in English-speaking lands, a dessert pie was known as a *pudding in a coffin,* the crusts were often of so heavy a dough that the filling (which was indeed a pudding) would be scooped out separately. But as they became pies of the sort that we know today—taking a name which had previously belonged to main course meat dishes in pastry—the crust became as desirable as the rich filling. The crusts of chocolate pies took on various aspects, being sometimes of pastry and sometimes of crumbs, which themselves might be of chocolate. So before going into the recipes for individual chocolate pie fillings, let us give you several crusts that you may use with whatever fillings strike your fancy.

PIE DOUGH

All pastry dough must be handled quickly and lightly; for best results it should be kept as cold as conveniently possible during the mixing. The use of a pastry blender (or two knives) will prevent the warmth of the hands from melting the shortening, but an expert cook can achieve the best results by working with the fingertips. The feel of the dough indicates its quality, as does the look of it: before the ice water is added the flour-shortening mixture should be fluffy and pebbly.

Too much flour makes for a tough pastry, while too much liquid makes for a soggy one. Butter is the essential shortening for dessert pies for its flavor (save in sweetened crusts) accents and enriches the filling, but the texture of the finished crust will be better if butter is used in combination with some vegetable shortening (not oil). Chilling the pastry dough after blending will also make it lighter and more tender. Several hours of chilling is better than none but 12 to 24 hours is recommended. The dough should be wrapped in wax paper to prevent its drying out. If really well wrapped, pastry dough will keep for several weeks in the refrigerator. Then, too, unbaked pie shells may be frozen.

FOR A ONE-CRUST 8- OR 9-INCH PIE

1½ cups sifted all-purpose flour
¾ teaspoon salt
½ cup shortening (butter and lard, half-and-half, *or* butter and vegetable shortening)

3 tablespoons ice water (approximately)

Measure sifted flour, then resift with salt into a cold mixing bowl. Quickly cut half of the combined shortenings into the flour with a pastry blender or two knives until the mixture is mealy. Add remaining shortening and cut in (or work lightly with the fingertips) until it is broken into small pea-size pellets, evenly distributed throughout. Sprinkle the dough with ice water and toss it together with two forks until it binds. As soon as it is moist enough throughout to hold together in a ball under gentle pressure, wrap it in wax paper and chill.

When ready to use, place the ball of dough on a very lightly floured board. Roll out to between ⅛- and ¼-inch thickness with a lightly floured roller, rolling from the center of the dough outward in different directions and lifting the roller to make each new roll. Do *not* pull the roller back and forth. Work quickly. Cut dough roughly in a circle 2 inches larger than the diameter of your pie dish. Place circle of dough in dish and trim edges; flute with fingertips if desired. Chill until ready to bake or fill.

Unbaked under-crusts have a way of becoming soggy with juicy fillings, so before adding filling, brush upper surface of shell either with unbeaten egg white or melted butter.

TO BAKE AN UNFILLED PIE SHELL

Prick bottom crust in several places with a fork or fill with dried beans to prevent its rising to an uneven shape or buckling. If beans are used, remove them from shell a couple of minutes before the full baking time is over. Bake at 450° F. for about 12 minutes.

To prevent a prebaked crust from becoming too brown when a subsequent filling must be baked for a brief period, place the entire pie (pie dish and all) in an extra pie dish of the same size before putting it in the oven.

Some pies, as we mentioned before, are made with a shell which itself contains chocolate; in such cases the pastry dough is usually also sweetened. A chocolate crust is particularly good with a plain cream pie filling or a coconut cream or butterscotch or a rich custard with sliced bananas. But it may be used for a chocolate filling as well . . . in which case you might try the one for the Plantation Pie (page 176) or the Chocolate Rum Cream (page 176).

CHOCOLATE PASTRY

To the ingredients for the One-crust Pie (page 172) add 4 tablespoons cocoa and 3 tablespoons powdered sugar. Combine these with flour and salt and sift together into cold bowl before working in the shortening. Proceed as directed.

This Chocolate Pastry may be rolled ¼-inch thick, cut in fingers and baked by itself at 450° F. for 12 minutes. Sprinkle with either plain powdered sugar or a mixture of cinnamon and powdered sugar while still hot from the oven and serve as Chocolate Shortbreads.

Crumb crusts are perhaps more widely used for chocolate pies in this country than ones of regular pastry dough. The ease of making them is by no means the least of their attractive features, but it is by no means their only attractive feature. They are very good crusts, indeed.

Crumb crusts may or may not be baked before filling, but if *not* baked, then they should be thoroughly chilled so that the melted butter that is used to bind the sweet crumbs will have a chance to set. And when they are baked (300° F. for 15 minutes as a rule), then they should be thoroughly cooled before the filling is poured in. They must be firmly, fully, evenly packed in the pie dish, whether baked or not. And the best way to insure this is to spread the crumb mixture as evenly as you can by hand and then press it into place by putting an empty pie dish of the same size over the crumbs and forcing them into shape.

A BASIC CRUMB CRUST FOR A 9-INCH SHELL

1 cup cookie or wafer or sweet cracker crumbs (vanilla or chocolate wafers, graham crackers, gingersnaps, zwieback)

¼ cup melted butter
2 tablespoons sugar
Spices and flavorings as desired

Combine in mixing bowl and spread in pie dish as directed above.

NUT-CRUMB CRUST

Add finely chopped nuts as desired (almonds, pecans, walnuts) and decrease cookie crumbs by an equal amount.

ORANGE-CRUMB CRUST

Add 2 tablespoons grated orange rind to basic mixture.

ORANGE-CHOCOLATE CRUST

Add 2 tablespoons grated orange rind and 2 ounces melted bitter chocolate. Blend carefully. Do *not* bake.

SPICE-CRUMB CRUST

Add ½ teaspoon cinnamon and ½ teaspoon ginger, *or* ½ teaspoon cinnamon and ¼ teaspoon cloves or allspice.

Other special kinds of pie shells are made for special pies. There is a Meringue Shell, for instance, for the Angel Pie (see index). And for those who like their chocolate to be a candy, there's a Chocolate Candy Shell made like the Colettes (see index). Here the candy shell is used for a Cream Pie with Pistachios.

CREAM PIE WITH PISTACHIOS IN A CANDY SHELL

For the shell:

1 6-ounce package semisweet
  chocolate bits
2 tablespoons butter, melted

2 tablespoons confectioners'
  sugar

Cut a 12-inch square of aluminum foil and press it into shape in a 9-inch pie dish. Fold the corners over the rim of the dish to hold it securely in place. Sprinkle bottom of foil-lined pan with melted butter. Add chocolate bits. Place pan in oven at 250° F. and leave about 5 minutes or until chocolate is soft enough to spread. Remove from oven. Sprinkle chocolate with sugar. Using the back of a teaspoon, blend sugar, chocolate and butter, spreading it over the inner surface of pan as you do so. It will not be smooth, but no matter. Spread about halfway up rim. Refrigerate 30 minutes or until chocolate is set. Very gently lift foil out of pan with chocolate crust inside. Peel off foil. Return crust to pie dish and keep cold until needed.

For the filling:

1 envelope gelatin
½ cup cold milk
6 egg yolks
1 cup sugar

1 pinch salt
½ cup sweet Marsala
1 cup heavy cream

Moisten gelatin with cold milk. Beat the egg yolks with sugar and salt until very thick and lemon colored. Place gelatin mixture over hot water in top of double boiler and cook until gelatin is completely dissolved. Pour slowly over beaten yolks, beating as you do so. Return to double boiler and cook until very thick, stirring constantly. Slowly stir in the Marsala. Cook 3 to 4 minutes, still stirring. Cool completely. When custard is cold, whip cream until stiff and fold into mixture. Chill until it is too thick to pour but not quite set. Spoon the mixture unevenly into the chocolate pie shell so that it mounds at the center. Sprinkle with ⅛ cup chopped pistachio nuts and decorate edges of pie with bitter chocolate curls. Chill at least one hour before serving.

We are ready now for the fillings which give the pies their proper names. Each recipe will recommend or specify a type of shell to use but the choice, within limits, is yours, whether pastry or crumb, plain, spice, nut, chocolate, or candy. The only rigid control comes from whether or not the filled shell needs baking. And bear in mind that *an 8-inch pie as a rule serves 6, while a 9-inch pie serves 8.* Pies of extra-special richness may serve more.

This pie seems the richer for having whipped cream folded into the chocolate mixture.

PLANTATION PIE

1 9-inch prebaked pie shell
3 ounces bitter chocolate
1 tablespoon butter
1½ cups milk
1 cup sugar

¼ teaspoon salt
3 tablespoons flour
2 eggs
1 teaspoon vanilla
½ cup heavy cream

Melt chocolate with butter in top of double boiler over hot (not boiling) water; blend, then set aside. Scald 1 cup of the milk in another double boiler. Combine sugar, salt and flour; blend with remaining ½ cup cold milk. Pour into hot milk and cook, stirring constantly, until thickened. Beat eggs and slowly pour into hot mixture, stirring as you do so. Cook 5 minutes over low heat, stirring from time to time. Remove from heat and stir in vanilla. Cool. Stir in chocolate-butter mixture. Whip cream until stiff and fold into cold chocolate mixture. Pour into prebaked shell and chill. Serve with a topping of additional whipped cream if desired.

For a delicious variation, cover the bottom of the baked pie shell with sliced bananas just before adding the filling.

The following Chocolate Rum Cream Pie is richer still:

CHOCOLATE RUM CREAM PIE

1 9-inch prebaked pie shell
1 cup milk
⅛ teaspoon nutmeg or mace
2 eggs, separated
⅓ cup plus 1 tablespoon sugar
1 generous pinch salt
2 teaspoons plain gelatin

2 tablespoons cold water
4 tablespoons rum
8 ounces milk chocolate
3 tablespoons cold water
1½ cups heavy cream
½ teaspoon vanilla

Heat milk with nutmeg or mace in top of double boiler. Beat egg yolks with ⅓ cup sugar and salt until thick and lemon colored. Slowly pour the hot milk over the egg yolks, beating as you do so. Return to double boiler and cook until thick, stirring constantly. Remove from heat. Moisten gelatin with 2 tablespoons water. Stir into hot custard and continue to stir until gelatin is dissolved. Place top of double boiler in bowl of cold water and cool quickly, stirring frequently. Add 3 tablespoons of the rum. When the mixture is very thick, beat the egg whites until stiff and fold in gently. Pour into pie shell and chill.

Melt chocolate with 3 tablespoons water in double boiler; cool. Beat cream until stiff. When chocolate is cold, add the remaining spoonful of rum and fold in half of the whipped cream. Beat the remaining half with the extra 1 tablespoon sugar and vanilla. Spread the vanilla cream evenly over the chilled pie. Cover the cream with the chocolate mixture. Chill at least 1 hour before serving.

For many years Mary was factotum-extraordinary of the Hirsh household in Dallas. This is her special chocolate pie made with corn syrup and sour cream.

BIG MARY'S CHOCOLATE PIE

1 9-inch prebaked pie shell
4 ounces sweet chocolate
2 eggs, separated
¼ cup light corn syrup

1 cup sour cream
¼ teaspoon salt
1 cup heavy cream
1 tablespoon powdered sugar

Melt chocolate in top of double boiler over hot (not boiling) water; set aside. Beat egg yolks until thick and lemon colored. Add to cooled chocolate and blend. Add syrup, sour cream and salt. Blend thoroughly. Beat egg whites until stiff and fold into mixture. Pour into pie crust and chill several hours. Whip cream and sweeten with powdered sugar. Spread over surface of chilled pie 1 hour before serving. Sprinkle with grated bitter chocolate if desired.

The texture of this Black Satin Pie is perfectly described by its name. It was a favorite in the White House during the Kennedy days.

BLACK SATIN PIE

1 9-inch prebaked pie shell
12 ounces semisweet chocolate
   bits
¼ cup milk
¼ cup sugar
1 pinch salt

4 eggs, separated
1 teaspoon vanilla
½ pint whipped cream, lightly
   sweetened, as desired
Bitter chocolate

Combine chocolate, milk, sugar and salt in top of double boiler; cook gently until chocolate is melted and the mixture is smooth. Stir frequently. Remove from heat and cool slightly. One by one, beat in the egg yolks, beating well after each addition. Beat all together until very thick. Add vanilla. Beat egg whites until stiff and fold gently into the chocolate. Pour into prebaked shell and let the pie stand at room temperature 3 hours before serving. If this pie is chilled (which it may be for holding purposes), remove it from the refrigerator 1 hour before serving. Top with sweetened whipped cream just before it goes to the table. Add a grating or curls of bitter chocolate if desired.

Chocolate Angel Pie requires a meringue crust. The crust, in fact, is what makes the pie "angel."

CHOCOLATE ANGEL PIE

2 egg whites
⅛ teaspoon salt
⅛ teaspoon cream of tartar
½ cup granulated sugar
½ cup chopped pecans, very fine
1 teaspoon grated orange rind
½ teaspoon vanilla

8 ounces German sweet chocolate
2 tablespoons water
1 teaspoon vanilla
1 tablespoon orange liqueur
1 cup heavy cream

Beat egg whites with salt and cream of tartar until they begin to hold peaks. Gradually beat in the sugar and continue beating until the meringue is stiff and glossy. Fold in chopped nuts, orange rind and ½ teaspoon vanilla. Blend lightly but thoroughly. Spread meringue over bottom of lightly greased 8-inch pie dish; build up sides to ½-inch above rim of pan. Bake at 300° F. for about 50 minutes. Do not brown too much. Let cool completely.

Melt chocolate with water in the top of a double boiler over hot (not boiling) water. Remove from heat and cool until thick. Stir in vanilla and liqueur. Whip cream until stiff. Fold into cold chocolate. Pour into meringue shell and chill 2 hours before serving. Serves 6 to 8.

This pie, appropriately named Heavenly Daze, also has a meringue crust. Its filling is considerably richer than that of the Angel Pie; and to add to the richness there's a topping of whipped cream, which gives it a gala appearance.

HEAVENLY DAZE

4 eggs, separated
1 pinch salt
¼ teaspoon cream of tartar
1 cup sugar
8 ounces dark sweet chocolate

4 tablespoons cold water
2 teaspoons rum
2 cups heavy cream
½ teaspoon vanilla
Bitter chocolate

Beat the egg whites until they begin to hold peaks, then beat with salt and cream of tartar until just stiff. Gradually beat in the sugar and continue beating until the meringue is thick and glossy. Spread evenly over bottom of lightly greased 9-inch pie dish; build up sides at least ½ inch higher than bottom. Bake at 275° F. for 1 hour. Remove from oven and cool completely.

Melt chocolate with water in the top of a double boiler over hot (not boiling) water. Beat the egg yolks until thick and then blend with the chocolate. Add rum. Whip 1 cup of the cream until stiff and fold into chocolate mixture. Pour into pie shell and chill 4 hours.

One hour before serving, whip remaining cup of cream and flavor with vanilla. Spread over top of pie. Sprinkle bitter chocolate curls around rim. Chill until time to serve.

Though it calls for cream cheese, this pie is not a cheesecake. It is as rich as cheesecake, however, and should be served either after a relatively light dinner or in small portions.

CHOCOLATE CREAM CHEESE PIE

1 chilled 9-inch graham cracker crumb crust	¼ teaspoon salt
	1 teaspoon vanilla
6 ounces semisweet chocolate bits	2 eggs, separated
	1 cup heavy cream
6 ounces cream cheese (2 3-ounce cakes)	¼ cup additional sugar
	Whipped cream
½ cup sugar	Maraschino cherries

Melt chocolate in top of double boiler over hot (not boiling) water; set aside. Soften cream cheese at room temperature and blend with sugar, salt and vanilla. Beat in egg yolks, one at a time, beating well after each addition. Stir in chocolate. Chill until very thick, then beat again until smooth. Whip cream until stiff and fold into the chocolate. Whip the egg whites until they form soft peaks and then, gradually, beat in the additional sugar. Fold into the chocolate also. Pile in prepared 9-inch shell. Chill until very cold. This is even better if placed in the freezer a while but it should not be frozen. Decorate around edge of pie with rosettes of whipped cream piped on with a pastry tube and in the center of each put a whole or half maraschino cherry.

Chiffon pies are made with a bit of gelatin in the filling and this enables them to be made higher and lighter than other pies. This Almond Mocha Chiffon Pie has a special almond crust.

ALMOND MOCHA CHIFFON PIE

¼ cup (⅛ pound) butter
1½ cups crushed chocolate
    wafers
¼ cup finely chopped almonds,
    not blanched
2 tablespoons powdered sugar
1 envelope gelatin
¼ cup cold, strong black coffee
1 cup sugar
½ teaspoon salt

1½ ounces semisweet chocolate
1¼ cups hot coffee
3 eggs, separated
1 cup heavy cream
1½ teaspoons vanilla
¼ teaspoon cream of tartar
1 tablespoon powdered sugar
¼ cup chopped or slivered
    toasted almonds

Melt butter and combine with wafer crumbs, nuts and sugar. Blend thoroughly. Pat into 9-inch pie plate. Bake at 350° F. for 10 minutes. Cool.

Soften gelatin in cold coffee. Combine half of the sugar, the ½ teaspoon salt, and chocolate with hot coffee. Cook over low heat until chocolate is melted. Beat the egg yolks until thick and lemon colored. Add a few spoonfuls of the hot coffee mixture, then pour slowly into the remaining hot mixture, beating as you do so. Cook over low heat, stirring constantly, until thickened. Remove from heat. Add gelatin and stir until dissolved. Cool until almost set; whip until smooth with rotary beater. Mixture should be very light and foamy. Whip half of the cream until stiff and add 1 teaspoon of the vanilla. Fold into the chocolate mixture. Whip the egg whites with cream of tartar until they hold soft peaks; gradually beat in the remaining ½ cup sugar. Continue beating until thick and glossy. Fold into the chocolate also. Pour into chilled shell and refrigerate several hours. One hour before serving, whip remaining ½ cup cream and sweeten with powdered sugar. Add remaining ½ teaspoon vanilla. Spread over top of pie. Sprinkle with toasted almonds. Keep chilled until needed.

Black bottom pies have two kinds of filling, a light and a dark, the dark, of course, going on the bottom, in this case in a prebaked 10-inch pastry shell.

CHIFFON BLACK BOTTOM PIE

1 prebaked 10-inch pastry crust
For the dark filling:
    4 teaspoons cornstarch
    ½ cup sugar

For the light filling:
    1 tablespoon gelatin
    ¼ cup strained orange juice
    3 egg whites

¼ teaspoon salt
2 cups milk
4 egg yolks, beaten
1½ cups semisweet chocolate bits
¾ teaspoon vanilla

⅓ cup sugar
1 teaspoon rum (or to taste)
½ cup heavy cream
2 tablespoons curaçao
Grated sweet chocolate

Combine cornstarch, sugar and salt and blend with cold milk. Cook in top of double boiler over direct heat, stirring constantly with a wooden spoon, until thick and smooth. Place over hot water and cook 10 minutes, stirring frequently. Beat egg yolks until lemon colored. Add several spoonfuls of the hot mixture and blend. Combine with rest of hot mixture and cook over hot water 2 minutes, stirring constantly. Remove from heat. Measure 1½ cups of this hot custard into a bowl, add chocolate bits and let stand over hot water (away from heat) until chocolate is melted. Add vanilla. Add additional pinch of salt if needed. Spread in prebaked pastry shell and chill.

Soften gelatin with orange juice. Add to remaining custard and stir over hot water until dissolved. Cool. Beat egg whites until they form soft peaks, then beat in ⅓ cup sugar. Add rum to remaining custard mixture. When cold and very thick, fold in the egg whites. Pour over chocolate filling and chill 3 hours. Before serving, whip cream and flavor with curaçao or other orange liqueur. Spread this over pie. Sprinkle with grated sweet chocolate and keep chilled until needed.

The following chocolate pies are made with fillings that require baking. Some, however, are made in prebaked shells. If the pie shell that you use is well done and brown to begin with, you can minimize further browning by placing the pie dish inside another of equal size or in a shallow pan with a skimming of water. It will help, too, if your prebaked crust is colder than the filling. Some further browning is inevitable, and it is best, for such pies, to use shells that are just barely done.

First on the roster of these pies is this Macaroon Crumb Pie which, for good measure, is finished with a meringue.

MACAROON CRUMB PIE

1 prebaked 9-inch pie shell
8 dry macaroons, crushed
1 ounce sweet chocolate, grated
2 cups hot milk
3 eggs, separated

1½ tablespoons sugar
¾ teaspoon vanilla
1 pinch salt
3 tablespoons additional sugar

Crush the macaroons to crumbs of equal size. Melt chocolate in hot milk; combine with crumbs and cool. Beat egg yolks until light with 1½ tablespoons sugar; add vanilla and the macaroon mixture. Pour into pie shell and bake at 375° F. for 15 minutes. Meanwhile beat egg whites with salt and additional sugar until stiff. Spread over pie at the end of 15 minutes, return immediately to oven and bake until meringue is a golden brown. Cool and chill before serving.

Milk chocolate bars make this one of the richest pies you'll ever eat.

CANDY BAR PIE

1 9-inch prebaked pie shell
3 eggs, separated
⅓ cup sugar
¼ teaspoon salt
2½ tablespoons cornstarch
1 tablespoon butter, softened

2 cups milk
½ teaspoon vanilla
1 teaspoon rum
2 ounces plain milk chocolate
   bars
2 tablespoons additional sugar

Beat the eggs with sugar until light; add salt, cornstarch and butter. Blend thoroughly. Scald milk and pour into egg mixture, beating as you do so. Pour into top of double boiler and cook, stirring constantly, until smooth and thickened. Cool and add flavorings. Spread bottom of pie with broken bits of chocolate bars. Pour on the cooled custard. Beat the egg whites until stiff and gradually beat in the additional sugar. Cover custard to edge of pie with the glossy meringue. Bake at 300° F. for 15 minutes. Cool and chill before serving.

This Chocolate-Apple Pie is reputedly of Viennese origin.

CHOCOLATE-APPLE PIE

1 9-inch unbaked pie shell	1 ounce bitter chocolate, grated
3 eggs, separated	1 tablespoon brandy
1 cup sugar	1 teaspoon vanilla
1 tart apple, peeled, cored and grated	1 pinch salt

Beat the egg yolks with the sugar until thick and lemon colored. Add grated apple and chocolate. Blend. Add brandy and vanilla. Beat egg whites with the pinch of salt until stiff but not dry. Fold into apple mixture. Pour into unbaked pie shell. Bake at 350° F. for 25 to 30 minutes. Cool before serving.

This Double Chocolate Pie has a chocolate-pecan filling with a kind of baked-on chocolate frosting.

DOUBLE CHOCOLATE PIE

1 9-inch unbaked pie shell	½ cup chopped pecans
2½ ounces bitter chocolate	6 tablespoons milk
½ tablespoon butter	1 teaspoon vanilla
¾ cup sifted flour	For the topping:
3¼ teaspoons baking powder	1½ ounces bitter chocolate
¼ teaspoon salt	1 cup water
9 tablespoons sugar	⅔ cup sugar

Melt chocolate with butter in the top of a double boiler over hot (not boiling) water; cool. Combine flour, baking powder, salt and sugar. Sift together. Add chopped nuts. Slowly add milk and vanilla; blend. Add chocolate mixture and blend until smooth. Pour into unbaked pie shell.

Combine chocolate with water and sugar in saucepan and cook over low heat, stirring constantly, until sugar and chocolate are melted. Allow mixture to come to a full boil without stirring. (Stirring will cause the syrup to crystallize.) Cook 1 minute. Remove from heat. Gently spoon this mixture over the chocolate filling. Bake at 375° F. until done, about 20 minutes. Serve warm or cold with lightly sweetened, rum-flavored whipped cream or vanilla or banana ice cream.

Plain pecan pies are candy-rich as a rule, and you might think that a Chocolate Fudge Pecan Pie (especially one from Texas) might have just too much candy-richness. But this one, to offset the sweetness, has a dash of lemon juice.

CHOCOLATE FUDGE PECAN PIE

1 10-inch unbaked pie shell
3 ounces bitter chocolate
3 tablespoons butter
4 eggs
2 cups sugar

1 pinch salt
½ teaspoon lemon juice
1 cup chopped pecans, not too fine

Melt chocolate with butter in top of double boiler over hot (not boiling) water; cool. Beat eggs until light, then beat again with sugar. Add butter-chocolate mixture and blend. Stir in salt and lemon juice. Add nuts. Pour into unbaked pie shell and bake at 375° F. for 30 minutes. The pie should be set around the edge by this time but still be somewhat soft at the center. It will thicken as it cools. Remove from oven and let come to room temperature. Do not chill. Serve with lightly sweetened whipped cream or vanilla ice cream.

Chocolate Cheesecake needs no introduction. This one is baked in a 9-inch springform pan instead of a pie dish, and its crust should be made of 2 cups crumbs (vanilla wafers, graham crackers or zwieback) and ⅓ cup of melted butter (see page 174). It should be thoroughly chilled before filling.

CHOCOLATE CHEESECAKE

1 prepared crumb crust in 9-inch springform
12 ounces semisweet chocolate
½ cup strong black coffee
1 teaspoon vanilla
3 8-ounce packages cream cheese

4 eggs, separated
½ cup sugar
½ cup additional sugar
1 cup heavy cream
Powdered sugar
½ teaspoon vanilla
Bitter chocolate curls

Melt chocolate with coffee in top of double boiler over hot (not boiling water); blend thoroughly. Stir in vanilla. Add cream cheese, bit by bit, and stir until melted and smooth. Beat egg yolks with sugar until thick and lemon colored. Combine with cheese mixture and blend. Beat the egg whites until they form soft peaks and then gradually beat in the additional ½ cup sugar. When stiff, fold them gently into the cheese batter. Pour into chilled crust in springform pan. Bake at 350° F. for 1 hour. Turn oven off and let cake cool in oven with the oven door open. When cold, refrigerate several hours. One hour before serving, remove sides from pan. Whip cream and sweeten to taste with powdered sugar; flavor with vanilla. Pile on top of cake. Refrigerate until needed or let stand at room temperature as desired. Garnish with bitter chocolate curls just before serving.

Most tortes are cake-like affairs, but some, like the Schaum Torte, are meringues and others, though cake-like in consistency, turn out to be pies. This version of the Linzer Torte even has a lattice crust for a finish.

LINZER TORTE

1 cup (½ pound) butter	½ teaspoon cinnamon
1 cup sugar	½ teaspoon cloves (or allspice)
2 teaspoons grated lemon peel	3 tablespoons cocoa
2 eggs	¼ teaspoon salt
1½ cups sifted flour	Raspberry jam
1 cup ground almonds	

Cream butter thoroughly with sugar and lemon peel. Add eggs and beat until thick and very light. Add all the other ingredients (except the raspberry jam) and beat until smooth. Chill 30 minutes. Roll between two sheets of wax paper to ¼-inch thickness. Cut a circle of dough 1 inch larger than a 9-inch pie dish and line the dish. Trim edges. Roll remaining dough to ½-inch thickness again and cut into strips ¾ to 1 inch wide and of a length to make a lattice on top of pie. Spread lower crust with raspberry jam to come almost to top of dish. Arrange lattice strips on top. Trim edges again. Bake at 300° F. for 1 hour.

Tartes in France are usually fruit filled, rectangular in shape and made of a free-standing, molded pastry. In this country, however, tarts are little, round, open-face pastries made sometimes with fruit fillings, and sometimes with creams and custards. They are pretty desserts to serve, these Mocha Fudge Tarts being a good example.

MOCHA FUDGE TARTS

8 partly prebaked tart shells in muffin tins	¼ teaspoon salt
	½ cup chopped walnuts
6 ounces semisweet chocolate bits	1 14-ounce can sweetened condensed milk
1½ cups vanilla wafer crumbs	Whipped cream
1 tablespoon instant coffee	

Melt chocolate in top of double boiler over hot (not boiling) water; cool. In a mixing bowl, combine crumbs, coffee, salt and chopped nuts. Add condensed milk and blend thoroughly. Combine crumb mixture with chocolate and blend. Fill tart shells about ⅔ full of mixture and bake at 375° F. for 12 minutes. Serve warm or cold with whipped cream.

These Chocolate Nut Tartlets make a marvelous finish for a buffet supper. And, as they must chill for 24 hours, there's a practical angle to their use as well.

CHOCOLATE NUT TARTLETS

⅔ cup sugar
1¼ cup ground almonds
6 tablespoons sifted flour
3 egg whites
3 ounces semisweet chocolate, grated coarsely

2 tablespoons confectioners' sugar
4 teaspoons hot water
⅛ cup sweet butter
2 egg yolks
¼ cup sliced almonds, toasted

In a mixing bowl combine sugar, ground almonds, flour and one of the egg whites (unbeaten); work to a dough. Roll out to ⅛-inch thickness on a lightly floured board and cut in circles to line 24 greased muffin tins. Pat into tins gently. Bake at 300° F. for about 20 minutes, or until lightly browned. Let shells cool in the tins. When cold, turn out carefully and arrange on a large cookie sheet.

Combine chocolate, confectioners' sugar and water in the top of a double boiler and cook over hot (not boiling) water until the chocolate is melted, stirring frequently. Remove from heat. Add butter and egg yolks. Beat 15 minutes with an electric beater at medium speed. Beat the remaining egg whites until stiff and fold into the chocolate mixture. Beat another 15 minutes with the beater. Fill prebaked shells. Chill overnight. Garnish with toasted almonds before serving. Serves 24.

Breads and Such

Chocolate breads, for the most part, are chocolate cakes, and the only discernible difference between them is in the matter of their sweetness and richness. Many are actually eaten as cakes, and some as specialties which, if not sweet in themselves, make up for it by the addition of a syrup or sauce, chocolate waffles, for instance. Those that are eaten as breads are served at such times and such meals where their sweetness seems in order. Many are tea breads or supper breads; some are served with breakfast. Typical, in this country at least, is this Chocolate Nut Bread.

CHOCOLATE NUT BREAD

6 cups sifted flour
1 teaspoon salt
2 cups sugar
6 teaspoons baking powder
½ cup cocoa

2 eggs
2 cups rich milk
1 tablespoon butter, melted and cooled
1 cup chopped pecans
1 cup ground pecans

Combine flour, salt, sugar, baking powder and cocoa; sift together into a mixing bowl. Beat eggs with milk. Add liquid to the dry ingredients and blend. Add butter, chopped nuts and ground nuts; mix thoroughly. Divide dough evenly between two greased loaf pans. Let stand in a warm place 30 minutes. Bake at 325° F. for 1 to 1¼ hours or until bread is done (it will pull from the side of the loaf pans). Turn out on a rack to cool. Let stand 24 hours before slicing. Serve with sweet butter, cream cheese and strawberry jam mixed with a little orange marmalade.

A fine Italian "bread" is this *Pinza Bertoldese,* the chief flavor of which is apricot jam.

PINZA BERTOLDESE

5 cups sifted pastry flour
2 envelopes yeast
5 tablespoons lukewarm water
1 cup mixed candied fruits diced or chopped very fine
1 cup chopped almonds

¼ cup cocoa
2 cups apricot jam
6 tablespoons softened butter
2 tablespoons honey
2 tablespoons dark rum

Sift 1 cup flour into a mixing bowl. Dissolve yeast in 3 tablespoons warm water. Combine flour and yeast, blend and let stand covered in a warm place (75° F.) until doubled in bulk. In another mixing bowl place the remaining 4 cups flour. Make a well at the center and pour in the risen dough and the remaining warm water. Work the flour into the dough, adding a little more warm water if needed. The dough when finished, and with all of the flour absorbed, should be on the soft side of stiff but still manageable. Cover and let stand in a warm place 2 hours.

Now punch down the dough with your fist. Bit by bit work in the fruits, nuts, cocoa and jam. Add softened butter. Blend. Shape dough into a ring by hand and place on a greased baking sheet. Again let it rise—2½ hours in a warm place. Bake at 400° F. for 1 hour. Meanwhile warm the honey and blend with rum. As soon as the bread is taken from the oven, brush it evenly all over with the rum mixture. When all is absorbed, serve warm or cold as desired. Marvelous with hot chocolate.

Mandelbrot is a German almond bread. This particular version is made with a chocolate center.

MANDELBROT

3 eggs
¾ cup sugar
1 tablespoon orange juice, strained
1 teaspoon grated orange peel
1 teaspoon almond extract

2¾ cups sifted flour
2 teaspoons baking powder
6 tablespoons melted butter
½ cup chopped almonds
¼ cup cocoa

Combine eggs and sugar in a mixing bowl and beat until thick and lemon colored. Add orange juice, grated peel and almond extract. Blend. Combine flour and baking powder, then sift together. Fold half of the dry ingredients into the egg mixture with the melted butter. Then add the remaining flour mixture and beat half a minute. Separate ¼ of the dough and add to it the chopped almonds and cocoa. Blend thoroughly. Form into a roll about ½ inch in diameter. Roll out the remaining dough ½-inch thick and as long as the cocoa roll. Wrap the flat sheet of dough around the roll and seal the joint by pressing gently together. Cut the whole roll in half crosswise. Place the two pieces side by side with a space between on a buttered baking sheet. Bake at 325° F. for 30 minutes. Now remove rolls from oven and slice ½-inch thick while still hot. Lay the slices cut-side up on a buttered baking sheet, return them to the oven at 325° F. and bake 5 minutes longer. Serve hot or cold.

This Sunday Brunch Treat is a real chocolate bread, without any embellishments. Serve it with sweet butter and jelly.

SUNDAY BRUNCH TREAT

1 envelope granular yeast
¼ cup lukewarm water
¼ cup sugar
2 tablespoons butter, melted
¾ teaspoon salt

1 egg
3 cups flour
¼ cup cocoa
1 cup milk, or as needed

Dissolve yeast in warm water with 2 tablespoons of the sugar. In a mixing bowl combine the butter, salt and remaining sugar. Add egg and beat well. Add dissolved yeast and blend. Gradually work in the flour and cocoa, adding as much milk as is needed to make a medium soft dough. Knead lightly until smooth, then place in a buttered bowl to rise (covered) in a warm place — 75° F. — until doubled in bulk, about 2 hours. Turn out on a floured board and form into a loaf. Place in greased loaf pan and let rise until doubled in bulk again, about 1 hour. Bake at 350° F. for about 45 minutes. Turn out of pan onto a rack when done. Serve while still warm with a quantity of sweet butter.

Pumpernickel often has a bit of chocolate added to its dough to give it a darker, richer brown and to increase its richness of taste.

PUMPERNICKEL

2 packages dry yeast
½ cup lukewarm water
1 ounce bitter chocolate, grated
1 teaspoon sugar
1½ tablespoons salt
¼ cup dark molasses

1 cup mashed potatoes, unseasoned
2 cups cold water
7 cups rye flour
½ cup corn meal
2 cups whole-wheat flour, approximately

Soften yeast in ½ cup warm water. Combine chocolate, sugar, molasses, mashed potatoes and cold water in a large saucepan. Bring to a boil and blend. Remove from heat and stir until chocolate is melted. Cool to lukewarm. Add yeast and blend. Add all of the rye flour and all of the corn meal and 1 cup of whole-wheat flour. Mix dough thoroughly with your hands. It should be stiff and workable. Let it stand for 10 minutes.

Now sprinkle breadboard with about ⅓ of the remaining whole-wheat flour. Turn dough onto board and knead for 10 minutes. Transfer dough to a large, greased bowl. Turn it in the bowl so that it is greased all over. Cover and let stand in a warm place (75° F.) until volume is increased by ½. Sprinkle board with half of what now remains of the wheat flour. Turn out dough and knead for 3 to 5 minutes. Return dough to greased bowl, cover again and once more let it rise until volume is increased by half. Sprinkle board with all the remaining wheat flour, turn out dough once more and knead gently, blending all the loose flour into the dough. Divide in halves. Mold each half into a ball. Place each ball in a greased 1 quart round baking dish. Brush top of each with cold water. Let rise 30 minutes. Bake at 375° F. for 1¼ hours or until done (the bread will give a dull thud when rapped by your knuckles or the handle of a knife). During the baking brush the tops of the loaves three times with milk. Cool on a rack when done. Serve in thin slices.

This Coconut Tea Ring makes a marvelous treat at tea or supper, or between meals or as a midnight snack.

COCONUT TEA RING

2 cups sifted flour
3 teaspoons baking powder
½ teaspoon salt
¼ cup butter (½ stick)
1 cup milk, approximately
2 tablespoons melted butter

3½ ounces semisweet chocolate, grated
1⅓ cups shredded coconut, moist
2 tablespoons sugar
¼ teaspoon cinnamon
Powdered sugar

Combine flour, baking powder and salt, then sift together. Cut in the butter as you would for pastry, then add milk bit by bit to make a medium soft dough. Roll out into a rectangle about 10 x 6½ inches on a lightly floured board. Brush with melted butter. Sprinkle with chocolate, coconut, sugar and cinnamon. Roll up jelly-roll fashion the long way. Moisten the edge and seal. Form gently into a circle on a greased baking sheet and bake at 375° F. for about 40 minutes. While still hot, sprinkle with powdered sugar and serve immediately.

Chocolate muffins are nearly indistinguishable from chocolate cup cakes, but they *are* muffins, delectable with tea or supper or light snacks of any kind.

CHOCOLATE MUFFINS

2 ounces bitter chocolate
¼ cup butter (½ stick)
⅓ cup sugar
1 egg

1 cup milk
2 cups sifted flour
4 teaspoons baking powder
½ teaspoon salt

Melt chocolate over hot (not boiling) water; cool. Cream butter and sugar together until light and fluffy. Add chocolate and blend. Beat egg with milk; sift the dry ingredients together. Add dry ingredients and milk mixture alternately to the butter mixture, blending after each addition. Do not beat. When just blended, fill greased muffin tins ⅔ full of the batter and bake at 400° F. for about 25 minutes. Serve as soon as possible. Makes 12 to 18, depending on size.

Among the most popular of the chocolate breads in this country are chocolate doughnuts. These are flavored with lemon.

CHOCOLATE DOUGHNUTS

1½ ounces bitter chocolate	3¾ cups sifted flour
5 tablespoons butter	4 teaspoons baking powder
1 cup plus 2 tablespoons sugar	½ teaspoon salt
2 eggs	1 teaspoon grated lemon rind
1 cup milk	1¼ teaspoons vanilla

Melt chocolate with butter over hot (not boiling) water; cool. Beat sugar with eggs until thick and lemon colored. Add chocolate and milk to egg mixture; blend. Combine flour, baking powder and salt; then sift together. Add dry ingredients, lemon rind and vanilla to batter. Stir until well mixed. Chill dough thoroughly. Roll dough to ¼-inch thickness on a lightly floured board. Cut out with doughnut cutter and fry in deep fat at 370° F. for 1½ minutes on each side. Remove from fat with perforated skimmer. Have ready at hand a good-sized pot of boiling water. Completely immerse the doughnut in water momentarily, just in and out. Place doughnuts on a very lightly greased cookie sheet and slip into the oven at 375° F. for several minutes to crisp. Dredge in powdered sugar while still hot. Cool on rack if desired. Do *not* pile on top of one another until completely cold. Makes 3 dozen.

Chocolate waffles make a wonderful dessert at an informal supper. Here are two ways to make them, similar insofar as ingredients are concerned, but different as to finished products.

CHOCOLATE WAFFLES #1

2 ounces bitter chocolate	1½ cups sifted flour
½ cup (¼ pound) butter	2 teaspoons baking powder
1 cup sugar	1 generous pinch salt
2 eggs, separated	1¼ teaspoons vanilla
½ cup milk	

Melt chocolate over hot (not boiling) water; cool. Cream butter and sugar until light and fluffy. Add egg yolks and beat until smooth and thick. Add milk and blend. Sift the dry ingredients together and stir into the batter. Add chocolate and vanilla. Beat thoroughly. Beat egg whites until stiff and fold in gently. Bake in an oiled and heated or otherwise prepared waffle iron. Dust with cinnamon-sugar and serve with sweetened whipped cream or the following sauce:

For the sauce:

2 ounces bitter chocolate
⅓ cup hot water
1½ cups sugar
1 tablespoon butter

¾ cup cream
1 pinch salt
1 teaspoon vanilla

Melt chocolate in the water over low heat. Add sugar, butter, cream and salt. Blend. Place over hot water and cook for 10 minutes, stirring frequently. Add vanilla. Serve either hot or cold over *hot* waffles. For 6.

CHOCOLATE WAFFLES #2

2¼ ounces bitter chocolate
4 tablespoons butter
½ cup plus 2 tablespoons sugar
3 eggs, separated
1½ cups sifted flour

3 teaspoons baking powder
¼ teaspoon salt
1¼ cups milk
¾ teaspoon vanilla

Melt chocolate over hot water and cool. Cream butter and sugar until light and fluffy. Add egg yolks and beat until thick and smooth. Add chocolate and blend. Combine the dry ingredients and sift together. Add dry ingredients and milk alternately to the batter. Beat egg whites until stiff and fold in gently. Add vanilla. Bake as directed above. Serve with the same chocolate sauce or sweetened whipped cream or simply with melted butter and sifted powdered sugar. Serves 6.

Candies
and Confections

Of the 360,000 tons of cocoa beans brought into the United State two years ago (the last available figure), it is safe to say that more than half—probably a good deal more that half—were used in the manufacture of candy and similar confections. No other country comes close to such a mountain of candy.

Good candy, though relatively easy to make, requires care and attention and a certain know-how . . . as with anything good, for that matter. Its quality may be affected by the weather or the moisture in a room or the altitude. It may be completely changed by the slightest change in cooking temperature, by stirring or not stirring, even by jiggling the pot. The vagaries of candy-making have been treated in books and pamphlets for two hundred years and more in every language of the Western World. The East, though it has its sweets to be sure—and very sweet sweets at that—has never gone in for candy as the West has done.

Trial and error will probably be your most important guide in candy-making, but a few general do's and don'ts may be helpful:

When butter is called for in any candy recipe, always use *sweet* butter. And if butter is included as an ingredient in any amount at all, butter the insides of your cooking pot before beginning to prevent the candy syrup from boiling over.

Always use a pot considerably larger than you would ordinarily for the same amount of ingredients. This also tends to keep the candy from boiling over.

Cover the pot for the first two or three minutes so that steam will form and wash down the sides of the pot, removing any grains of undissolved sugar that may remain there.

Always stir, if you must stir at all, with an absolutely clean, long-handled, wooden spoon.

Sugar, which has an ornery character when exposed to heat, is the chief troublemaker for the would-be confectioner. When all goes well in the cooking and cooling process, sugar contributes to the velvet texture of the candy, but when anything at all goes awry, sugar crystallizes, making the candy grainy. Any speck of sugar introduced after the cooking has begun will tend to "grain" the whole batch. If the candy does start to sugar, add a bit of water and begin the cooking again.

When a candy syrup has cooked to the required temperature, remove the pan from the heat without shaking it; and do not stir or beat the candy until it has cooled to at least 110° F. You may cool it quickly by immersing the pan gently in a bowl of cold water, or you may gently pour it out onto a buttered marble slab or buttered platter. But if you do, do not scrape the pan, for the syrupy mass that adheres to the bottom of the pot will have been exposed to greater heat than the rest of the syrup and, hence, will have a greater tendency to crystallize.

The easiest and surest chocolate candy is that which requires no cooking, such as this chocolate fondant.

UNCOOKED CHOCOLATE FONDANT

½ cup (¼ pound) sweet butter
1 pound confectioners' sugar
½ cup cocoa
¼ cup heaviest cream

1 scant teaspoon curaçao
¼ teaspoon vanilla
1 cup additional confectioners' sugar

Cream butter until soft, then gradually work in the 1 pound sugar and ¼ cup of the cocoa. Bit by bit, add cream, curaçao and vanilla. Work the mixture quickly and thoroughly by hand, kneading and turning and folding it. When smooth, shape into 1-inch balls. Sift additional cup sugar with the remaining cocoa. Roll the balls in this mixture to coat them evenly all over. Arrange on wax paper and chill until hardened. You may eat them as they are, of course, or you may dip them in a chocolate coating, and in case you find this a discouraging process, bear in mind the exasperating advice that practice makes perfect.

CHOCOLATE COATING

For this, to begin with, you need a dry day so far as the weather is concerned, and an indoor temperature of about 68° F. The room you work in, furthermore, should be free from drafts.

Melt 1 pound bitter or bittersweet chocolate *very* slowly in a 1½-quart double boiler *over* (not touching) hot (not boiling) water. Stir the chocolate until it reaches 130° F. on your candy thermometer (and unless you have a candy thermometer, you may as well forget most candy). Remove from heat and let cool to about 88° F. on the thermometer. And from now on, keep the temperature of the water beneath the chocolate at about 90° F. While chocolate is melting, let your candy centers (the filling) come to room temperature. And have ready a candy rack with ¼-inch mesh screen, beneath which you should have a platter to catch the drip, which may be remelted at a later date.

Now, one by one, immerse the centers in the coating. Lift them out straight up with a candy fork. Let them drain in midair a moment, then lay them on the rack with a space between. Cool. Store in a covered container in the refrigerator, with wax paper between layers, until needed.

In virtually all countries where candy is made, there is some use of cut-up or chopped fruits and nuts in combination with melted chocolate. Such candy may be simple in the extreme or relatively sophisticated. Among the latter are these Greek *Troufes Sokolata.*

TROUFES SOKOLATA

2 cups sweet milk chocolate bits
2 cups ground walnuts
1 cup ground pecans
  (or hazelnuts)
½ cup ground almonds
1 cup powdered sugar

2 tablespoons warm cream
  (more or less)
2 teaspoons dark rum
1 teaspoon vanilla
  Whole blanched almonds as
  needed

Melt the chocolate in a saucepan set over (not in) hot water. When completely melted, add walnuts, pecans, almonds and sugar. Blend. Bit by bit add warm cream and flavorings. If still too stiff to mold, add more warmed cream. Blend after each addition. Roll into balls of 1 tablespoon each. Top with a whole or halved blanched almond and allow to cool until set. Makes 6 to 7 dozen.

The truffle seems to have loaned its name almost universally to small delicacies. Our Chocolate Truffle, however, is far less complex in the matter of ingredients than that of Greece.

CHOCOLATE TRUFFLES

½ cup (¼ pound) sweet butter
¾ cup plus 2 tablespoons
  powdered sugar
6 ounces bitter chocolate, grated

1 pinch salt
4 tablespoons heavy cream
Cocoa

Cream butter and sugar together and then cream with the grated chocolate and salt. Bit by bit, add the cream. Work until smooth. Roll into small balls of any desired size (but all alike) and roll lightly in cocoa. Store in a covered container with wax paper between layers. Makes about 3 dozen.

In France, on the other hand, chocolate truffles have great elegance, not only in their name—*truffes de chocolat Maréchal de Plessis-Praslin* —but in the manner of their making. They require *praline,* which itself takes its name from the ducal family (whose name with somewhat less elegance was also attached to one of the most famous murder trials in French history).

TRUFFES DE CHOCOLAT MARÉCHAL DE PLESSIS-PRASLIN

2¼ cups dark brown sugar,
  packed
1 cup water
½ cup rum
2 cups cashews
7 ounces bitter chocolate

¼ cup sweet butter
  (4 tablespoons)
¼ cup strained honey
½ cup cocoa
½ cup confectioners' sugar
1 teaspoon cinnamon

Combine sugar, water and rum in a heavy-bottomed saucepan, bring to a boil and cook to the hard-crack stage, 295° F. on your candy thermometer. Meanwhile spread cashews evenly on a buttered cookie sheet. When the syrup is done, pour it over the nuts. Let this harden. Then break it in pieces and put it through the fine blade of your food grinder.

In a double boiler over hot (not boiling) water, melt the chocolate with butter and honey. Blend. Add the powdered praline. Form mixture into small, rather uneven balls about 1 inch in diameter. Blend cocoa, sugar and cinnamon. Roll the balls in this mixture to coat them evenly all over. Store in an airtight container with wax paper between layers. Makes about 50.

Mixtures much like that of the Greek truffles have been used in candies in all countries. In Hungary, you find *Ordogpirulka,* Devil's Pills. In this country there is a confection known as heavenly hash (not to be confused with the heavenly hash of Texas, which is a kind of fruit compote).

HEAVENLY HASH

8 ounces bitter chocolate
4 ounces dark sweet chocolate
1 small package (about
   5 ounces) miniature
   marshmallows

1 cup chopped pecans
1 cup chopped candied cherries

Melt the two chocolates together over hot (not boiling) water. Combine the other ingredients in a mixing bowl. Pour the hot, melted chocolate over the marshmallow mixture and blend. Pour all together into a buttered 8 x 8-inch pan. Cool, then cut into squares as desired. Makes about 5 dozen 1-inch squares.

Sweetened condensed milk is often used in candy-making. In Brazil, *Ela E Eu* (She and I) is made simply of grated chocolate and sweetened condensed milk combined and rolled into small balls which, subsequently, are coated with chocolate sprills. In this country we use condensed milk for such delights as these Butter Balls.

BUTTER BALLS

6 ounces milk chocolate
1½ teaspoons butter
½ teaspoon cinnamon
6½ tablespoons sweetened
   condensed milk

1 pinch salt
½ teaspoon vanilla
¼ cup finely grated semisweet
   chocolate
½ cup cocoa

Melt milk chocolate over hot (not boiling) water. Add butter, cinnamon, condensed milk, salt and vanilla; blend. Pour mixture out onto a buttered platter and let stand for 2 hours. Now sprinkle with grated chocolate. Mold into small balls, pressing the chocolate into the mixture. Roll each in cocoa to coat it evenly all over. Store in an airtight container with wax paper between layers. Makes about 3 dozen.

SWEET CHOCOLATE DROPS WITH PISTACHIOS

8 ounces sweet chocolate	1 egg yolk
1 cup milk	1 pinch salt
2 tablespoons flour	½ cup powdered sugar
¼ cup sugar	½ cup chopped pistachio nuts

Melt chocolate over hot (not boiling) water; cool. Combine milk, flour, sugar, egg yolk and salt in top of double boiler; beat well, then cook until smooth and thickened, stirring constantly. Remove from heat and cool. Add cooled chocolate and blend. When thick enough to handle, form into small balls. Combine powdered sugar and chopped nuts and roll the balls in this mixture to coat them evenly all over. Store in airtight container with wax paper between layers. Makes about 3½ dozen.

Candied and preserved fruits, rinds, and nuts may be coated with chocolate to make delicious confections. Candied cherries, candied pineapple, candied orange peel, to name a few, are easy to make, allowing, of course, for the peculiarities of chocolate itself. Pitted dates and prunes may be dipped and coated, too. These Stuffed Chocolate Figs are especially good.

STUFFED CHOCOLATE FIGS

1 pound large, soft dried figs	½ teaspoon dark rum
½ cup heavy cream	2 ounces additional sweet
4 ounces sweet chocolate, grated	chocolate
¼ teaspoon vanilla	

Cut the stems from the figs and make a slit down one side of each. Widen this pocket with the knife or your finger. Set the fruit aside. Heat the cream in the top of a double boiler and add the grated chocolate. Stir until chocolate is melted. Add vanilla and rum. Remove from heat and cool. When very thick, fill the figs with this mixture. Then press the slits gently together and shape the figs as desired. Melt the additional chocolate in double boiler. Dip each stuffed fig in this to coat it halfway. Let them dry on racks. Then put each fig in a little fluted paper cup.

These Chocolate Taffy Apples have been favorites with Hirsch children for several generations.

CHOCOLATE TAFFY APPLES

1 cup brown sugar, packed
¼ cup white corn syrup
¼ cup milk
1 ounce bitter chocolate

2 tablespoons butter
4 Jonathan apples, washed and dried
4 wooden skewers

Combine sugar, syrup, milk and chocolate in the top of a double boiler. Place over direct heat and cook to the hard-ball stage, 250° F. on your candy thermometer. Stir several times to prevent sticking. Add butter and cool 3 minutes.

Now place over hot water to keep at this same temperature. Push a skewer into the core of each apple through the stem end. Then, holding skewer, dip apple to coat completely. Lift out, then dip again to coat top. Twirl once or twice in air to remove excess. Prop upright over greased sheet of wax paper to cool completely.

Fudge is always a favorite, and an excellent and very easy fudge can be made with sweetened condensed milk, as in the following:

DOUBLE SWEET FUDGE

2 8-ounce packages sweet chocolate bits
½ teaspoon salt

2 teaspoons vanilla
1⅓ cups sweetened condensed milk

Heat chocolate over hot (not boiling) water until partially melted. Remove from heat and stir until entirely melted. Add remaining ingredients and stir until thoroughly blended. Spread in greased 8 x 8-inch pan. Chill until firm and cut in squares as desired. Makes about 4 dozen pieces about 1-inch square.

Sour Cream Fudge is also delicious. This particular version has the added richness of chopped walnuts.

SOUR CREAM FUDGE

2½ cups dark brown sugar
3 ounces bitter chocolate,
  grated
1 cup sour cream

1 pinch salt
¼ teaspoon vanilla
½ cup finely chopped walnuts

Combine sugar, chocolate and sour cream in a saucepan and cook over moderately high heat, stirring, until the sugar is completely dissolved. Lower heat, cover and cook 2 minutes without stirring; uncover and cook without stirring until the mixture reaches 238° F. on your candy thermometer, the soft-ball stage. Remove from heat and cool. When the fudge reaches 110° F. start beating and continue until it starts to thicken. Add pinch of salt and vanilla. Beat until it begins to lose its sheen, add nuts, blend and pour into a buttered 8 x 8-inch pan. Cool and cut into squares as desired. Makes 3 to 4 dozen pieces.

This Marshmallow Fudge, made with evaporated milk, is easy, virtually foolproof, and delectable as well—a rare combination.

MARSHMALLOW FUDGE

1⅔ cups sugar
2 tablespoons butter
½ teaspoon salt
⅔ cup evaporated milk

1½ cups semisweet chocolate bits
2½ cups miniature marshmallows
1 cup chopped pecans
1¼ teaspoons vanilla

Combine sugar, butter, salt and evaporated milk in a saucepan. Cook, stirring constantly, until sugar is melted and the mixture starts to bubble. Reduce heat to low and cook at a slow boil 8 minutes without stirring. Remove from fire. Add chocolate, marshmallows, pecans and vanilla. Beat until the marshmallows are melted. Pour at once into a greased 9 x 9-inch pan. Cool and cut into squares as desired. Makes 5 to 6 dozen pieces.

Divinity Fudge has a different texture from plain fudge because of the corn syrup it contains. It should not be confused with the divinity that is made with egg whites and dropped from a teaspoon to cool on wax paper in irregular shapes. Divinity Fudge, like regular fudge, is cooled in a pan, then cut into squares.

DIVINITY FUDGE

2 ounces bitter chocolate
2 cups sugar
1 cup milk
1 teaspoon white corn syrup
¼ teaspoon salt

2 tablespoons butter
1 teaspoon vanilla
1 cup chopped nuts (pecans or walnuts)

Combine chocolate, sugar, milk, corn syrup, salt and butter in a 3-quart saucepan, stir until thoroughly blended, then place over direct heat. Cook, stirring constantly, until the mixture comes to the boil; then cook without stirring until it reaches the soft-ball stage, when your candy thermometer will register 238° F. Remove from heat and let cool, without stirring, until 110° F. Add vanilla and beat until the candy loses its sheen. Add nuts and blend. Pour into a greased 8 x 8-inch pan and cool completely. Cut into squares as desired. Makes about 5 dozen pieces.

MAPLE NUT FUDGE

2 cups maple sugar
2 teaspoons light corn syrup
1 cup milk
2½ ounces bitter chocolate
2 tablespoons butter

1 pinch salt
¾ teaspoon vanilla
½ cup chopped walnuts or pecans

Combine sugar, syrup, milk and chocolate in a good-sized saucepan and bring to a boil over moderate heat, stirring constantly. Cover and cook 2 minutes without stirring; uncover and—still without stirring—cook to the soft-ball stage, when your candy thermometer will register 238° F. Remove from heat and cool to 110° F. Add butter, salt and vanilla. Beat until thick and creamy. When the fudge begins to lose its sheen, add nuts and pour into a buttered 8 x 8-inch pan. Cool. Cut into squares as desired. Makes about 5 dozen pieces.

This Cream Cheese Fudge follows a somewhat different procedure.

CREAM CHEESE FUDGE

4 ounces bitter chocolate
2 teaspoons butter
2 cups light cream
4 cups sugar
5 tablespoons light corn syrup

¼ teaspoon salt
1 3-ounce package cream cheese
1½ teaspoons vanilla
2 cups chopped pecans

In a good-sized saucepan, melt the chocolate with the butter over hot water. Add cream, sugar, syrup and salt; blend. Bring to a boil over direct, moderate heat, stirring constantly. Cover and cook 2 minutes without stirring. Uncover and cook to soft-ball stage (still without stirring), when your candy thermometer will register 238° F. Remove from heat and cool to 110° F. Add cheese cut in small bits and vanilla. Beat until thick and creamy. When the fudge loses its sheen, add the nuts. Pour into a buttered 9 x 13-inch pan. Cool, then cut into squares as desired. Makes 8 dozen pieces.

Cooked fondant is the base of many candies and makes the soft creamy center of most that are chocolate-dipped (page 196). The procedure must be followed precisely, and special care must be taken in wiping away the sugar crystals that form on the sides of the pan.

CHOCOLATE FONDANT

2 cups sugar
1¼ cups water
2 tablespoons light corn syrup

1½ teaspoons vanilla
2 ounces bitter chocolate

Combine sugar, water and corn syrup in a saucepan. Cook over moderately low heat, stirring constantly, until the sugar is dissolved. Cook gently, without stirring, until the syrup reaches the soft-ball stage, 238° F. on your candy thermometer. Wrap a damp cloth around the tines of a fork and carefully wipe the sides of the pan to remove all sugar crystals. The cloth should be quite wet but not a bit drippy. If the sides of the pan have any heavy residue of sugar, change the wrapping a couple of times so that the pan is wiped clean. Don't simply spread the sugar. Pour the hot syrup immediately on a cold, wet platter or marble slab. With a spatula start immediately turning the fondant up and over on itself from around the edges. Work quickly. Then beat it as it starts to thicken and continue to beat until it is thick and creamy. Add 1 teaspoon of the vanilla and blend. Store in a covered jar in the refrigerator 2 to 3 days to ripen.

To use the fondant, measure out 1 cup. Melt chocolate over hot (not boiling) water and cool. Knead the cooled chocolate into the fondant. Add remaining ½ teaspoon vanilla and blend. Flatten with a spatula in a pan and cut into squares as desired.

Caramels, like fudge, are easy enough to make, provided that the temperature is watched and the procedure followed to the letter.

MOLASSES CARAMELS

1 cup half-and-half (cream and milk)
1 cup grated bitter chocolate
1 cup white sugar
1 cup dark brown sugar, packed

1 cup unsulphured molasses
1 tablespoon butter
1¼ teaspoons vanilla or rum
1 pinch salt
1½ cups chopped walnuts or pecans (optional)

Combine cream, chocolate, white sugar, brown sugar and molasses in a saucepan and cook over moderately high heat, stirring constantly, until the sugar is dissolved. Reduce heat and cook without stirring until the syrup reaches 248° F. on your candy thermometer. Remove from heat. Cool to 110° F. Add butter, flavoring and salt and blend. Thoroughly blend in nuts if desired and pour into a lightly buttered 8 x 8-inch pan. Cool. When cold turn out on wax paper and cut into squares as desired. Wrap each square in wax paper.

These French Caramels involve a slightly different procedure and should have a creamier consistency.

FRENCH CARAMELS

1 cup sugar
¾ cup light corn syrup
3½ ounces bitter chocolate

¼ teaspoon salt
1½ cups cream
¼ teaspoon vanilla

Combine sugar, syrup, chocolate and salt in a good-sized saucepan with ½ cup of the cream. Cook over moderately high heat, stirring constantly, until the sugar is dissolved. Reduce heat and cook to soft-ball stage stirring occasionally—238° F. on your candy thermometer—and add another ½ cup cream. Bring to 238° F. once more, stirring from time to time, add the remaining cream, blend and then cook to 248° F. without stirring. Remove from heat and cool. Add vanilla. Pour into buttered 6 x 6-inch pan. When cold, turn out on wax paper and cut into squares as desired. Let these dry for 3 to 4 hours, then wrap each in wax paper. Makes about 3 dozen pieces.

Special Christmas candies and ones for other festivals and occasions are made the world over. And though we doubt the wisdom of the Japanese and others who, of late years, have been making greeting cards of chocolate, we do recommend the use of imagination in devising candies and other similar confections that will add to the spirit of some celebration. Such, for instance, are these little Chocolate Bells that are made in Greece at Christmas time.

CHOCOLATE BELLS

1 pound sweet milk chocolate
1 pound ground walnut meats
3 cups powdered sugar
4 tablespoons cream

1 tablespoon grated orange rind
3 tablespoons rum
Additional powdered sugar

Cut or break up the chocolate and put it in a mixing bowl. Place the bowl over hot water and, when the chocolate is melted completely, add the other ingredients—walnuts, 3 cups sugar, cream, orange rind and rum—and mix thoroughly. Cool if necessary. Mold into little bells (a simple enough operation). Roll these in powdered sugar and store in tightly covered containers with wax paper between the layers. Makes 3 to 4 dozen.

Chocolate with Meat
and Other
Main Dishes

Chocolate, in small quantities, is used in many meat and fowl dishes in Mexico and Central America. Incorporated in a sauce or with natural pan juices, it adds a very special richness and color. Though its taste as chocolate seems to disappear in such cases, it has a way of accenting and enriching other flavors, and it acts as a thickener as well.

The *Molé* sauce of Mexico, used with birds of all kinds, is undoubtedly the most frequently copied of all the dishes that utilize chocolate in this way. It is a marvelous creation and the presence of chocolate among its ingredients is rarely suspected save by those who have had similar dishes. This sauce should not be thought of as the only dish of this sort. In fact, quite the reverse, it should be a point of departure for the use of chocolate in a host of dishes in similar ways, or ways suggested by it. Chocolate is excellent in a wide variety of stews, for instance; it is good in gravies and sauces, particularly in brown gravies for beef, or gravies for pork. A small amount can be added to meatballs and meat loaves. It is good in soups, especially those, other than cream soups, that have mushrooms. Just bear in mind that a very small amount of chocolate will make a great deal of difference, a minute quantity in many cases. It acts as a catalyst for other flavors and, if the amounts specified seem so small as to be not worth bothering about, you will discover they do make a great difference. Thereafter let your imagination be your guide. It should lead you to much gastronomic pleasure, which may well seem the greater for having been personally devised.

TURKEY MOLÉ (PAVO MOLÉ)

1 8-pound turkey
1 large onion
2 whole cloves
1 bay leaf
  Cold water
  Salt to taste
12 almonds, browned in butter
1 slice stale bread, toasted
1 heaping tablespoon raisins
1 tablespoon grated bitter
  chocolate
¼ teaspoon ground cloves
3 tablespoons dried red chili
  pulp

¼ teaspoon ground aniseed
1 teaspoon ground cinnamon
6 tablespoons chicken fat or
  lard
1 medium onion, chopped
1 clove garlic, minced
2 tablespoons flour
3 cups tomato sauce
3 cups stock from turkey
  (see below)
  Salt to taste
1 tablespoon toasted sesame
  seeds

Cut turkey into portions as you would a chicken for fricassee. Place in large heavy pot with onion stuck with whole cloves, bay leaf and cold water to cover. Add salt to taste. Bring to boil, reduce heat and simmer gently until turkey is tender. Let cool in broth. Remove from pot and cut up the meat (light and dark) into sizeable chunks or slices. Measure off 3 cups of the broth and reserve. Return turkey skin and bones to remaining broth and cook down to use as soup.

Put the almonds, bread, raisins and chocolate through the fine blade of a food chopper. Combine with ground cloves, chili pulp, aniseed and cinnamon. Blend. In a very large, heavy skillet melt the fat and add onion and garlic. Cook until golden brown. Add the flour and let that brown lightly also. Add the nut mixture and blend. Stir in the tomato sauce and cook gently five minutes. Add the reserved turkey stock, blend and cook 5 minutes longer. Correct seasoning with salt. Add cut-up turkey and cook gently until very thick. Serve in a deep, heated platter with the sesame seeds sprinkled over all.

This same sauce will give you a delectable beef stew if you will change the procedure slightly. Substitute canned chicken broth for the turkey stock, in the first place. Use lean, boneless beef cut in 1½-inch cubes instead of the turkey. And lastly, do not add the chocolate until the last 5 minutes of cooking.

To proceed, combine the ground ingredients (except chocolate) with the spices and chili pulp. Brown onion and garlic in the fat. Then, *before* adding the flour, brown the beef on all sides. Add ground mixture, tomato sauce and, after the five minutes of cooking, the broth. Cook gently until meat is tender. Add chocolate, blend and cook 5 minutes longer. Serve as directed above.

Meatballs are also very good made with a *Molé* sauce. For this particular dish the proportions are somewhat different from those above and vinegar is added, and a considerable amount of minced fresh parsley.

MEATBALLS WITH MOLÉ SAUCE

2 pounds ground beef,
    preferably chuck with a little
    fat
1 teaspoon salt
3 tablespoons flour
2 to 3 tablespoons olive oil
    or lard
1 large onion, chopped
2 cloves garlic, minced

1 teaspoon cinnamon, ground
¼ teaspoon ground cloves
¼ teaspoon ground cumin
1 tablespoon vinegar
1 tablespoon tomato paste
1 teaspoon sugar
2 cups beef or chicken broth
½ ounce bitter chocolate, grated
¼ cup minced fresh parsley

Season the meat with salt, shape into balls 1½ inches in diameter and dredge them evenly in the flour. In a large heavy skillet, heat the fat or oil and brown the meatballs on all sides over moderately high heat. Remove meat from pan when browned; add onion and garlic and let brown over low heat. Add spices, cumin, vinegar, tomato paste, sugar and blend. Add stock and cook 2 to 3 minutes. Add meatballs, reduce heat to very low and simmer gently 1 hour. Turn from time to time. Stir in chocolate and about half of the parsley. Cook 5 minutes. Turn meat and sauce into a deep, heated platter, top with remaining parsley and serve immediately.

Dried beans of all kinds are good with chocolate, too. Or, if you want an easier dish, you can use the canned beans instead, red kidney beans, garbanzos, black beans, or even white beans.

RED KIDNEY BEANS WITH GREEN PEPPERS

3 cans red kidney beans
    (or 2½ cups dried)
1 cup tomato sauce
1 cup finely chopped onion
1 clove garlic, minced
½ cup chopped, seeded green
    pepper

1 tablespoon grated bitter
    chocolate
2 teaspoons salt
½ teaspoon rosemary
1 tablespoon chili powder
¼ teaspoon hot pepper sauce

Combine all ingredients in a greased, not-too-deep baking dish. Blend thoroughly. Bake 1 hour at 350° F. Serve from baking dish. For 6.

Picadillo à la Catalana is a Spanish dish of beef and beans with tomatoes and ripe olives and a flavoring of sherry. In Central America and in the West Indies a bit of chocolate is often added to good effect.

PICADILLO A LA CATALANA

1 pound ground or finely minced beef round

3 tablespoons olive oil

1 medium onion, chopped

1 clove garlic, minced

½ cup sliced, pitted ripe olives (Spanish, if available)

1 cup canned garbanzos

½ cup raisins

2 cups canned tomatoes with part of their juice drained away

1 teaspoon salt

¼ teaspoon each marjoram and thyme

1 tablespoon grated chocolate

1 teaspoon sugar

2 tablespoons brown sherry

Brown the meat in the oil over moderate heat; add the onion and garlic and cook until golden. Add olives, garbanzos, raisins, tomatoes, salt and herbs. Blend. Cook over low heat 1 hour, stirring from time to time. Add chocolate and sugar. Cook 5 minutes. Stir in the sherry. Serve with slices of French bread or hard rolls that have been sautéed until golden brown in additional olive oil.

A Madeira sauce is the classic sauce to serve with ham of any kind. We suggest that you try it with a bit of chocolate.

MADEIRA SAUCE

Ham skin with fat trimmed away
Ham bone or knuckle of veal
2 tablespoons butter
6 shallots, minced (or scallions)
2 tablespoons flour
1 cup red wine (bordeaux or burgundy)

1 10½-ounce can beef gravy
1 tablespoon (scant) grated chocolate
⅓ cup red currant jelly
¼ cup Madeira
Minced fresh parsley

Place a good-sized piece of ham skin and the ham bone in a heavy pot and cover with cold water. Bring to a boil, skim, reduce heat and simmer 3 hours. Strain broth. Return to clean pot and reduce over moderately high heat to 2 cups.

Melt butter in skillet. Sauté shallots until limp. Do *not* brown them. Sprinkle with flour, blend and cook 1 minute. Add reserved broth, red wine and gravy. Bring to boil, reduce heat and cook 20 minutes. Pass through sieve, pressing the shallots through at the same time. Return to fire. Add chocolate and jelly. Blend. Add Madeira. Heat thoroughly and remove from fire. Sprinkle with minced parsley before serving with ham, pork or any rare beef. Makes about 1 quart.

Index

Detroit City Ordinance 29-85, Section
29-2-2(b) provides: "Any person who
retains any library material or any part
thereof for more than fifty (50) cal-
endar days beyond the due date shall
be guilty of a misdemeanor."